BEYOND DIGITAL PHOTOGRAPHY

Transforming Photos into Fine Art with Photoshop and Painter

Cher Threinen-Pendarvis and Donal Jolley

Peachpit Press

Beyond Digital Photography:
Transforming Photos into Fine Art with Photoshop and Painter
Cher Threinen-Pendarvis
Donal Jolley

Peachpit Press
1249 Eighth Street
Berkeley, CA 94710
(510) 524-2178
(510) 524-2221 (fax)
Find us on the web at www.peachpit.com
To report errors, please send a note to errata@peachpit.com

Peachpit Press is a division of Pearson Education.

Peachpit Press editor: Karyn Johnson
Cover design: Mimi Heft and Donal Jolley
Front cover illustration: Cher Threinen-Pendarvis
Back cover illustrations: Cher Threinen-Pendarvis and Donal Jolley
Book design, art direction and layout: Cher Threinen-Pendarvis
Copy editor: Jennifer Eberhardt Lynn
Technical editor: Elizabeth Meyer
Proofreader: Linda Seifert
Indexer: Joy Dean Lee
Production and prepress manager: Jonathan Parker
Peachpit Press production editor: Hilal Sala

This book was set using the Minion and Myriad type families. It was written and composed in
InDesign CS3. Final output was computer to plate at CDS, Medford, Oregon.

ISBN 13: 978-0-321-41021-4
ISBN 10: 0-321-41021-1

0 9 8 7 6 5 4 3 2 1
Printed and bound in the United States of America.

To our Creator,
from whom all inspiration comes.
To my husband, Steven,
for your friendship, kindness and love.
To my dear friend, Linnea Dayton,
I am eternally grateful for your encouragement.
— Cher Threinen-Pendarvis

To my bride, Beth, my treasure in life.
To my children, coneheads and putzes all.
To my mom, Kay Pauling, always in my thoughts.
To my dad, Donal C. Jolley, my yardstick.
To my stepfather, Crellin, I so miss you.
To my friend, Karen Cohen, for the next step.
— Donal Jolley

Acknowledgments

This book has been in progress for more than four years—and it's been a memorable journey.

Our special thanks go to John Derry, one of the fathers of Painter and a long-time colleague and friend. During the early stages of the book, John offered important inspiration, encouragement and help. Heartfelt thanks also go to our dear friend and colleague Linnea Dayton, who shared her enthusiasm, wisdom and guidance.

Warmest thanks go to our talented friend Jack Davis, for writing the wonderful foreword for the book. Jack's work always inspires artists to push themselves to new levels. A special thank you goes to the gifted designer John Odam, for his inspiration and friendship. John designed the clever sidebar icons. A warm thank you goes to the talented photographer Melinda Holden, who shot the portrait of Cher at the easel.

We'd like to thank those who worked "behind the scenes" on *Beyond Digital Photography*. We're grateful to Elizabeth Meyer for her helpful technical reads. Warmest thanks go to Jennifer Eberhardt Lynn for her helpful copy editing; Linda Seifert for her careful proofreading;

Joy Dean Lee for her detailed indexing; and production manager Jonathan Parker for his thorough production and prepress expertise. Jonathan's calm assurance during deadlines is sincerely appreciated.

Special thanks go to our friends at Peachpit Press. A sincere thank you goes to Nancy Ruenzel for understanding the vision and for her support of the book. Our special thanks go to Karyn Johnson, who gave wonderful editing feedback through the development of the project. Our warmest thanks go to Mimi Heft for the beautiful cover design and to the rest of the publishing team for their support. Thank you, Peachpit, for the opportunity to write this book.

Our sincere thanks go to the great people at Adobe—Tom and John Knoll, Mark Hamburg, Chris Cox and to Jerry Harris (PixelPaint co-creator and creator of the Brush engine in Photoshop 7), and the rest of the team for creating such an awesome program.

Our warmest thanks go to the brilliant creators of Painter—Mark Zimmer, Tom Hedges and John Derry—for creating such an incredible program.

Our sincere thank you goes to Heather Anderson, Rob MacDonald, and Steve Szoczei, the Program Manager, Product Manager and User Experience Designer for Painter, respectively, and to Public Relations Manager Kelly O'Dwyer Manuel, for their support.

A big thank you goes to the wonderful folks at Wacom for their incredible pressure-sensitive tablets that help us artists unlock the creative power of Painter and Photoshop. Our special thanks go to Don Varga for his support of this book. A warm thank you also goes to the Wacom folks that we've enjoyed working alongside at the trade shows and conferences—Peter Deitrich, Weston Maggio, and the rest of the Wacom team.

Cher sincerely thanks Donal for his friendship, for coming aboard the book as co-author during the book's development, and for sharing his enthusiasm and creativity. Donal is a true pleasure to work with. A heartfelt thank you goes to Cher's special "coworkers:" to her husband Steve, for his loving encouragement and patience; and to Pearl, Sable and Marika, the close companions who keep her company in the studio. Warm thanks go to dear friends Lisa Baker, Carol Benioff, Susan Bugbee, Elaine Chadwick, Linnea Dayton, Jack and Jill Davis, Mary Envall, Skip Frye, Michelle Jacquin, Donal Jolley, Julie Klein, Elizabeth Meyer, Janine Rees, Julie Roulette, and Mike and Luann Younes who shared sincere encouragement and prayers. Thanks for checking in while we worked, and for the fun lunch breaks that were shared in the water at favorite surf spots.

Donal's biggest thanks goes to Cher for the honor of working with her on the project, and for her patience as she took this newbie author under her wing. Donal also thanks his greatest love, Beth, and their kids Hannah, Aryn, Kristen, Mark and Sean for their patience. Donal could never have done this without his mentors: Donal C. Jolley, Judy Atwater, Cher Threinen-Pendarvis, Jack Davis and Linnea Dayton. For helping him stay sane through the rough patches Donal is truly blessed to have had Alfie Meek, Linnea Dayton, Cher, Pat Swindall and Paul Joiner—all incredible people and unwavering friends.

Finally, we both would like to thank all the other family, friends, and colleagues who have been so patient and understanding during the development of this book.

About the Authors

PHOTO: MELINDA HOLDEN

Award-winning artist and author, Cher Threinen-Pendarvis, has always worked with traditional art tools. Cher is a native Californian and her artwork is a reflection of the inspiring travels she has made over the years with her family around the Pacific Rim—Hawaii, the Philippines, Japan, and China, to name a few. Her mother, Wanda, was also an artist and their times of sitting together and drawing on location was especially inspiring to Cher as she developed her interest in plein-air painting. A pioneer in digital art, Cher has created illustrations using the Macintosh computer for more than two decades. She has been widely recognized for her mastery of Painter, Photoshop and the Wacom pressure-sensitive tablet, and has used these electronic tools since they were first released. Exercising her passion for Painter's artist

tools, Cher has worked as a consultant and demo-artist for the developers of Painter. Her artwork has been exhibited around the world and her articles and art have been published in many books and periodicals. Cher holds a BFA with Highest Honors and Distinction in Art, specializing in painting and printmaking, and she is a member of the San Diego Museum of Art Artist Guild. She has taught Painter and Photoshop workshops around the world, and is principal of the consulting firm Cher Threinen Design. Cher is the author of all editions of *The Painter Wow! Book* and *The Photoshop and Painter Artist Tablet Book: Creative Techniques in Digital Painting*.

To learn more about Cher, please visit her web site at www.pendarvis-studios.com.

Art has always been an integral part of Donal Jolley's life. The son of a nationally recognized artist, he grew up to the familiar scents of the studio and in the company of accomplished contemporary artists. His introduction to the art world was not in a classroom with facts and tutorials, but with the molding of the heart of an artist.

Donal is a self-taught artist. A fourteen-year career in fine commercial printing saw him working with well-known designers, and he often found himself teaching them how to get from concept to ink on paper when technical issues required advanced training.

When Apple revolutionized the print world, Donal's life was changed as well. After learning the basics of Photoshop 2 and other design applications, he changed his career path to digital art and design. He was certified to teach digital design at the college level in the state of California, and spent several years teaching Photoshop and Illustrator to students and professionals alike.

Donal is also a cartoonist and spends a lot of time working with children. His true passion is volunteering his time and talents with the Children's Hospital of Atlanta where he interacts with patients and their families as they endure the stress involved with illnesses and injuries.

Donal lives in Johns Creek, Georgia with his wife and children. Watson, his African Grey parrot, is his constant studio companion and Wacom pen destroyer.

To learn more about Donal, please visit his web site at www.donaljolley.com.

Foreword

In art, the hand can never execute anything higher than the heart can imagine.

—Ralph Waldo Emerson

There is nothing worse than a sharp image of a fuzzy concept.

—Ansel Adams

Balance is always one of the most difficult states for an artist to achieve, especially one who lives in the digital age.

Good art always has its germination in creative passion. Passion without technique, and without craftsmanship and control over one's artistic tools can be desperately stunted. Conversely, mastery of technology without a vision worth sharing, is a decorative meal without nutrition or taste.

Creativity and Craftsmanship are key components of the artist's balancing act. The skills used to execute the tools at hand extend the vision that is within the heart.

Enter Stage Right: Cher Threinen-Pendarvis. The consummate artistic tightrope walker! Cher is an absolute master of the digital medium, and a painter so passionate you couldn't stop her from creating art on a daily basis if you tried!

I've known Cher for a zillion years, both of us starting to do digital painting back when computer art was one-bit and the computers themselves were wood-burning! In addition to our art, both of us also share an intense love for the sea and the riding of her waves (which you will experience in much of Cher's work), that continues to this day. But what has always struck me about Cher is her ability to balance out the completely bohemian drive

to paint and draw, with a "geeky" technical prowess of the digital tools—especially her drive to share *both* of these passions, these gifts, these ways of looking at the creative life, through her wonderfully intimate writing and teaching.

In your hands is the consummation of Cher's and her coauthor, Don's, incredible ability to share these two sides of the digital painter's coin. Here you will find everything from setting up your computer studio, to help choosing what makes a great composition, to practicing step-by-step real-world art projects in both of the artist's essential software packages—Photoshop and Painter—to printing out your masterpieces after they have come to life.

The authors have done this sharing of the complete creative process is such a way that it is highly accessible, completely enjoyable and entirely inspirational. In this

book you will *play* . . . and *work* (another balancing act that Cher excels in) and thus you will walk away from your sessions in this virtual classroom empowered to put into passionate practice what you have just experienced first-hand from these two Masters.

You have a gift in your hands. Enjoy it. Consume it. Master this balancing act of Craftsmanship and Creativity, and take up your stylus and continue down this wonderful adventure that is the Artistic Life!

Vaya con Dios,
Jack H. Davis

Award-winning artist, photographer and author of numerous books on the digital creative process.

AdventuresInPhotoshop.com

Contents

About the Authors vi

Foreword viii

Introduction xii

1

Getting Started 1

Setting Up the Studio with Hardware and Software **2**

Photoshop Basics for Photographers and Painters **6**

Painter Basics for Photographers and Painters **16**

Gestural Expressiveness Using a Wacom Tablet **25**

2

Painting for Non-Painters 28

Creating Pop Art **30**
  Photoshop and Painter

Using Filters for an Impressionist Watercolor Look **38**
  Photoshop

Flexible Auto-Painting for an Impressionistic Treatment **46**
  Photoshop and Painter

Simplifying a Photograph to Achieve a Hand-Rendered Result **54**
  Photoshop and Painter

Using Filters for a Realist-Style Oil Treatment **62**
  Photoshop

Creating a Bold, Graphic Woodcut Look **68**
  Photoshop and Painter

3

Emphasizing the Subject 78

Subduing a Busy Background and Adding Painterly Brushwork **80**
  Photoshop

Brushing in Sharp Focus **88**
  Photoshop and Painter

4

Adding Texture to Photographs 98

Taming the Art History Brush **100**
  Photoshop

Creating a Dry Media Textured Look with Pastels **110**
  Photoshop and Painter

Painting a Textured Black-and-White Study **118**
  Photoshop and Painter

5

Emulating the Look of Watercolor 124

Soft, Diffused Painting with Digital
Watercolor and Blenders **126**
  Photoshop and Painter

Extraordinary Watercolors from Ordinary
Pictures **136**
  Photoshop

6

**Achieving Acrylic and Oil-Painted
Looks 146**

Using Real Bristle Brushes for a
Quick Acrylic Study **148**
  Photoshop and Painter

Using Chiaroscuro Lighting in an
Oil Painting **156**
  Photoshop and Painter

Turning Noise into Beautiful Digital Oils **168**
  Photoshop

Using the Artists' Oils for an Expressive,
Old Masters Style **180**
  Photoshop and Painter

7

**Creating Abstract Art from
Photographs 190**

Going Abstract: Bright Colors and Loose
Strokes **192**
  Photoshop

Painting an Abstract Mixed Media Work **198**
  Photoshop and Painter

8

Composition and Collaging 204

Simulating Reality Using Compositing,
Masking and Color Layers **206**
  Photoshop

A Painter's Sense of Composition **218**
  Photoshop and Painter

Index 228

Introduction

Pink Ginger Sky, *was painted using custom Pastels brushes, over Charcoal Paper in Painter.*

Photographers and artists who attended our classes and at conferences over the years asked for this book: They are the inspiration for *Beyond Digital Photography*. Some students came from a conventional drawing and painting background and desired to make the transition from traditional to digital tools. Others had no experience with drawing and painting, but wanted to learn the principles of good composition, color theory and art history, as well as to gain practice with digital painting. Some artists wanted to combine their art with photography. Still others came from a business perspective and were looking to combine photographs with painting and other digital effects and develop new ways to enhance their art or photography business.

Who This Book Is For. *Beyond Digital Photography* offers inspiration and exciting creative techniques, and ideas for creative expression that cannot found elsewhere. This book is written for professional photographers, commercial illustrators and artists of all levels. With today's digital art tools and hardware you can become immersed in the creative process in much the same way that you can using conventional materials.

This book is an expressive journey that involves combining photography with drawing and painting. This is not a quick trick book, but a book where the authors take the reader by the hand and demonstrate the creative process in a conversational manner. The book assumes that you have a grasp of basic digital photography principles. Some of the projects will touch on setting up the camera for a specific shot, or making a print of an image, but digital cameras and final output are not be discussed in detail. Our book assumes that you will already have a basic understanding of basic digital photography and printing. The focus is on creative concepts, theory and technique.

The Photographer's Digital Tools. With the invention of photography, artists were able to develop a keener

Thoughts in Blue, created with wet edged brushes and Pattern features in Photoshop.

eye as they captured their visions with a camera. The lessons in this book can be performed on digital photographs or on scans of photographic film or prints. Although this book has been written for those readers using Photoshop CS2 through CS4 and Painter 9 through 11, the lessons are all presented in a way that can be applied to future releases of the software.

Photoshop is an essential tool for photographers who want to do retouching, compositing, color correction, painting and more. If your interest is primarily painting, then Painter is an essential tool because of its incredible natural media brushes, and the tactile feel of the paint. The portability between Photoshop and Painter is very excellent and they complement one another.

Approach. This book is not a replacement for the documentation that ships with Photoshop and Painter, and it doesn't address every feature in the software. Instead, it focuses on concepts, such as creative composition in your photographs, enhancing the center of interest and painting styles inspired by old masters.

In Chapter 2 of this book you'll have an opportunity to express yourself using different filter and effect recipes with Photoshop and Painter. In Chapter 3, you'll discover projects that will give you practice with applying various kinds of brushwork effects to your photographs, as well as ideas for emphasizing the subject. In subsequent chapters you'll find projects that will help you enrich your compositions—for instance, applying natural media textures to your photographs, applying watercolor washes, acrylic and oil looks, mixing media, building collage compositions and more.

The projects in the book are presented with color illustrations that are created by the authors. These illustrations are intended to show you how to apply the techniques to use in your own work. Feel free to take off from here with your own creative explorations. We hope you enjoy the artwork, creative thought processes, and techniques in this book.

How to Use
This Book

The chapter table of contents shows a thumbnail of the featured image, project titles, page numbers and software used.

The chapter overview is located facing a chapter table of contents and gives a summary of what you'll learn in the project.

Beyond Digital Photography has a simple design so that you can easily read through the development of an art project. Each chapter begins with a chapter overview and chapter table of contents, for a taste of what you'll learn in the chapter. The chapter table of contents also tells you which programs are used in the projects. At the beginning of each project, you'll find an author introduction that shares inspiration for the art and a summary of the creative process.

Sprinkled throughout the book projects, you'll find three kinds of sidebars. The sidebars are identified by an artist palette, an eye and a paint can. The artist palette identifies

a conceptual tip from an artist-author, the eye identifies a sidebar about Photoshop, and the paint can denotes a Painter-related sidebar. In a few places, the eye or the paint can icon is used with the artist palette to identify an artist tip that also has information about Photoshop or Painter. In other cases, you'll find the eye and the paint can icons used together to represent a tip covering both Photoshop and Painter.

Where possible, creative artistic concept or technical information is separated into mini-technique sidebars identified by a heading, such as "Nondestructive Dodging and

Burning" on page 94. These sidebars are also identified by the warm gold background used on the small sidebars.

Do you use Windows or Mac? Photoshop and Painter work similarly on the Windows and Mac platforms. Since we're both Mac users, we've created the screen shots using the Macintosh OS X systems that we work with. And just to make sure that the project instructions work with both Windows and Mac, we've tested them using both platforms, and we've included key commands for both Windows and Mac users.

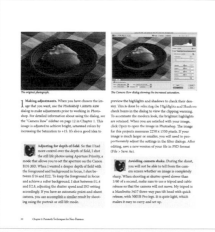

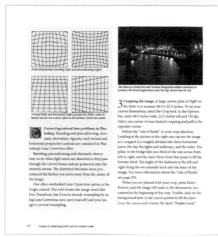

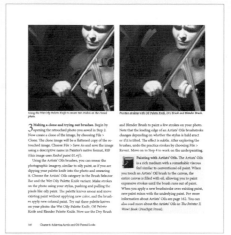

The Artist's tips are identified by artist palette icons.

The Photoshop tips are identified by eye icons.

The Painter tips are identified by paint can icons.

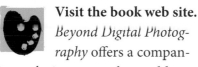 **Visit the book web site.** *Beyond Digital Photography* offers a companion web site at www.beyonddigitalbook.com, where we will offer updates and some of the images used in the projects. You will find either the original raw files or in some cases, very similar photographs. The exercises are written in a general way, however, so you can apply the steps to your own photographs. You will also find a few custom brushes used in the exercises, although we hope you will still go through the rewarding steps of building the brushes yourself.

An opening spread showing the project title and personal artist's introduction.

Setting Up the Studio with Hardware and Software

2

Photoshop Basics for Photographers and Painters

6

Painter Basics for Photographers and Painters

16

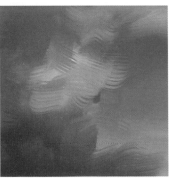

Gestural Expressiveness Using a Wacom Tablet

25

1

GETTING STARTED

All artists need tools and an environment in which to work. Before we dive into the projects that make up the majority of this book, we'll give you some ideas for setting up your studio with hardware and software. We'll also discuss some important concepts such as pixels and resolution. This chapter also covers Photoshop and Painter basics for artists and photographers. Finally, we'll give you some tips for using a Wacom tablet.

Setting Up the Studio with Hardware and Software includes information about the cameras, computers and software that are used for the projects in the book. This section offers useful tips about printing your images in the studio, and discusses working with pixels and resolution.

Photoshop Basics for Photographers and Painters offers an overview of the interface and describes the tools and features that are used most often in the book, including the Colors, Layers, and Brushes palettes, Art History features, as well as some insight on organizing your workspace.

Painter Basics for Photographers and Painters gives an overview of the workspace, including the tools and features that are used in the book projects, including the Colors, Layers and Brush Selector Bar palettes as well as the Photo-Painting system. Additionally, ideas for efficiently organizing the palettes on your screen are offered.

Gestural Expressiveness Using a Wacom Tablet gives an orientation on the Wacom Intuos tablet, and describes setting up a pressure-sensitive tablet, including customizing important settings. To help those new to the tablet and pen prepare for the painting projects in the book, Chapter 1 concludes with some practice exercises.

Setting Up the Studio with Hardware and Software

The Apple Cinema Display, keyboard and Wacom Intuos4 tablet and pen.

A digital photographer's studio is not complete without a fast computer, an excellent, high-resolution monitor, Adobe Photoshop, Corel Painter and a great-quality pressure-sensitive tablet.

The software and tablet perform well on both Windows and Mac platforms. We use Macintosh G5 and Mac Pro computers. Photoshop and Painter are power-hungry programs, so a computer with a fast processor speed, a fast hard disk and at least 2 GB of RAM is recommended.

For the care of your eyes and for the quality of your images, buy the highest-quality display that you can afford. (You'll need a minimum of 20 inches and a video card that supports millions of colors.) Cher's studio has a 23-inch flat panel Apple High-Definition Cinema Display and a LaCie 22 Electron Blue with a hood. The hood is helpful for doing color correction and retouching. When arranging your studio, it's a good idea to set up your display away from the bright light of a window. Consider using low lighting in your studio so you can concentrate on the work you are doing on screen without distractions.

For painting, a Wacom Intuos4 pressure-sensitive graphics tablet or a Cintiq 21UX is recommended. The Intuos line of tablets offers pressure-sensitivity, as well as tilt and bearing recognition. The Intuos4 also senses rotation when a special Art Pen is used. The Cintiq 21UX is a sophisticated pen-sensitive screen that allows working directly on the artwork with the pen. For more information and for practice exercises for creating artwork with Wacom tablets, see pages 24–27.

To shoot digital photos with the utmost creativity and flexibility, a high-quality digital SLR is recommended. Some of the cameras used in the book projects are the Canon Digital Rebel XT, Canon EOS 20D, Canon EOS 5D and Nikon D200.

For safely backing up your files, plan to invest in a large external hard drive such as the LaCie Big Disk Extreme 500 GB or 1 TB (terabyte) desktop hard drive. A CD or DVD burner is also recommended for keeping archives of your work.

A fine art print was made of Danubis Afterglow *using the eight-color Epson Stylus Pro 4880 on Hahnemuehle William Turner paper.*

 Fine art printmaking in the studio. If you want to proof your own images or make fine art prints in your own studio using archival inks and fine art papers, there are many excellent alternatives.

Today's desktop inkjet printers deliver beautiful color prints. The affordable HP printers (such as the HP Photosmart Pro B8850 and DesignJet 130) and the Epson printers (the Epson Stylus Photo 1400 and the Epson Stylus Pro 4880, for instance) are good printers not only for pulling test prints before sending images to a fine art service bureau, but also for use in experimental fine art printmaking.

The Epson Stylus Pro 4880 ships with an eight-color UltraChrome K3 pigmented inkset and handles media up to 17 inches wide with an unlimited length. It can handle heavier substrates, up to cardboard 1.5 mm thick. Capable of printing on virtually any media, the 4880 Pro produces water-resistant prints, especially

when used with Epson's UltraSmooth Fine Art Paper, Watercolor Paper Radiant White or Velvet Fine Art Paper. Using a unique three-level black system, the Epson Stylus Pro 4880 produces professional black-and-white prints from color or grayscale image files.

Many traditional art papers are manufactured for digital printmaking—for instance, Arches, Innova, Museo, Somerset, Concorde Rag and Hahnemuehle's fine art papers, which are available from companies such as Cone Editions Inkjet Mall, Charrette Corporation or Digital Art Supplies. Also, check out the artist-grade canvases available from Digital Art Supplies, located on the Web at www.digitalartsupplies.com.

You can order larger exhibition-quality prints from digital printmaking studios and service bureaus such as Cone Editions Press, Green Flash Photography and Trillium Press. For more information on printmaking and archiving, check out *The Painter Wow! Book* (Peachpit Press).

Working with Pixels and Image Resolution

The original photograph used for Afternoon Light and Shadow Play *in Chapter 2.*

Digital photos are bitmap images composed of pixels. Pixels are square elements arranged in a grid that builds the image file. The resolution of an image is determined by the number of pixels per inch (ppi).

Resolution is a term that describes the number of pixels, or the amount of data in a bitmap (raster) image file. Pixel-based images are resolution dependent, which means that quality can suffer if the image resolution is too low for the size and method of printing that is used.

How will you present your photo?
Before shooting your digital photo, it's a good idea to plan ahead: How will you use your final image? Will it appear in a book or magazine that is printed using offset printing? Will it be printed on an inkjet printer at a fine art service bureau? Will you

print your image on your own studio inkjet? Take the output method into account when you are setting up to shoot photos, and also later when you are preparing to build a collage file or create a digital painting.

Resolution for offset and screen printing. This book was printed using a four-color commercial offset printing process. The images shown in the lessons were prepared at a resolution of 300 pixels per inch. To be printed on an offset press, the square pixels are converted into a grid of round dots for half tones. The (half tone) line screen used for this book is 150 lpi (lines per inch).

To determine the file size you should begin with, find out the line screen needed for the process used by the commercial printer. Typical line-screen resolutions are 56 lpi

(screen printing), 85 lpi (newspaper), 133 lpi, 150 lpi and 200 lpi (magazines and books). If your line screen is 150 lpi, it's recommended that you multiply the line-screen number (150) by 2. Two is a conservative factor to use, and this would create an image resolution of 300 ppi.

The New dialog in Photoshop showing the dimensions and the resolution.

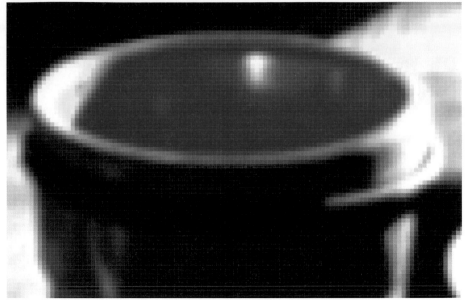

A detail of the photograph viewed at 300%.

A 1600% enlargement of a detail of the photograph showing the grid of pixels.

Resolution for inkjet printing.
When creating an image file to print on an Epson 4800 Pro, it's recommended to set up the file at its final dimensions (for instance, 20 x 16 inches), with a resolution between 150 300 pixels per inch. There is no significant improvement in quality with settings higher than 200 pixels per inch.

Prior to creating an image file that will be printed at a fine art service bureau, speak with your service bureau to find out the equipment requirements. Service bureaus use equipment from different manufacturers—for instance, Epson or Hewlett-Packard. The printing equipment might require different resolutions, and some might request that you convert your RGB file to CMYK color mode.

 Resizing versus resampling. *Resizing* changes the physical dimensions of a file, without changing the number of pixels in the file. *Resampling*, however, uses a process called *interpolation* to increase or decrease the number of pixels. Resampling can cause softness, loss of detail and artifacts in a file. You can avoid resampling by capturing a digital photo at a resolution large enough for its end use. It's recommended not to resample "up" more than 10%. Resampling down is less harmful to the file, but some sharpening might be needed. During interpolation, Photoshop remaps pixels to enlarge or reduce the size of the image. When an image is enlarged, new pixels are manufactured. Pixels are discarded when a file is resampled to a smaller size.

The illustrations below show the Image Size dialog in Photoshop (Image > Image Size). Painter has a similar dialog (Canvas > Resize).

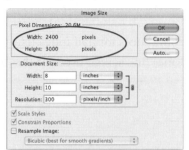 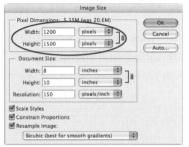

Resizing an image. Note the deselected Resample check box (left). Resampling using Bicubic interpolation (right).

Photoshop Basics for Photographers and Painters

Rather than focus on the nuances of every tool in Photoshop, this section focuses on the basics of Photoshop with photographers and painting in mind. Here, you'll find information and tips about brushes and tools to use for retouching and applying painted effects to your images. This section includes an overview of the interface, information about the Brushes palette, Color palettes, Layers palette, cloning tools, helpful tips for artists and ideas for customizing your Photoshop workspace.

Let's begin with an overview of the Photoshop interface. By default, the Toolbox displays 22 tools. Some tools contain a small arrow in the lower-right corner. If you click and hold the tools with these arrows, additional tools will appear and you can change the tool by selecting a new tool.

The Options Bar is a context-sensitive palette at the top of the Photoshop screen that shows the settings for the current tool. In the upper-right of the Options Bar, you'll notice a docking area where you can store often-used palettes.

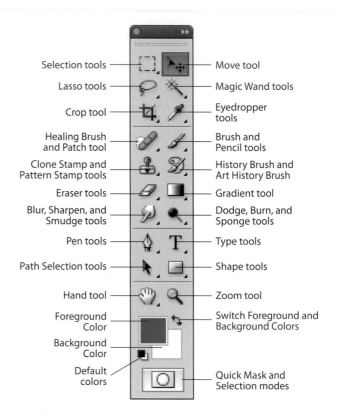

The Toolbox with a focus on the painting, toning and cloning tools to use when working with photographs.

THE PHOTOSHOP WORKSPACE

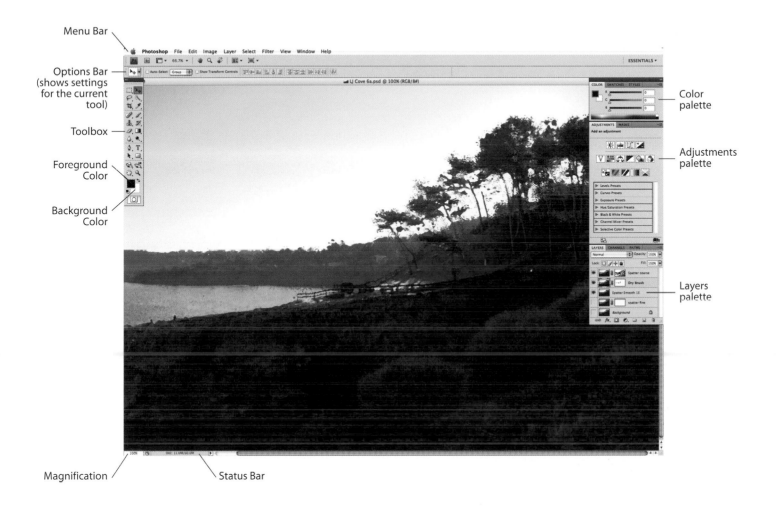

Menu Bar

Options Bar (shows settings for the current tool)

Toolbox

Foreground Color

Background Color

Color palette

Adjustments palette

Layers palette

Magnification

Status Bar

Exploring the workspace. When Photoshop CS4 is first opened, three palette groups are docked on the right in the Essentials workspace. The Color palette displays sliders that you can adjust to mix color, or you can choose a color by clicking in the Color Bar at the bottom of the palette. The Adjustments palette allows you to create an Adjustment Layer with a click and also access adjustment presets. The Layers palette allows you to store and manage elements that float above your image background.

The magnification of the document is displayed in the lower-left corner of the Photoshop window (100% magnification displays your image with the most accuracy). The Status Bar lets you view the Document sizes, Scratch sizes, Timing information, and Efficiency information. On the following pages are the primary tools used for combining painting and artistic effects with photography.

For Sanctuary in Morning Light, *a series of artistic filters was applied to layers, and then the imagery was combined using layer masks for a dry brush oil look.*

Helpful palettes. Use the Layers palette to organize the floating elements in your images, and to apply masks and Adjustment Layers to the elements. For flexibility, you can paint individual elements on their own layers if you like and then hide or show them or move them around.

With the Color palette, you can choose color. Click in the Color Bar to choose a color or use the sliders.

The History palette allows you to click back in history states and can function as a multiple undo alternative. History gives flexibility that suits your workflow.

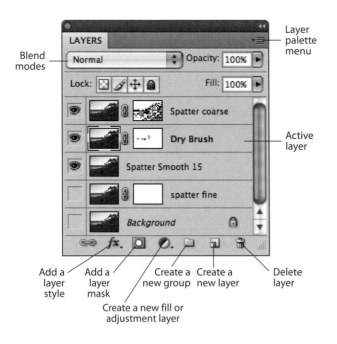

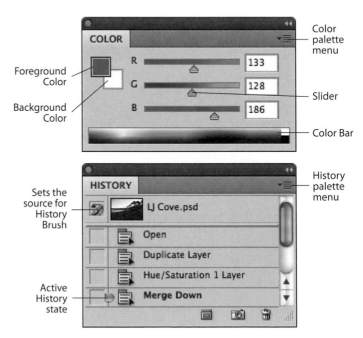

When creating Night on the Seine, *noise and film grain filters were applied to the image, and then the Smudge tool was used in combination with Wet Media brushes on layers to push pixels around, for the look of an oil painting.*

The Brushes palette. With the Brushes palette, you can chose a preset brush or create your own and save it as a new brush preset. You can use the brush presets with the Brush and Pencil tools; the Clone Stamp and Pattern Stamp tools, The History Brush and Art History Brush tools; the Dodge, Burn, and Sponge tools; and the Blur, Sharpen and Smudge tools.

On the left of the palette, under Brush Tip Shape, are the names of windows where more frequently used controls are located.

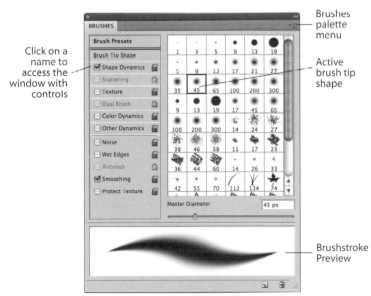

Click on a name to access the window with controls

Brushes palette menu

Active brush tip shape

Master Diameter 45 px

Brushstroke Preview

The Brush Presets window.

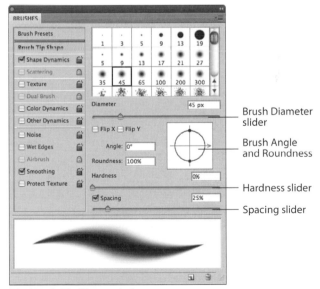

Brush Diameter slider

Brush Angle and Roundness

Hardness slider

Spacing slider

The Brush Tip Shape window.

This detail of Children of the Tuileries *shows painting with the Art History Brush tool and the Charcoal Flat brush preset.*

HELPFUL CLONING AND PAINTING TOOLS

The Art History Brush and the History Brush are cloning tools that use a specified history state or snapshot as source material.

The Art History Brush is a painting tool that automatically applies stylized strokes with a mouse-click. Automated strokes can also be applied by dragging the mouse or painting with a stylus. The strokes are based on the imagery of a source (history state or snapshot) chosen in the History palette. You can simulate a broad range of painting styles by experimenting with different brush tips, stroke Styles, Opacity, Mode and Tolerance settings. For techniques using the Art History Brush, see "Subduing a Busy Background and Adding Painterly Brushwork" on page 80 and "Taming Photoshop's Art History Brush" on page 100.

The History Brush tool paints by restoring the specified source imagery, based on the history state or snapshot that is selected in the History palette.

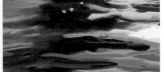 **Adding depth to oily brushwork.** You can build depth into your brushwork using the Lighting Effects filter. Open the file you want to enhance and choose Filter > Render > Lighting Effects. In the Style menu, choose the 2 O'clock Spotlight and drag in the preview window to size the spotlight to fit your image. For a warm look (below right), use the default cream-yellow light and ambient light colors. In the Texture Channel pop-up menu, choose a channel with good contrast (the blue channel is used here.) For a raised look on the lighter areas, select the White is High check box. For relief, adjust the Height slider to your taste. (Try 50% for a subtle look.)

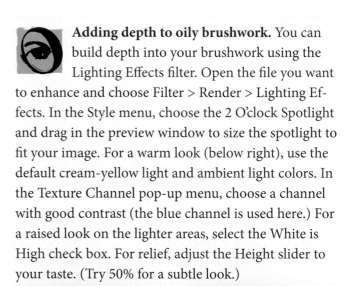

Detail of Night on the Seine, *before effect (left) and after (right).*

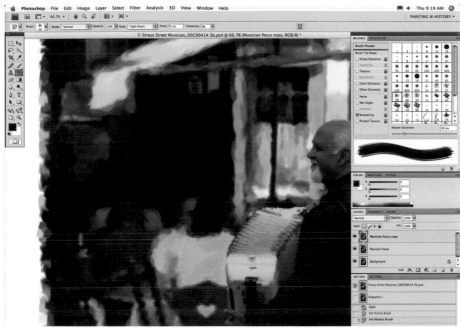

The Painting workspace for Jovial Street Musician, *with the Brushes, Color, Layers and History palettes available.*

CUSTOMIZING A PHOTOSHOP WORKSPACE

Photoshop CS4 ships with several helpful workspaces, for instance, Basic, Color and Tone, Painting and Proofing. Choose Window > Workspace > Painting. Close the palettes that you won't need, and open others—for instance, the History palette is opened here (Window > History), and save your own palette layout by choosing Window > Workspace > Save Workspace. (The custom Painting History workspace is shown above.) If you are using an earlier version of Photoshop, simply open the palettes that you need from the Window menu.

Docking palettes. The palettes are designed to snap together to help you keep your workspace tidy. You can create your own combinations of palettes, for instance. Try dragging the Color palette into the Layers palette group. You can dock frequently used palettes up against the upper-right area of the Options Bar.

Preferred painting cursors. You can set the painting cursors to display the shape of the brush tip at the size it's being used. Choose File > Photoshop Preferences > Cursors. Set the Painting Cursors to Full Size Brush Tip for most uses. When you're working with a tiny brush (just a few pixels), it can be difficult to see

the tiny brush if you are not viewing using a high magnification. Then it's helpful to temporarily switch the painting cursor back to Standard.

Setting Painting Cursors to Full Size Brush Tip.

A Quick Look at Photoshop Camera Raw

This photograph was taken using RAW mode with a high-quality JPG preview.

The corrected RAW file shows considerably more detail and truer color.

High-end digital cameras capture far more information than most people realize. Using the JPG or TIF format option saves space on the memory card, but the results can't compete with the capabilities inherent to a raw format where exponentially more data is recorded.

There are many proprietary raw formats used by camera makers, such as Nikon's NEF and Canon's CRW and CR2. When you shoot, your camera captures the same data no matter what format setting you choose. With non-raw formats, the camera's software processes this information on the fly and makes educated guesses about what to keep and what to permanently discard. Once the camera writes the file to the card, a lot of very useful data is lost forever.

Photoshop Camera Raw is useful in that it translates the proprietary raw file into a color space where the human eye perceives how best to interpret such things as white balance, detail, tonal response and much more.

Writing about everything Camera Raw is capable of doing in four pages is like painting a house with a single gallon of paint. Here only the most pertinent panels for digital painting are touched upon.

Opening a file with Camera Raw. There are two ways of opening a file using Camera Raw. The first is from within Adobe Bridge. Using Bridge to find the folder in which your raw files reside is easy for anyone familiar with a computer file management system. If you are not familiar, consult the Help menu. Navigate to your image file, select the RAW file and click on the Open in Camera Raw icon, which looks like a lens aperture.

The preview JPG was corrected in Photoshop. The lack of information and already clipped ends limits the amount of editing possible.

Tool Bar

Preferences button

Preview window

Zoom controls

File name

Dialog title

Clipping Warnings

Histogram

Panel Icons

Panel settings—the Basic panel is displayed here.

Clicking on the panel icons shows the settings for the selected panel.

Main control buttons

The Photoshop Camera Raw interface with the Basic panel.

The other way is to open the file in Photoshop. Make sure your preferences are set to use Camera Raw to open supported file formats. Choose Photoshop > Preferences > File Handling and make sure the Prefer Adobe Camera Raw for Supported Raw Files check box is selected.

Using the Basic panel. The Basic panel is the most complicated and important panel in Camera Raw. Here you find most of the controls needed for basic correction to your colors and tones.

In the figure above, you find the White Balance menu at the top of the Basic panel. Generally speaking, the As Shot option is adequate for most

shots, but if you have a particularly difficult fix ahead of you, consider selecting Auto.

Use the Exposure slider to set the highlights in your photo. Exposure affects the image dramatically because a disproportionate amount of image data is found in the lowest "stop." Keep an eye on the shadows when adjusting the exposure as increased noise and even posterization is a by-product of heavy changes.

The Recovery slider brings back highlight detail lost due to clipping—the point at which your data exceeds the limits of available gray levels at both ends.

The Fill Light slider is helpful for revealing detail in the shadow areas.

Look out for haloing in high-contrast areas during heavy application.

The Blacks slider determines the shadow clipping point in your image. The default setting of 5 is acceptable, but you may find reducing this number provides a more pleasing result.

Brightness is another slider that yields dramatic results. It is used to adjust the midtones without clipping either the shadow or highlight ends. While you can dramatically remap your tones into the shadow and highlight areas, the clipped pixel values remain at the same points.

The Contrast slider moves tones away from the midtone, with values under 50% going lighter, and values above darkening in proportion.

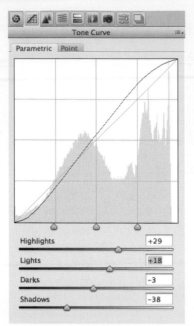

The Tone Curve panel.

Vibrance (above) and Saturation (below) are separately applied at 100% in this comparison.

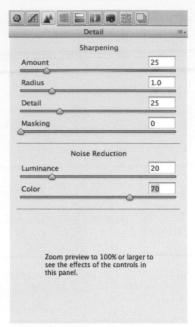

The Detail panel.

The Clarity slider adds clarity to your image through midtone sharpening. Similar in some respects to Unsharp Masking in Photoshop, it is far more complex and targeted.

The Vibrance slider is a variation of the next slider, Saturation. Vibrance and Saturation are both used to brighten colors in comparison with their original intensity. Hues become more or less intense depending on your setting. Saturation changes are global, while Vibrance works to saturate less-saturated pixels to a far greater degree than already saturated pixels. Vibrance has a wonderful ability to leave skin tones alone, so adjustments don't make the people in your shots appear freakishly colorful.

The Tone Curve panel. Clicking the Tone Curve tab reveals the Tone Curve panel, similar to the Curves panel in Photoshop. This panel has two tabs: Parametric and Point. Parametric is usually all you'll need, but more specific adjustments can be made using the Point panel.

The Detail panel. The Detail panel is divided into two parts: Sharpening and Noise Reduction. Pressing the Alt/Option key while using any sharpening slider will show you how your changes affect the sharpening, and it is important to zoom in to at least 100% to accurately gauge your results. The first slider, Amount, is just as it suggests. It determines the

amount of sharpening applied and ranges from 0 (none) to 150 (max). Although you can use it by itself, the effect significantly changes when used with the other sharpening settings. The Radius slider simply determines, in pixels, how far from the edges in your photo the sharpening is applied. The Detail slider enables you to control the extent to which every sharpening slider is applied, and the Masking slider produces a mask much like a layer mask (although you can't see it) and limits the size, and therefore number, of the edges affected by your changes.

Noise is an ever-present issue in digital photography. Camera Raw's Luminance and Color Noise

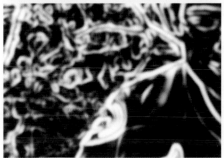

Pressing Alt/Option while using a Sharpening slider toggles a mask preview of the change.

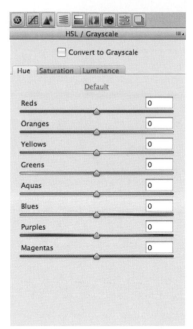

The HSL/Grayscale panel.

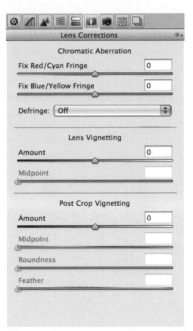

The Lens Corrections panel.

Reduction sliders reduce noise according to luminosity and color. Color is self-explanatory: the reduction is limited strictly to the color portion of the image. To oversimplify, luminosity means the light to dark part of your image in grayscale form. You can see Luminance noise by converting an image to Lab mode. Choose Image > Mode > Lab color and click on the Lightness channel on the Channels palette; then look for the noise.

The HSL/Grayscale panel. The Hue, Saturation and Luminance panels divide color into eight different ranges. If you study the panel, you will notice the first slider starts in red, the colors move through the rainbow, and finally return to magenta at the bottom. You can target specific colors to subtly change hue, be more or less saturated, or be a brighter or darker shade of the same hue.

The Lens Corrections panel. Finally, the Lens Corrections panel rounds out the list of panels most important to what we cover in this book. The Chromatic Aberration sliders are used to minimize or totally correct one type of problem that occurs when light passes through a lens and focuses on your camera's sensor. Occasionally, one color channel is rendered at a different size from the other two plates and under close

inspection appears as color fringes. Camera Raw scales the offending channel to get rid of most of the fringing.

The Defringe pop-up menu is the last Camera Raw control we'll cover. It "cleans up" leftover fringing. The default Off setting leaves the leftover fringing alone, while the Highlights Edges and All Edges options evaluate edges throughout the image and further reduce the fringing by making the pixel hues more consistent with surrounding color. Some chromatic aberration is fixable, and it is best done prior to writing the finished file, but if it's done now, there's no benefit to further correction in Photoshop.

Painter Basics for Photographers and Painters

This section focuses on the basics of Painter for photographers and painters. Here you'll find an overview of the interface; information about the Colors palette and the Mixer, Brush Selector Bar and Brush Controls palettes; the Photo-Painting system; helpful tips for photographers; and ideas for customizing your Painter workspace and more!

The default Toolbox displays 18 tools. Some tools contain a small arrow in the lower-right corner. If you click and hold the tools with these arrows, additional tool icons will appear and you can change the tool by selecting a new tool. The Property Bar is a context-sensitive palette at the top of the screen that shows the settings for the current tool.

Painter's brushes are designed to work their best with a good-quality tablet. The brushes can interpret sensitive movements of your hand—pressure, tilt, bearing angle (direction) and more.

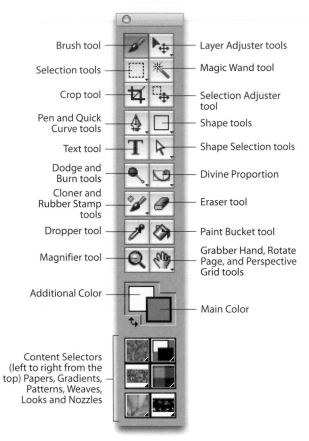

Brush tool — Layer Adjuster tools
Selection tools — Magic Wand tool
Crop tool — Selection Adjuster tool
Pen and Quick Curve tools — Shape tools
Text tool — Shape Selection tools
Dodge and Burn tools — Divine Proportion
Cloner and Rubber Stamp tools — Eraser tool
Dropper tool — Paint Bucket tool
Magnifier tool — Grabber Hand, Rotate Page, and Perspective Grid tools
Additional Color
Main Color
Content Selectors (left to right from the top) Papers, Gradients, Patterns, Weaves, Looks and Nozzles

The Toolbox with emphasis on the painting, toning, color and cloning tools

Using Brush Tracking. Before you begin to paint, it's essential to set up the Brush Tracking so you can customize how Painter interprets the input of your stylus, including parameters such as pressure and speed. Choose Edit > Preferences > Brush Tracking, or Corel Painter > Preferences > Brush Tracking and make a representative brushstroke in the window. For instance, if you plan to use both light and heavy pressure, while painting slowly for a while and then quickly, try to make a brushstroke in the window that would include all of these factors.

THE PAINTER WORKSPACE

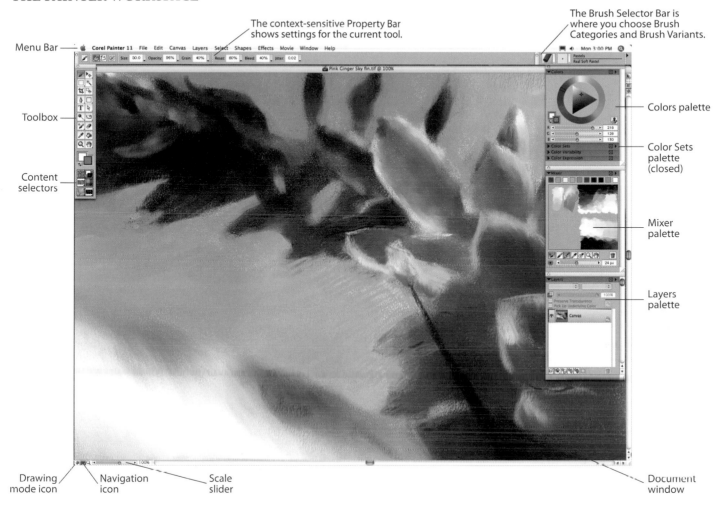

The context-sensitive Property Bar shows settings for the current tool.

The Brush Selector Bar is where you choose Brush Categories and Brush Variants.

Menu Bar

Toolbox

Content selectors

Colors palette

Color Sets palette (closed)

Mixer palette

Layers palette

Drawing mode icon

Navigation icon

Scale slider

Document window

Navigating the workspace. When you first launch Corel Painter 11, two palette groups are docked on the right side of the screen. The palettes are displayed here using the default layout (Window > Arrange Palettes > Default). The open palettes are used in most of the projects in the book.

The first palette group includes the Colors, Mixer and Color Sets palettes. The Colors palette displays a Hue

Ring and Saturation/Value Triangle that you can adjust to mix color. Nested with the Colors palette are the Mixer and Color Sets palettes. With the Mixer, you can mix paint, just as you would on a traditional artist's palette. Color Sets are useful for storing colors that you want to use again.

The second palette group includes the Layers and Channels palettes. The Layers palette allows you to

store and manage elements that float above your image background. You can use the Channels palette to store your masks (alpha channels).

The magnification of the document is displayed in the lower-left corner of the Painter window (100% magnification will display your image with the most accuracy). The Scale slider lets you dynamically magnify or reduce your image.

For Rachel, *a Brightness/Contrast layer was applied for more dramatic contrast, and then a layer mask was used to isolate the effect.*

Helpful palettes. Use the Colors palette to choose color. Click in the Hue Ring to select a hue and mix tints and shades of the color using the Saturation/Value Triangle. If you'd like to hide the RGB/HSV sliders, from the Colors palette menu, choose Hide Color Info. The Mixer palette lets you mix color similar to the way you would mix paint on a conventional artist's palette. New in Painter 11, the Colors palette and Mixer are dynamically resizable, as described on the next page.

You can organize the elements in your paintings using the Layers palette. Layers give you the flexibility to paint elements on their own layers, hide them, show them and reposition them. Layer masks can be added to layers, giving you the capability to hide and show portions of layers and combine the elements into exciting compositions.

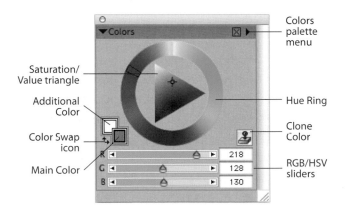

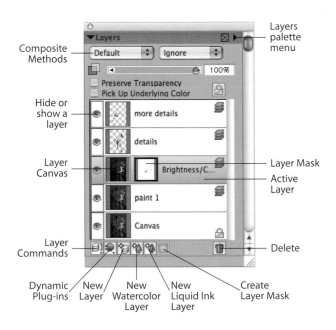

In Wood, Sea, Sky, *Chalk, Pastels and Blenders brushes were used when painting over a photo collage. The Real Soft Pastel brushwork can be seen in the clouds.*

The Brush Selector Bar. Painter ships with a stunning variety of natural-media brushes. Use the Brush Selector Bar to choose brush categories and brush variants. To choose a new brush category, click on a name in the list. In the Brush variant menu, click on a variant name to choose a brush variant. The triangle to the right of the

Brush Variant icon opens a pop-up menu that allows you to choose a variant—in this case, the Real Soft Pastel variant of Pastel.

Using the enhanced Colors palette and Mixer. For even more accuracy when choosing and mixing colors, the Colors and Mixer palettes are resizable in Painter 11. With the Colors palette, you can enlarge the palette up to 800 pixels and adjust colors using the Hue Ring, Saturation/ Value Triangle or sliders. When you enlarge the Mixer palette, more Mixer swatches appear. To enlarge the Colors or Mixer palette, click on the title bar and drag the palette away from its palette group. To resize it, click on the bottom-right corner and drag. When you've finished choosing and mixing colors, reduce the palettes to their original sizes so they occupy less area on your screen.

The Brush Selector Bar with the Brush Category pop-up menu open.

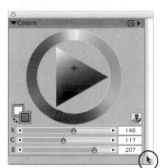

Resizing the Colors palette using the lower-right corner.

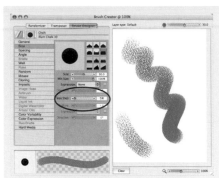
The Brush Creator and its Size section.

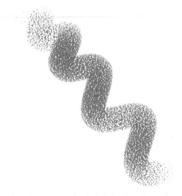
Stroke drawn with the default Blunt Chalk.

Stroke drawn with the custom Blunt Chalk.

WORKING WITH BRUSHES

Painter ships with literally hundreds of amazing natural-media brushes. To familiarize yourself with them, open a practice file and try out the variants in each brush category.

These exercises will give you a peek at what's going on "under the hood" so that you can begin to customize brushes. To try out the brush settings, begin by choosing the Brush tool in the Toolbox and opening the Brush Creator in Painter 8 (Window > Show Brush Creator) or in Painter 6, 7, IX, X and 11, open the Brush Controls by choosing Window > Show Brush Controls > Show General. (If you're using the Brush Controls, you'll also need to open the General and Size sections.) For detailed information about customizing brushes, check out *The Painter Wow! Book* (Peachpit Press).

Choosing a brush and painting a stroke. In the Brush Selector Bar, choose the Chalk category and the Blunt Chalk 30 variant. Apply varied pressure to your stylus while painting a squiggly brushstroke. You'll notice that the default brush reveals more grain with less pressure.

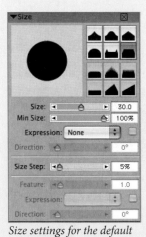
Size settings for the default Blunt Chalk.

Setting the brush to change its stroke width. In the Size section (of the Brush Controls), set the Min Size to 35%; then set the Expression pop-up menu to Pressure. Make another squiggly stroke, and you'll see the thickness of the stroke change based on the pressure that you apply.

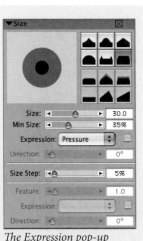
The Expression pop-up menu is set to Pressure.

Adding thick paint to a new version of Shower at Sunset Point, *using the Palette Knife, Thick Bristle and Smeary Round variants of Impasto.*

ACHIEVING THE LOOK OF THICK PAINT

With traditional impasto painting, the paint is applied thickly, giving a three-dimensional appearance to the paint on the canvas. Painter achieves the look of impasto by the simulating the highlights and shadows on the paint.

To try out impasto painting, choose the Impasto brush category in the Brush Selector Bar and then experiment with the variants. For an oily feel, try the Smeary Round and Round Camelhair variants of Impasto. Impasto brushes can be substituted for some of the brushes used in the acrylic and oil painting projects—for instance, "Using Chiaroscuro Lighting in an Oil Painting" on page 157 in Chapter 6 and "Painting an Abstract Mixed Media Work" on page 198 in Chapter 7.

Two sets of controls affect the height and the depth of Impasto. The first is the Surface Lighting dialog. Surface Lighting controls the global appearance of Impasto on the image. To open Surface Lighting, choose Canvas > Surface Lighting. With Impasto, subtle settings are important. For instance, an Amount setting of 20% will give the appearance of thick paint without overpowering

the rendering of your subject. A low Shine setting is also recommended.

The second set of controls allows you to adjust the depth of individual Impasto brushstrokes and other settings. Choose Window > Brush Controls > Impasto. Experiment with the Depth slider to adjust the depth of strokes. For more information about using Impasto, check out the Help menu in Corel Painter.

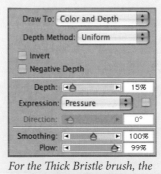

For a natural look, use a small to moderate Amount setting (try 20%).

For the Thick Bristle brush, the Depth slider is set to 15%.

Exciting Real Hard Media Brushes

Adding textured strokes with the Real Soft Chalk for a new version of the Pink Ginger Sky *image.*

The Real Hard Media brushes in Painter 11 simulate the feel of conventional mark-making tools and are great for drawing from scratch or for embellishing photos.

The feel is most noticeable with drawing tools such as the Real Pencils, Real Pens, Real Chalk and Real Pastels. These brushes are scattered throughout existing brush categories—for instance, the Pencils and Chalk. With these brushes you can tilt your stylus on the tablet to shade with the side of the pencil, chalk or pastel.

To begin trying out the Real Hard Media brushes, choose the Pencils category and then choose the Real 6B Soft Pencil variant. Hold the stylus tip more vertical for drawing and tilt it to the side for shading. Have fun doodling and practicing with the Real 6B Soft Pencil and then try out the other Real Pencils.

With the Real Pens, the quicker you sketch, the thinner the lines will be. When you draw slowly, the lines become thicker, just as when a conventional pen moves slowly across a drawing surface.

With the Markers brush category, color intensifies with each new stroke of the Marker brush as color builds up. If you paint a continuous stroke, the shade remains the same until the stylus is lifted and a new stroke is drawn over existing color. These brushes can be substituted into projects such as "Creating a Dry Media Textured Look with Pastels" on page 111.

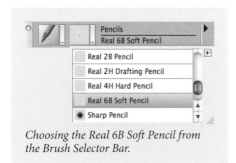

Choosing the Real 6B Soft Pencil from the Brush Selector Bar.

Doodling with the Real 6B Soft Pencil. Tilt the Real Pencil to shade with its side.

Black Real Variable Width Pen strokes (left) and blue Flat Rendering Marker strokes (right).

Detail of the final auto-painting Impression: Peace.

EXPLORING THE PHOTO-PAINTING SYSTEM

The Auto-Painting system features in Painter IX.5, X and 11 allow you to transform photographs into painted looks by applying automatic strokes that incorporate stroke style, pressure and direction. For those not yet practiced with painting by hand, Auto-Painting helps build a painted look. Using sliders in the Auto-Painting palette, you can adjust Pressure, Length, Rotation, and Brush Size to get the brushstrokes you desire. In the illustration from Chapter 2 above, detail was softened using the Smart Blur feature on the Underpainting palette and then Auto-Painting was used to add brushwork on layers.

Open a photograph that has a strong center of interest and good contrast. Choose File > Open, navigate to choose your photo and click Open. To open the Auto-Painting system palettes, from the Window menu, choose Show Auto-Painting. For more detailed information about automated painting in Painter, see the technique "Flexible Auto-Painting for an Impressionist Treatment" on page 46.

 Using the Cloner and Rubber Stamp tools. Cloning tools are similar to other Brush tools, except that clone tools take their color information from a clone source instead of from the Colors palette.

When you select the Cloner tool in the Toolbox, the Brush Category in the Brush Selector Bar switches to the Cloners and the Colors palette "grays out," because color will be sampled from a clone source instead of the Colors palette. The Cloner tool can be used to clone within a document or among multiple documents. The Rubber Stamp tool is ideal for retouching or repairing an area of an image. With the Rubber Stamp tool, you can copy a portion of your image from one area to another by setting the source and destination points.

To set a source point for the Cloner or Rubber Stamp tools, choose the tool you want to use and then Alt-click/Option-click. Move the cursor to the area you want to repair and then begin painting.

A palette layout often used for painting. Notice the custom palette with brushes and canvas texture.

CUSTOMIZING THE PAINTER WORKSPACE

Painter has tools that allow you to set up your workspace for various kinds of projects. For instance, you can build a custom palette to store your brushes, tools and commands. You can also create and save a workspace for painting that includes the Colors and Mixer palettes and a different one for collage work that might include the Layers and Channels palettes.

Making your own custom palettes. For *Moon Over Lennox*, shown as a detail above, a custom palette was created with brushes and a texture.

To create your own custom palette, choose a brush variant (try the Real Oils Short variant of Real Bristle Brushes) and drag it from the Brush Selector Bar. A small palette with the brush automatically appears. Drag the lower-right corner to expand the size of the palette. Choose another variant and drag and drop it onto the palette. To add a paper texture, drag a paper texture from the Paper Selector onto your palette (Coarse Cotton Canvas is used here). To save and name your palette using the Organizer, choose Window > Custom Palette > Organizer and enter a name for your palette.

Saving a custom palette layout. For more intuitive painting, it's helpful to simplify your workspace by closing palettes that you don't need while painting. Begin with the default palette layout by choosing Window > Arrange Palettes > Default. If you're not using layers, you might need only the Colors and the Mixer palettes. Continue arranging the palettes that you need for your project. To save a custom layout, choose Window > Arrange Palettes > Save Layout. Name your layout in the Palette Layout dialog and click OK.

Gestural Expressiveness Using a Wacom Tablet

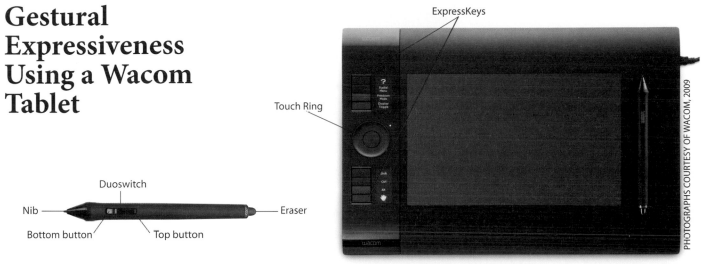

ExpressKeys

Touch Ring

Duoswitch

Nib

Bottom button

Top button

Eraser

The Intuos4 Grip Pen

The Intuos4 M (medium-sized) tablet shown with the pen.

THE WACOM INTUOS4 TABLET

Painter and Photoshop brushes do not perform to their full potential with just the software and a mouse. The beautiful Painter and Photoshop images that you'll see in the book projects could not have been created without a professional pen tablet.

The Intuos4 tablet steps up with 2,048 levels of pressure, allowing amazing sensitivity, and more creative control with your brushes. The Intuos line of tablets sense subtle variations in your wrist and arm movements—such as tilt and bearing—that other tablets do not. The Intuos4 Grip Pen features a new Tip Sensor capable of sensing just a single gram of pressure, allowing you to express the most subtle nuances of your hand movements. Additionally, the Intuos4 offers a resolution of 5,080 lines per inch, giving exceptional accuracy while navigating and drawing.

Important features of the Intuos4 tablet are described in the photo above. The Intuos4 is ambidextrous, which means it can be set up for right-handed or left-handed use. The example above is configured for a right-handed artist.

At its default settings, the side switch on the pen shaft performs the same standard functions as the right and left buttons on a mouse, however, like nearly everything on a Wacom tablet, can be customized to perform a myriad of other time-saving short-cut functions.

To get started, install the tablet software and then connect your tablet to your computer using the USB port. The software automatically maps the tablet to your screen. The pages that follow cover important Wacom software panels and offer some fun exercises for practicing with your tablet.

Sensitive, expressive brushwork in Moon Over Lennox, *made possible with Painter's brushes and a custom pressure curve in the Wacom software.*

CHOOSING SETTINGS FOR YOUR TABLET AND STYLUS

Three main software panels are covered in this short overview and, with the exception of the Pen panel, default settings are described. Each of the panel settings can be customized for your own working style.

Adjusting the feel of the Pen. Open the Wacom software and then open the Pen panel by clicking on the stylus icon on the Tool row (the Grip Pen is chosen here). The Tip Feel is the most important control for painters because its settings affect how Photoshop and Painter interpret the pressure that you apply to the tablet. Tip Feel controls the hardness or softness of the pressure curve. The harder the pressure curve, the firmer you'll have to press on the tablet to make a brushstroke appear on your screen, and the less sensitivity and variation will appear in the stroke. Also, with a softer curve, you'll be able to draw by applying much less pressure.

Using the ExpressKeys. The Intuos4 tablet features an ambidextrous design that you can set up for right-handed or left-handed work. In the Tool area, click the Functions button to open the ExpressKeys panel. The ExpressKeys allow you to modify a tool (for instance, a brush) with your secondary hand while you draw with your primary hand.

Using the Touch Ring. By default the Touch Ring is set up to allow you to quickly zoom in and then zoom back out while painting. Turn the wheel clockwise to zoom in and counterclockwise to zoom out. In the center of the Touch Ring is the Radial pop-up menu which gives access to commands. To access it, an ExpressKey must be set to Radial Menu, as shown in the illustration in the previous column.

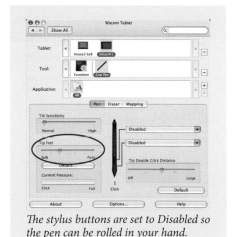

The stylus buttons are set to Disabled so the pen can be rolled in your hand.

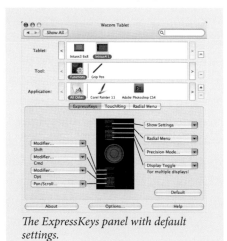

The ExpressKeys panel with default settings.

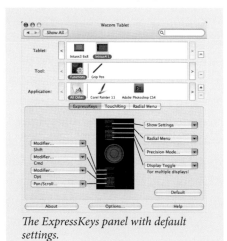

The Touch Ring panel with default settings.

Practicing with a Tablet, Painter and Photoshop

If you're a new tablet user, try out these exercises prior to moving on to the book projects. If you are working in Painter, customize Painter to your hand by setting Brush Tracking. See page 16 for information about Brush Tracking.

Here, the Artists' Oils brushes are used to loosely work over a photograph. After cloning the photo, brushstrokes are painted over the clone and then the brushwork is refined. The final image, Danubis Afterglow, *can be seen in "Using the Artists' Oils for an Expressive, Old Masters Style" on page 180.*

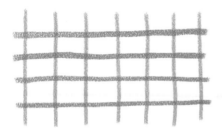

Strokes drawn with the Real Soft Chalk variant of Chalk. In Painter, choose the Chalk category and the Real Soft Chalk variant from the Brush Selector Bar. Hold the stylus upright and pull vertical strokes. Then tilt the stylus at an angle and draw wider horizontal strokes.

Painting coiled strokes using the Real Filbert variant of Digital Watercolor. In Painter choose the Digital Watercolor category and the Real Filbert variant. Practice drawing loose, coiled strokes and then draw them from the opposite direction.

Painting squiggly strokes using the Real Tapered Bristle variant of Real Bristle Brushes. In Painter choose the Real Bristle category and the Real Tapered Bristle variant. Tilt your stylus slightly and paint a series of expressive curved strokes.

Drawing horizontal and vertical strokes with the Chalk 36 preset. In Photoshop choose the Chalk 36 preset from the Brushes palette. Pull vertical strokes, and then horizontal strokes.

Painting coiled strokes with a Spatter brush. In Photoshop choose the Spatter Brush 39 preset. Practice sketching coiled strokes and then draw them from the opposite direction.

Painting squiggly strokes with the Oil Medium Wet Flow Brush in Photoshop. Choose the Oil Medium Wet Flow Brush and then practice painting loose, squiggly strokes.

Creating Pop Art

Photoshop and Painter **30**

Using Filters for an Impressionist Watercolor Look

Photoshop **38**

Flexible Auto-Painting for an Impressionistic Treatment

Photoshop and Painter **46**

Simplifying a Photograph to Achieve a Hand-Rendered Result

Photoshop and Painter **54**

Using Filters for a Realist-Style Oil Treatment

Photoshop **62**

Creating a Bold, Graphic Woodcut Look

Photoshop and Painter **68**

2

PAINTERLY TECHNIQUES FOR NON-PAINTERS

This chapter is written for photographers who are not yet comfortable with painting by hand and for those who want to explore filter recipes. These projects offer recommendations for taking photographs that will be appropriate for applying painterly techniques. In them, you'll learn how to create a painterly look for your images using filters, layers, masks and blend modes.

Creating Pop Art shows how to shoot a still life, apply filters in Photoshop to suggest dabs of paint and add linear interest, and blend the layered effects. More creative pop art looks are then explored using Painter.

Using Filters for an Impressionist Watercolor Look teaches composition design for a watercolor look by way of a creative recipe using the Palette Knife, Photocopy and Watercolor filters, and Blend modes in Photoshop.

Flexible Auto-Painting for an Impressionistic Treatment shows how to use Painter's Auto-Painting and cloning features to add a variety of brushstroke sizes to layers. Then, layer masks are used to selectively combine areas of the layers.

Simplifying a Photograph to Achieve a Hand-Rendered Result examines how Photoshop can reduce fine photographic detail. A creative alternative in Painter is shown at the end of the project.

Using Filters for a Realist-Style Oil Treatment features Photoshop's Adjustment layers for enhancing saturation in the photograph. Then the Dry Brush and Spatter filters are used to build up a painted look on layers. Layer masks are employed to hide and show areas of the filtered layers.

Creating a Bold, Graphic Woodcut Look teaches how to use Painter's powerful Woodcut effects and layers to build a creative color woodcut from your photograph. A creative variation is explored using Painter.

Pie, Please

Creating Pop Art

Here are six photos from the still life shoot. The close-up photo of the pie in the upper-right corner has good focus, composition and lighting—making it the best candidate for the Pop Art look.

Many examples of the Pop Art movement celebrate "commonplace" items by showing close-up views of everyday subjects that many people take for granted. This project was inspired by a favorite artist of mine who worked during the Pop Art movement, Wayne Thiebaud. He painted desserts, gumball machines and other items in a straightforward way with reverence for the subject.

You can create a Pop Art look by applying various filters in Photoshop to your photographs. In this project we'll look at the Paint Daubs and Accented Edges filters in detail, and use a variety of Blend modes to achieve bold effects.

For the shoot, I chose brightly colored heart cakes and a slice of lemon meringue pie and then set them on colorful Fiesta plates for a period look. When I set up the scenes, I arranged the still life subjects so that the diagonally cast shadows would complement or counter balance the design in the tablecloths. I set my camera to shoot in Camera Raw format using Aperture Priority so that I could easily set the aperture and adjust for the depth of field. Then I shot the subject from various angles using a tripod.

What inspired me for this project was the play of light on the brightly colored pie plates and the intriguing shadows on the checkered cloth—they are both great elements to work with when creating a Pop Art image. Before shooting your own photos, get inspired by looking at the paintings and sculptures of master artists who worked in the Pop Art era, including David Hockney, Jasper Johns, Wayne Thiebaud, and Andy Warhol. When setting up your still life, choose a simple, everyday item and arrange it so that you have intriguing negative space around the subject and interesting shadows. As you compose your photograph, observe how the subject occupies the space within the frame. The negative space (the space around the subject) is very important in creating an intriguing, balanced composition.

After downloading your photos, view each photograph at 100% in the Camera Raw dialog to check the focus. The photograph chosen for this project has good focus, intriguing light shining through the translucent lemon pie and interesting shadow shapes on the plate and tablecloth. Let's begin!

The original photograph.

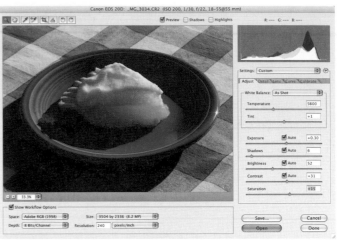

The Camera Raw dialog showing the increased saturation.

1 **Making adjustments.** When you have chosen the image that you want, use the Photoshop Camera Raw dialog to make adjustments prior to working in Photoshop. For detailed information about using the dialog, see the Camera Raw sidebar on page 12 in Chapter 1. This image is adjusted to achieve bright, saturated colors by increasing the Saturation to +15. It's also a good idea to preview

 Adjusting for depth of field. So that I had more control over the depth of field, I shot the still life photos using Aperture Priority, a mode that allows you to set the aperture on the Canon EOS 20D. When I wanted a deeper depth of field with the foreground and background in focus, I shot between f/16 and f/22. To keep the foreground in focus and achieve a softer background, I shot between f/1.4 and f/2.8, adjusting the shutter speed and ISO setting accordingly. If you have an automatic point-and-shoot camera, you can accomplish a similar result by shooting using the portrait or still life mode.

the highlights and shadows to check their density. This is done by selecting the Highlights and Shadows check boxes in the dialog to view the clipping warning. To accentuate the modern look, the brightest highlights are retained. When you are satisfied with your image, click Open to open the image in Photoshop. The image for this projects measures 2250 x 1550 pixels. If your image is much larger or smaller, you will need to proportionately adjust the settings in the filter dialogs. After editing, save a new version of your file in PSD format (File > Save As).

Avoiding camera shake. During the shoot, you will not be able to tell from the camera screen whether an image is completely sharp. When shooting at shutter speed slower than 1/60 of a second, make sure to use a tripod and cable release so that the camera will not move. My tripod is a Manfrotto 3437 three-way pan tilt head with quick release, with 3001B Pro legs. It is quite light, which makes it easy to carry and set up.

The adjusted image of the pie.

The working image with the Paint Daubs filter applied.

2 **Putting the image on a layer.** For the most flexible, nondestructive workflow, place a copy of the image on a new layer. To do this, click the Background layer and press Ctrl-J/⌘-J, and a new layer, titled Layer 1, appears in the Layers palette. To keep your file organized, it's a good idea to give the layer a descriptive name. (To rename the layer, click the layer name and when a cursor appears, type the new name.) For this project, the first layer was named Paint Daubs to reflect the name of the filter that is used.

3 **Simplifying the photograph.** Now, you're ready to begin applying filters. The first filter, Paint Daubs, will simplify the image and transform tiny photographic details into dabs of color. With the new layer active, choose Filter > Artistic > Paint Daubs. You will see your image appear in the Preview window, and it will be transformed dynamically as you adjust the settings. For a smooth look, choose Simple from the Brush Type pop-up menu. Adjust the sliders to your taste, but be careful of high Sharpness settings because a high sharpness can generate jagged edges on curves. The settings for this project are Brush Size: 20 and Sharpness: 5.

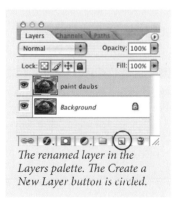

The renamed layer in the Layers palette. The Create a New Layer button is circled.

The Paint Daubs dialog shows the image transformed in the Preview window.

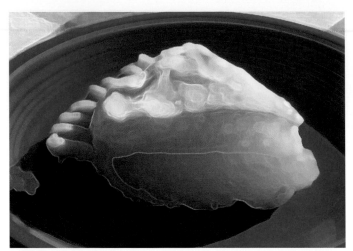

The image with Accented Edges applied. The Blend mode is Normal.

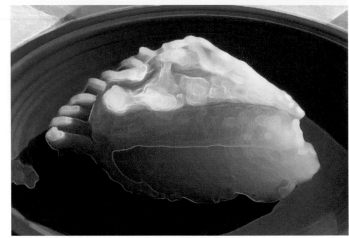

When Luminosity is used, the edge colors and brightness are more subtle.

4 Adding linear interest to the image. Now that your image is simplified, add linear details back into your image for more interest. Photoshop has several filters with which you can generate various kinds of line work, such as Accented Edges, Ink Outlines and Find Edges. For this image, Accented Edges is used. Make a copy of your Paint Daubs layer by dragging it to the Create a New Layer button in the Layers palette. From the Filters menu choose Filter > Brush Strokes > Accented Edges. For glowing light edges like those in the image above, increase the Edge Brightness to about 45 and then adjust the Smoothness to your taste. Set the Smoothness slider

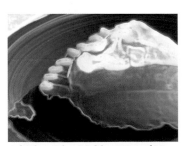

A higher Edge Width setting of 10 overpowers the image.

at a moderate setting like 5 to avoid jagged lines. Set the Edge Width so that the lines are thick enough to complement the image but not overpower it. (Try 3.) When you are pleased with the Preview image, click OK.

5 Blending the effects. Photoshop's Blend modes are extremely useful for blending layered elements with colorful transparency. To make the linear interest areas you created with the Accent Edges filter merge with the image and create a subtle look, try using the Luminosity Blend mode. Luminosity mode creates colors by using the hue and saturation of the underlying color and the luminance of the blend color. Other Blend modes—for instance, Soft Light and Hard Light—can also yield good results for a bright Pop Art look. Generally, Hard Light and Soft Light modes blend colors by darkening or lightening colors, depending on the underlying color value.

The Hard Light Blend mode yields bolder colors and darker shadows.

Good work! You've completed the steps for the featured Pop Art project. It's a good time to take a break, or you can leave your image open and continue on to the next page, where you'll learn about an additional technique.

Adding a Dark Linear Element to the Pop Art Image

The pie image with the Photocopy layer set to Vivid Light Blend mode.

Y ou can add filtered layers to achieve a variety of looks. To try out this concept, open the image that you created in Step 5 on page 34. You'll use the image as a starting point for this variation.

1 Copying the layer. The Paint Daubs layer has simple forms with broad areas of color and yields a pleasing image when combined with the linear elements produced by the Photocopy filter. Make a copy of the Paint Daubs layer by dragging it to the Create a New Layer button on the Layers palette. In preparation for the next step, set the Blend mode for the new layer to Normal.

A copy of the Paint Daubs layer before the Photocopy filter is applied.

2 Applying a Sketch filter. Select the layer copy and drag it to the top of the layer stack. Now choose Filter > Sketch > Photocopy. The objective is to achieve a strong line quality, without much texture in the image. (Try setting the Detail slider at 7, and the Darkness slider at 30.)

The Photocopy layer shows a nice line quality, achieved by using the settings above.

3 Setting the Blend mode. To achieve the result in the final image above, set the Blend mode for the new layer to Vivid Light. Generally, the Vivid Light mode blends by burning (increasing the exposure to darken) or by dodging (decreasing the light in areas for less exposure), depending on the colors in the blend layer and the underlying colors.

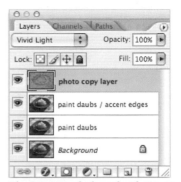

The Paint Daubs layer has been set to Vivid Light Blend mode and renamed.

Creating a
Pop Art Photo
Look in Painter

The images on this spread were inspired by Roy Lichtenstein, the eminent Pop Artist who often used half-tone dots in his work. He painted contemporary subjects including images inspired by comic books. In the first dot treatment, we'll use the appropriately named Pop Art Fill.

The first Pop Art image using the single layer with Pop Art fill, layered over the photo on the image Canvas. The Composite Method for the layer is set to Overlay.

1 Setting up layers. Open a photo in Painter. (For this image variation, I started with the adjusted photograph from Step 2). If the Layers palette is not open, open it by choosing Window > Show Layers. Place a copy of the image canvas onto a layer by choosing Select > All and then holding down the Alt/Option key and choosing Select > Float.

2 Applying the Pop Art Fill. You'll find a treasure trove of creative filters under the Effects menu in Painter. With the new layer selected in the Layers palette, choose Effects > Esoterica > Pop Art Fill. When the dialog appears, choose Image Luminance from the Using menu. To choose a new color for the fill, click the Dab Color swatch. When the Colors palette appears, choose a color (bright yellow-orange).

3 Blending the layers. To achieve the result in the final image above, set the Composite Method for the new layer to Overlay. The colors on the layer are combined with the Canvas colors and reflect the lightness or darkness of the original colors. Save your file in Photoshop format to preserve the layers. You will need them in the next technique. I named my file *Pie Pop Art Fill.psd*.

The original image of the pie.

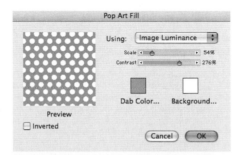

For small dots that fit the proportions of the pie image, try reducing the Scale from 100% to 54% and then set the Contrast at 276%.

The new layer is renamed Pop Art Fill Layer, and the Composite Method is set to Overlay in the Layers palette.

Using Painter for a Pop Art Graphic

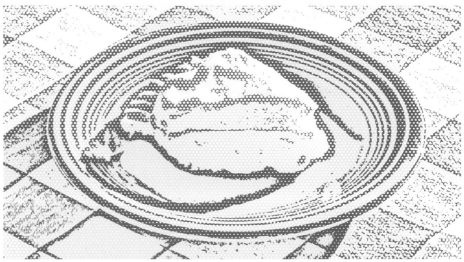

The contemporary Pop Art graphic on this page has a more linear look than the image on the left. I used Painter's Woodcut filter to create a line drawing and then composited this layer with the Pop Art Fill image from the facing page.

The final graphic Pop Art look, with the Pop Art Fill and Woodcut layers combined.

1 Creating a graphic variation. Begin this new image with the layered Pie Pop Art Fill.psd file from Step 3 of the facing page. Place a new copy of the image Canvas onto a new layer. Position the new layer above the Canvas and below the Pop Art Fill layer, and keep the new layer selected in preparation for the next step.

2 Building a line drawing layer. The Woodcut filter in Painter can create a black-and-white line drawing, which is ideal for this graphic effect. Now choose Effects > Surface Control > Woodcut. To create a black-and-white image, in the Woodcut dialog, deselect the Output Color check box. To reduce the texture and create smoother lines, try these settings: Black Edge: 40.09; Erosion Time: 20; Erosion Edge: 2.00, and Heaviness: 46%.

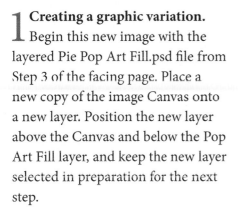

The Woodcut settings used for the drawing.

3 Combining the layers. To achieve the result in the image above, set the Composite Method for the Pop Art Fill layer to Hard Light to blend the layers. Hard Light mode multiplies or screens colors, using colors on the layer. The effect is dramatic with a black-and-white underlying layer like this one. Save your image. This file is named *Pop Art Woodcut. psd*. Good work!

The Pop Art fill layer is set to Hard Light mode.

Afternoon Light and Shadow Play

Using Filters for an Impressionist Watercolor Look

Photographs from the shoot. The photograph in the upper-right corner has good focus and an interesting composition—and is a good candidate for an Impressionist watercolor look.

Important ingredients for an Impressionist look include natural light, colorful shadows and an innovative composition. The composition and color in *Afternoon Light and Shadow Play* was inspired by the Impressionist style, and the image used came from a collection of late afternoon photos that were styled and shot at our rustic cottage. As you can see, the image in the upper-right is a good candidate because of the good focus, color and angled shadows.

In this project we will look at several Photoshop filters in detail and use them to build a watercolor look that includes texture and pencil sketch details. In conventional watercolor painting, I often begin by blocking in broad areas of color and tone using a large flat brush, leaving areas of white paper showing through to depict the brightest highlights. You can achieve a similar look using the process described in this lesson. The Palette Knife filter breaks up the image into broad areas of color that resemble puddles of paint. It also increases the contrast and creates white areas that enhance the look of the dappled light in a photograph. Then, Watercolor textures and details are applied to enhance the broad areas of color.

Two of my favorite Impressionist masters are Paul Cézanne—for his innovative composition—and Claude Monet—for his lively brushwork and sensitive color. (Look at the composition *Still Life with Fruit* by Cézanne, and *Still Life with Pears and Grapes* by Monet.) Plan your shoot for early morning or late afternoon to take advantage of the colorful long shadows, and arrange your items to build an interesting design. After downloading your images, view them at 100% to choose the best candidate. Now, let's get started!

Redesigning the composition to focus on interesting angles, shadows and objects to create a square format.

1 **Finessing a composition by cropping the image.** The original uncropped image in this project measures 2383 x 1544 pixels. If your file is larger or smaller, it may be necessary in Steps 3 and 5 to proportionately increase or decrease the settings in the Palette Knife filter and the Watercolor filter dialogs.

The photo above was saved in JPG format and was opened directly into Photoshop to begin the project. If you shot your images in Camera Raw, use the dialog to process your image. For information about using Camera Raw, turn to the Camera Raw sidebar on page 12 in Chapter 1.

Open your image in Photoshop. If your image is complex like the photograph above, you can create a simpler, stronger composition that will work better for a watercolor look by cropping it. In this image, the left side of the table with the cups and bowls and long shadows are good areas of focus.

For the purposes of this project, a square composition with an asymmetrical balance is used. The eye is drawn into the composition due to the strong diagonals of the table edge and the intriguing shadows leading off the table in a "V" from the lower-left corner of the image. The chair in the background, lit by the sunlight, helps the circular flow of the composition. Focusing on these elements in the photograph make it natural to create this unusual, square composition.

If your image needs cropping, choose the Crop tool in the Toolbox. Set the tool to its defaults by clicking the Clear button in the Options bar. Now, drag with the Crop tool to create a marquee around the area that you want to retain. When you have a composition that you like, double-click inside the marquee (or press the Enter or Return key) to accept the crop. Choose File > Save As and save your cropped image in PSD format, with a unique name so that you do not replace the original photo.

The new composition focuses on interesting angles and dynamic shadows.

The sketch built using the inverted Photocopy filter shows linear details.

2 Making a layer and generating a "sketch." In many of the projects in this chapter, detail is added near the end of the project, but in this project we start with a sketch, as many artists do when working with conventional media. For a nondestructive workflow, first, put a copy of the photo onto a layer, and rename this first layer Photocopy to reflect the filter.

Now you're ready to begin applying filters. The first filter, Photocopy, will transform the photograph into a white "sketch" on a dark background. With the new layer active, choose Filter > Sketch > Photocopy. Your image will appear in the Preview window, and it will be transformed dynamically as you adjust the settings. By default, the Photocopy filter creates edges around large dark areas, and the midtone values are translated to black or white. For this project, set the Detail slider at the minimum of 1 and the Darkness at the maximum of 50. To change the result into a black sketch on a white

background, choose Image > Invert, then choose Image > Adjustments > Auto Levels. The illustrations below show a comparison of Detail settings, after Image > Adjustments > Invert and the Auto Levels adjustments are applied. Click the eye icon to the left of the layer name to temporarily hide it while you work on the next step.

The Photocopy filter applied to the image, using a moderate Detail setting of 13 (left). The Detail setting of 1 yields a more linear result (right).

The photograph with the Palette Knife filter applied. The Photocopy layer is hidden in this illustration.

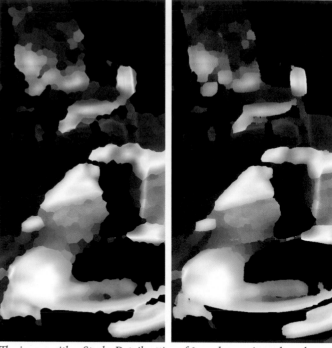

The image with a Stroke Detail setting of 1 produces a jagged result (left). The Stroke Detail setting of 3 achieves a smoother result (right).

3 Adding a layer and building broad areas of color. In preparation for the next step, put a new copy of the Background on to a layer by clicking on the Background layer and pressing Ctrl-J/⌘-J. Give the new layer a descriptive name to keep your file organized. Drag the new layer to a position under the Photocopy layer in the Layers palette. For this project, the second layer is renamed Palette Knife to reflect the name of the filter.

The Palette Knife filter transforms the photograph into broad areas of color. With the new layer active, choose Filter > Artistic > Palette Knife. Your image appears in the Preview window, and it is transformed as you adjust the sliders. You can adjust the sliders to your taste, but be careful of low Stroke Detail settings,

which can generate chunky blocks of color and jagged lines along curves (see the figure on this page). A higher Stroke Size setting will simplify the image and help to suggest large areas of paint that are applied with a palette knife or a large flat brush. The settings for this project are Stroke Size: 28, Stroke Detail: 3 and Softness: 5.

The adjusted Palette Knife filter layer has lighter midtones. The shadows now have a wider range of color and value.

The new layer with the Watercolor filter applied. The Sketch layer and Palette Knife layer are hidden in this illustration.

4 Making adjustments. The Palette Knife filter can intensify the contrast and shadows in an image. The photograph in this project already has dark midtones and shadows, and the deep valued areas are now darker. To create a lighter look overall, you can use a Levels Adjustment Layer. To make a Levels Adjustment Layer that will be grouped with and applied to the Palette Knife layer only (instead of the entire image), press Alt/Option, click the Create New Adjustment Layer button at the bottom of the Layers palette, and choose Levels from the pop-up menu. When the Levels dialog appears, lighten the midtones in the overall image by moving the middle Input slider to the left. Your image will dynamically update as you adjust the slider.

Using the middle Input slider to lighten the midtones.

5 Applying watercolor textures. Now that the photograph is broken up into large areas of color, add details and texture back into your image by using two different Watercolor filter layers. As before, click on the Background layer, press Ctrl-J/⌘-J to create another new layer and give your layer a descriptive name that will reflect the Watercolor filter to come (Watercolor Brush Detail layer for this project). Now choose Filter > Artistic > Watercolor. To achieve a smooth result similar to the look used here, the settings are Brush Detail: 8, Shadow Intensity: 0 and Texture: 1. When you are pleased with the Preview image in the Watercolor dialog, click OK. Drag the layer above the Palette Knife layer and turn off the visibility of the Watercolor layer for now.

Next, make another new layer from the Background layer. Position it above the first Watercolor layer in the Layers palette, and name it Watercolor Dark to reflect the settings to come. Choose Filter > Artistic > Watercolor,

The Watercolor Dark layer shows dramatic texture and darker details. In this illustration, the Blend mode is set to Normal.

Setting the Blend mode for the Watercolor Brush Detail 8 layer to Screen makes the image glow.

and when the dialog appears, use the filter to create darker shadows and texture detail using these settings: Brush Detail: 3, Shadow Intensity: 1 and Texture: 3.

Alternate watercolor looks. To finesse the watercolor look on your own images, experiment with the sliders in the Watercolor dialog. If you would like to achieve more detail, try a lower Brush Detail setting. See the comparison shown in these images.

The image on the left uses the Watercolor settings of Brush Detail: 1, Shadow Intensity: 1 and Texture: 1. For darker shadows and more texture, the image on the right uses Brush Detail: 1, Shadow Intensity: 8 and Texture: 3.

6 Blending the filtered layers. In this step, you will use Photoshop's Blend modes to combine the filtered layers into one beautiful image.

First, turn off visibility of all of the layers except for the Palette Knife layer, the Levels Adjustment Layer that is linked to it, and the Background layer. Set the Blend mode of the Palette Knife layer to Lighten to merge the broad areas of color in the Palette Knife layer with the photograph on the Background and create a subtle, lighter look. With the Lighten mode, colors darker than the blended layer color are replaced with a lighter value, and colors lighter than the blended layer color remain the same. The Lighten mode allows the puddles of color on the Palette Knife layer to replace areas of the photographic imagery for a more organic look.

Next, turn on the visibility for the Watercolor Brush Detail layer, and set its Blend mode to Screen. The Screen mode uses the nuances of the first Watercolor layer to

The visibility of the Watercolor Dark layer is turned on, and its Blend mode is set to Screen, yielding subtle texture.

The addition of the Photocopy layer with Blend mode set to Multiply and opacity reduced gives the image subtle linear detail.

enrich areas of the image, add a bit more detail and subtly lighten it. Now, turn on the visibility for the Watercolor Dark layer with the texture and set its Blend mode to Screen. This will add subtle detail and texture, and further lighten the image. You will notice that the dark detail areas in the image will be lightened and enhanced using the imagery in the layer.

Finally, turn on the visibility for the Photocopy layer, and set its Blend mode to Multiply. The Multiply mode will allow the white areas in the Sketch layer to appear transparent, and the underlying imagery will show through.

7 **Making final adjustments.** Now, make adjustments to your image that will finesse it. You can adjust the opacity of the Photocopy layer to your taste. In this project, the opacity of the Photocopy layer is reduced to 27%.

The Photocopy layer in the Layers palette with its Blend mode set to Multiply.

Finally, to suit the needs of your own photograph, experiment with the opacity of the Watercolor filtered layers and the Palette Knife filter layer. For this project, the opacity of the Watercolor Dark filter layer is set to 85%, whereas the Watercolor Brush Detail layer and the Palette Knife layer are set to 100%. Congratulations! You've completed this watercolor project.

Impression: Peace

Flexible Auto-Painting for an Impressionistic Treatment

Photographs from the shoot. The image in the upper-right is a good choice for this project because of its composition, and the sparkling light on the foliage and water.

In this project, we'll use the Auto-Painting system in Painter to build an Impressionistic treatment. In this technique, you'll use Auto-Painting to paint strokes of varying sizes onto layers and then combine them into one image by using masks.

While on a teaching assignment in Germany, I crossed the Rhine river to visit the historic city of Strasbourg, France, and photographed many of its magnificent buildings and parks. The photographs in this shoot were taken with a Sony Cybershot DSC-F505V camera with a Carl Zeiss zoom lens. My settings for the chosen photo are aperture: f/4, wide angle focal length: 7mm, shutter speed: 1/180, and ISO 100.

Compositional elements, such as the intersecting horizontals and verticals of the bridge and steeples (found in the image on the upper-right), are an example of classical composition using the Divine Proportion or Golden Section, in which a line or rectangle is divided into subdivisions; for instance, thirds or fifths. The horizontal line of the bridge is positioned at two-fifths and three-fifths. The vertical reflections on the water intersect the horizontal lines and lead the viewer's eye into the composition.

Impression: Peace was inspired by quiet walks along the Ill river that meanders through Strasbourg, and the work of the French Impressionist painter, Camille Pissarro. To get inspired before shooting, look at the paintings by Camille Pissarro such as *View from my Window, Eragny* and *Eragny-sur-Epte.* Pissarro often painted pastoral scenes, and usually began by roughing in a composition with loose, curved strokes applied from different directions. Then he painted smaller strokes on top to model the forms. When Pissarro sought more structure in his work, he experimented with Pointillism, a style that incorporates small over-lapping dots of paint. Now let's get started!

CP

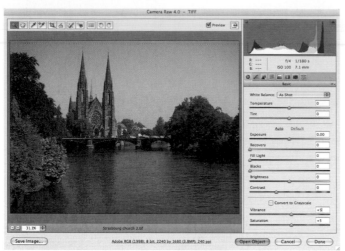

The photograph in the Camera Raw dialog with the adjustments applied.

The original photo (left). The image with Smart Blur applied shows less photographic detail (right).

1 **Making adjustments using Photoshop.** When you have chosen the image that you want, use the Camera Raw dialog to make adjustments in Photoshop. For more information about using the dialog, see the Camera Raw sidebar on page 12 in Chapter 1. To achieve brighter colors in the image in this project, increase the Vibrance and Saturation sliders to +5. You can preview the Highlights and Shadows to check their density. To preview them on your image, select the Highlights and the Shadows check boxes in the dialog to view the clipping warning. When you are satisfied with your image, click Open to open the image in Photoshop. The image for this project measures 2240 pixels wide. If your image is much larger, you will need to adjust the size of the brushes when using the Underpainting and Auto-Painting tools in Steps 2, 3, 4 and 5. Save your image using a new name to avoid replacing your original, and save it in Photoshop format for opening in Painter. This project uses the file name *Stras church sat.psd*.

2 **Simplifying and applying a vignette in Painter.** Open Painter and choose File > Open. Navigate to choose your photo and click Open. Open the Auto-Painting system palettes by choosing Window > Show Auto-Painting.

To make a clone image to use as a source for your painting, choose File > Clone and save your clone file in RIF format with a descriptive name by choosing File > Save As. (I named my file *Stras church underpaint.rif*.)

To build the underpainting, I used the Underpainting palette's Smart Blur feature to simplify the details in the photograph. Smart Blur lessens detail in the low-contrast areas, while preserving edges. (I set the Smart Blur slider to 75%). If your file is larger than 2240 pixels wide, you will need to increase the Smart Blur setting to achieve a similar effect. My image had good contrast and color so I left these settings as is. If you want to adjust the contrast or saturation in your image, use those sliders in the Underpainting palette. The preview will update on your

The image with the Smart Blur effect and the soft Jagged Vignette border applied.

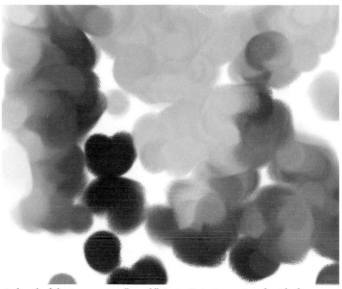

A detail of the in-progress "rough" Auto-Painting painted with the Captured Bristle using Color Variability and color from the Clone Source.

image. The illustrations on the previous page show the original image and the enhanced photo with the Smart Blur applied.

To apply a soft vignette to your underpainting, choose an option from the Edge Effect pop-up menu (I chose Jagged Vignette for this example) and then set the slider for your desired effect. (I set the Amount slider to 30%.) When your underpainting is as you like it, save your file.

The Underpainting palette with settings for the Smart Blur and Jagged Vignette.

3 **Roughing in strokes on a layer.** You can use Auto-Painting to build a hand-painted look. In this project you will use controls in the Auto-Painting palette to paint strokes of varying sizes and detail onto layers.

To set up your file for Auto-Painting, select your underpainting file and then choose File > Quick Clone. (The contents of the Canvas are deleted and Tracing Paper is enabled.) Choose File > Save As, giving it a descriptive name. I named my file *Stras church autopaint.rif*. So that you can see the strokes as they appear on the empty canvas, turn Tracing Paper off by pressing Ctrl-T/⌘-T.

Now, add an empty new layer to your file by clicking the New Layer button at the bottom of the Layers palette. At the top of the Layers palette, select the Pick Up Underlying Color check box and *make sure* that Preserve Transparency is disabled.

The renamed layer in the Layers palette. Pick Up Underlying Color is enabled.

The rough strokes are in progress in this illustration.

In this detail, you can see the final rough strokes on the layer.

Next choose the brush that you want to use for Auto-Painting in the Brush Selector Bar. I chose the Captured Bristle variant of Acrylics because it performs like a soft brush that smears subtly as the strokes are laid down. I customized it to incorporate Color Variability to add interest and expression to the image, and to make it look hand-painted. (Color Variability allows the Hue, Saturation and Value to vary with each stroke, within the range of settings that have been saved with the brush.) To add Color Variability to your brush, choose Window > Brush Controls > Show Color Variability. In the Color Variability panel, set the sliders as follows: H, 5%; S, 0% and V, 5%. In the Colors palette, enable Clone Color for the Captured Bristle by clicking the Rubber Stamp icon on the Colors palette.

Now, in the Auto-Painting palette, choose a Stroke style. For this example, I chose the Short Dab style for its natural look which would work well with the Captured Bristle brush. (This brush and stroke style is used throughout the painting process.)

For the rough stroke stage, I used these settings in the Auto-Painting palette: Randomness: 100% (applies strokes randomly for a natural look), Pressure: 100% (the amount of pressure applied), Length: 75% (the length of the strokes), Rotation: 180° (the rotation of the brush-strokes) and Brush Size: 100% (percentage of the actual brush size chosen). When the sliders are set, click the Play button (the small arrow) near the bottom of the Auto-Painting palette. You can click the Stop button or click in the image to stop the Auto-Painting process. Click the Play button again if want to add more strokes. When the rough painting is complete, save your file.

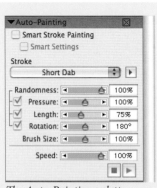

The Auto-Painting palette showing the settings for the Rough Strokes layer.

The medium strokes are applied to the new layer.

The finest strokes are applied to a new layer to build more detail.

4 Refining with smaller strokes on new layers. After the rough stage was complete, I added smaller brushstrokes. To begin this stage, add another new layer to your working file. (I named this layer medium strokes.) Set up the Auto-Painting palette to use a smaller brush size and to make shorter strokes, using these settings: Randomness: 100%, Pressure: 100%, Length: 75%, Rotation: 180° and Brush Size: 50%. With the sliders set, click the Play button, and then sit back and watch as Painter adds smaller strokes to the new layer.

The medium strokes are applied to the layer in this detail.

Now that the medium stage is complete, it's time to add even finer brushstrokes to the center of interest in your painting. To begin this stage, add another new layer to your working file. I named this layer Small Strokes. Next, set up the Auto-Painting palette to use a smaller brush size and to make shorter strokes, using these settings: Randomness: 100%, Pressure: 100%, Length: 50%, Rotation: 180° and Brush Size: 10%. Now that the sliders are set, click the Play button, and enjoy watching as Painter adds the finer strokes to the new layer.

The small strokes produce more detail, as shown in this example.

Painting the Small Strokes layer mask to cover the area around the center of interest with the church and bridge, revealing the Medium Strokes layer underneath.

In this detail, you can see the smaller strokes around the center of interest with the church and bridge and the larger strokes on the underlying Medium Strokes layer.

5 Combining imagery on layers using layer masks.
There are several ways to combine imagery on multiple layers, such as opacity, Blend modes and layer masks. For this technique I used 100% Opacity on all of the layers, Normal Blend mode, and masks on two of the layers. Take a good look at your image and decide which areas need detail and where you want the rough and medium strokes to appear. In this example, I began by masking areas of the Small Strokes layer so that only the center of interest, the church and a portion of the bridge and river, were shown with the smaller strokes.

Choose black and white in the Colors palette by clicking the back swatch (Additional Color) and choosing white in the Colors palette. Now, click the Main Color (the front

Black is chosen for the Main Color in the Colors palette.

swatch) and choose black. Target the Small Strokes layer and add a layer mask by clicking the Create Layer Mask button on the Layers palette. A layer mask filled with white will appear, click on the layer mask and you will see a black outline border appear around it.

Choose the Brush tool in the Toolbox, and in the Brush Selector Bar, choose the Airbrush category and the Digital Airbrush variant. (Use the Size slider in the Property Bar to size the brush to 100 pixels.) Paint on the layer mask by using the Digital Airbrush. As you add black to the mask, the imagery from the underlying layer appears.

In my image I wanted to hide portions of the Small Strokes layer to allow more of the brush work from

The Small Strokes layer mask is chosen in the Layers palette and is ready to paint.

In this example, the layer mask is painted on the Medium Strokes layer, to reveal the much coarser strokes on the underlying Rough Strokes layer.

You can see the larger, looser strokes on the foliage on the background and on the right in this detail.

the Medium Strokes layer to show through. To show only certain areas of the Small Strokes layer, activate it in the Layers palette and then click the Create Layer Mask button on the Layers palette. Using the Digital Airbrush, paint black color on the areas of the Small Strokes layer that you want to hide.

To reveal the larger, looser brush work on the Rough Strokes layer, target the Medium Strokes layer and add a layer mask. Decide which Rough Strokes areas that you want to reveal and paint those areas on the Medium Strokes mask. In the examples above, you can see the coarser strokes on the foliage on the edges of the painting. As you work

The Small Strokes layer mask with black paint. The Medium Strokes layer mask is now chosen in the Layers palette and is ready to be painted.

on the masking, you can move back and forth from the Medium Strokes layer and the Small Strokes layer to hide or reveal areas on the layers. (Remember to be careful to click on the layer mask thumbnail instead of the layer itself when switching between layers.) In the detail above, you can see the combination of small, medium and large strokes. When you're finished, save your file.

Good work! You've learned how to use Auto-Painting on layers to paint from your photo and how to combine layers with different stroke sizes into one image by using masks. Now, try the technique on a new image, using some of your own Auto-Painting settings.

The Small Strokes layer mask is chosen in the Layers palette. The black paint on the two layer masks hides those areas on the layers.

Maine Day in May

Simplifying a Photograph to Achieve a Hand-Rendered Result

Photos taken over two days offered a variety of choices. The lighthouse was a place I particularly liked, and I took the photograph with exactly this hand-rendered process in mind.

The realist Winslow Homer did not attempt to create precise detail in his works but instead chose to represent such things as leaves, cloth, plants, and wisps of hair with casual swipes of color, leaving these for the viewer to interpret. Complex details were reduced to larger fields of color and suggestive strokes, allowing the viewer's mind to fill in the missing information.

Simplifying a photograph to render a hand-rendered look does not require a perfect representation of the original, and not every image responds well to the process. While almost any photograph can render acceptable results, I prefer images of low-to-medium frequency for the simple reason that they respond more favorably to heavy applications of filters.

A chilly Maine vacation offered an opportunity to photograph many interesting places under a variety of conditions, many of which resulted in less-than-optimal quality. One sequence of shots provided excellent compositions, but the cloudy sky and lack of a tripod produced relatively poor exposures, void of vivid colors and perfect focus.

The shot of the lighthouse stands out as a good candidate for this process because of two key reasons: low frequency and a relatively small range of color. The low frequency prevents Photoshop's filters from becoming so noticeable, and the flaws from the poor shooting conditions are easily remedied using Camera Raw.

In most photographic settings you can shoot confidently using Aperture Priority mode, choosing to capture the depth of field and allowing the camera to determine shutter speed. In this circumstance, however, the camera required manual settings for both speed and aperture to capture the shot. The depth of field required a high f-stop and long exposure, but without a tripod any camera shake would throw the photograph out of focus. The neutral gray sky prevented me from increasing the ISO settings, because the higher it is set the more color noise is introduced, which is undesirable during this process.

Shooting with my Nikon D200, I left the ISO at 100 and selected my 17–85mm lens. An exposure of f/18 and 1/80 second was nearly two stops underexposed, just fast enough to stop the water motion.

The original exposure is nearly two steps underexposed. The neutral grays are highly susceptible to color noise.

The Camera Raw dialog showing basic adjustments.

1 **Opening the digital original.** The "as-is" exposure in the image above reveals a dark, low-contrast image. Highlight areas start in the low midtone range, with the fractal highlight at an extremely high 37%! An optimal starting point when opening the original in Camera Raw requires balancing three basic settings: exposure, brightness and contrast.

For this photo, using Camera Raw's Exposure and Brightness sliders is only subtly different. Increasing the exposure should be your first step. The Exposure slider is adjusted nearly one full stop, to +95. On a normal, full range exposure, changing the Exposure would affect highlights more than midtones and shadows, but because the highlights fall squarely in the midtone range the changes affect all tones equally.

Adjusting the Brightness slider to +.50 adjusts the range between the original highlight and shadow areas, resulting in greater midtone detail without blowing out either end. After this adjustment the spectral highlight (the whitest part of the image, usually a reflection) is considerably smaller than it would be if only the Exposure had been adjusted. A contrast adjustment of −4 improved the image by slightly reducing the difference between the dark and light ends. Later steps exaggerate the contrast of dark to light, so it is undesirable to have heavy shadow coverage at this point.

Noise suppression while opening the digital original is important and can even be used to soften the image prior to opening it in Photoshop or Painter. Gray is especially sensitive to color noise because it is made up of relatively equal values in each of the RGB channels. Brightly saturated pixels amongst neutral gray pixels stand out, and noise reduction techniques often produce blotchy grayish areas of color that are nearly impossible to eliminate.

Moving to the Detail panel, the Color Noise Reduction is set all the way to 100, whereas the Luminance is left alone to retain shape detail. With images that have less noise the noise reduction does not need to be so extreme, but even the best photos will most likely benefit from careful attention to the amount of noise.

Greater Color Noise Reduction can reveal distinctive stepping between colors and reduce smooth transitions between color fields. Because this has somewhat of a sharpening effect, and sharpening exaggerates noise, the sharpening slider is adjusted to zero.

The image is cropped and rotated at the same time.

Edits are painted directly onto the image.

2 **Cropping, straightening and original editing.** The first step once the file is open is to crop and scale it to the target output size, in this case 4200 x 3150 pixels.

Like many photographs, the horizon of the lighthouse photo requires a slight rotation. This is best done during the cropping process so that both can be done at the same time, resampling one time instead of two. Begin by opening your file in Photoshop. Select the Crop tool, and enter your desired dimensions and resolution in the Options bar, select a corner for your image and drag to the desired crop. Positioning the pointer slightly outside of the selection allows the image to be rotated, reverting back when the pointer is moved to a corner or inside the selection. When satisfied with the cropping, press Return. The cropped, rotated and scaled image now rests on a flattened layer titled background.

This is the optimal time to make large edits to add or delete elements within the image. The sign on the lighthouse door is eliminated by selecting the Eyedropper tool and clicking next to the sign to sample the gray color, then brushing over the area with the Soft Round 27 brush from the Brushes palette. The same process is used to roughen up the letters on the sign in the foreground.

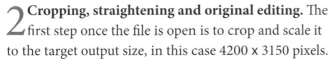 **Using Photoshop's Smart Objects.** Smart Objects are truly wonderful when used correctly. By making the background layer a Smart Object at the very beginning, then duplicating that layer when it is needed, future edits to the content of the Smart Object are automatically incorporated into each instance in which it is used.

To make the background a Smart Object, choose Filters > Convert for Smart Filters. Now, changes to this layer are done either by double-clicking on the layer on the Layers palette, or by using Layer > Smart Objects > Edit Smart Object. The Smart Object opens in a new window. Edit the layer as much as you like, then save and close the window.

Each instance of the layer is immediately updated, with the filter(s) applied. If you use this feature be sure to examine other layers and masks carefully to make sure no unexpected changes crept in!

Be careful not to expect to open files with Smart Layers in them using Painter. As of this writing, Painter does not support Smart Layers.

Dust and Scratches is applied to the Dust and Scratches 8/0 layer and set to Lighten mode on the Layers palette.

The Dry Brush filter produces a lot of painterly daubs, but lines such as the shadows between the planks suffer.

3 **Saving and applying layering effects.** Save the file by choosing File > Save As, and at the end of your file name, type the word *original.* Do this one more time, this time replacing *original* with *working.* This step ensures your access to the original file should you inadvertently alter the original working layer in future steps.

At this point you should have a single layer document, with the layer entitled *Background.* Rename this layer by double-clicking its title and typing *original.* Use Layer > Duplicate Layer to make a copy, then choose Filter > Noise > Dust & Scratches. Adjust the Radius slider to 8 and the Threshold to 0, then press Enter or Return. Dust and Scratches removes noise and small details without blurring the edges by averaging the colors in a given area, the size of the area determined by the Radius and the number of rendered colors by the Threshold sliders. On the Layers palette, set the Blend mode to Lighten and re-name it Dust and Scratches 8/0. Using the Lighten mode on the layer eliminates many of the original sharp, dark edges, softens the overall image and makes larger areas of pixels a more uniform color.

Once again, duplicate the layer titled original, then choose Filter > Artistic > Dry Brush. Setting a small

Brush Size (2), high Brush Detail (8), and the lowest Texture amount possible (1) results in a modified layer that does not look quite as computer rendered as it would with a bigger Brush size or higher Texture setting. Double-click on the layer's name and rename the layer Dry Brush 2/8/1. Because the Blend mode is set to Normal, it now becomes the lowest visible layer in the document, sitting above the original layer and below the Dust and Scratches 8/0 layer. The image has less detail and wider color fields than the original photograph. Save your file.

This comparison shows the difference between setting the Dust and Scratches on Normal (left) and Lighten (right) Blend modes.

Using Unsharp Mask produces a painterly white edge. A layer mask allows undesired white details to be reduced or eliminated.

A heavily blurred layer derived by combining all layers is set on Soft Light to produce a soft, watery effect.

4 **Softening and brightening.** A close look at a well done watercolor reveals how paper white is left when color fields almost butt one another, either by intent or accident. This effect is difficult to duplicate using Photoshop filters, so in an attempt to emulate it, select the Dry Brush 2/8/1 layer and copy it by choosing Layer > Duplicate Layer. Click and drag the layer's name on the Layers palette and drag it to the top of the stack. Choose Filter > Sharpen > Unsharp Mask, and drastically oversharpen. The sliders should be set to Amount:123, Radius:1.4 and Threshold:4. Again, in the Layers palette set this layer to Lighten. A white halo effect appears around different elements in the image. Rename this layer Sharpen 123/1.4/4.

Not all of the white detail on this layer is desirable. To remove unwanted white areas, apply a layer mask by clicking on the Add Layer Mask button on the bottom of the Layers palette. Choose a large, soft brush and paint black on the mask, eliminating excessive edges, especially around the windows and the waterline.

Finally, to soften the image and enhance colors, make a composite layer of the document by selecting the top layer and pressing Ctrl-Alt-Shift-E/⌘-Shift-Option-E. This merges every layer while keeping all the original layers intact. Apply a heavy blur to this new merged layer, somewhere around 40, by choosing Filter >Blur > Gaussian Blur. Rename the layer Gaussian 40, then set the layer mode to soft light.

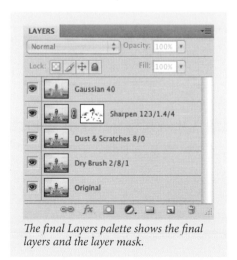

The final Layers palette shows the final layers and the layer mask.

Using Painter to Simplify a Photograph to Achieve a Hand-Rendered Result

The difference between the Camera Raw data (top) and the opened document (bottom).

The Smart Blur filter set at 50 preserves edges while reducing noise and excess details.

Painter often renders better results using high-frequency images than Photoshop by using this adaptation upon a process developed originally by Painter artist and developer John Derry. Images with lots of detail or noise tend to look overly filtered in Photoshop. This is also a danger to look out for in Painter, so resist the temptation to overindulge your filtering habit!

The source photograph for *The Mail Boat* shows how Painter's tools can be used to quickly produce pleasing results from an image that would not be as good a candidate for the Photoshop method of achieving a hand-rendered result.

1 Opening the document. The same issues of lighting, noise and gray balance as the lighthouse in the previous exercise exist in this original. Review Step 1 of "Simplifying a Photograph to Achieve a Hand-Rendered Result" on page 54. Instead of the settings used on the lighthouse image, increase Exposure to +1.4, the Brightness to +68 and the Contrast to +48. Open the image and then save the document in Photoshop's native .psd format.

In Painter, open your new .psd file by choosing File > Open. Resave it by selecting File > Save As, this time saving your document in RGB using Painter's native .rif format.

2 Shape simplification. Make any initial edits using the Chalk > Square Chalk variant. The dock was uncluttered by sampling nearby colors and painting directly onto the Canvas.

To make sure you have a ready copy of this "original," duplicate the canvas layer using Select > All and then Edit > Paste in Place. The new layer automatically becomes the target for editing.

Use the Window > Show Underpainting pop-up menu to open this powerful set of adjustment sliders. Set the Smart Blur filter to 50 to preserve edges while blurring fine detail and reducing the noise in the image.

The initial layer produced by the Woodcut filter.

The Glass Distortion creates nice edges and pencil like lines.

Adjusting Dye Concentration using Uniform Color creates global shifts in the image.

3 Adding non-photographic detail. Begin by using Select > All, then Edit > Paste in Place on your currently simplified layer. Choose Effects > Surface Control > Woodcut and deselect the Output Color check box. Set Erosion Time to 1, Erosion Edge to 2.0, and then move the Black Edge to a low value of 2.7. Adjusting the Heaviness slider upward increases the black coverage of the woodcut. Keeping the black coverage at 44% provides a good balance between too little and too many small details. The result is a relatively simple black-and-white layer without complex, distracting detail. Set the Composite Method to Multiply in the Layers palette.

4 Refining the linework with Glass Distortion. To refine the appearance of the Woodcut-generated linework, apply the Glass Distortion effect to very delicately thin them. Choose Effects > Focus > Glass Distortion and select Image Luminance from the Using pop-up. Select the Inverted check box to shrink the dark tonalities. With the Amount set to –.80, Variance to 1.0, and leaving the Direction at 0, move the Softness slider to 5.5. A higher Softness setting would not show any thinning, while too little forces the lines to become weak and ineffective. The Amount slider causes distortion so the lines are not quite aligned with color edges, so it should be used sparingly.

5 Adjusting color and contrast. At this point, you have two layers above the Canvas containing the original photograph: the Woodcut linework on top and the simplified color layer directly below. Select the simplified color layer. Choose Effects > Adjust Dye Concentration and set the pop-up menu to Uniform Color. Moving the maximum slider increases the amount of pigment present by multiplying existing values upon themselves. Darker areas will be affected more noticeably than lighter areas. For *The Mail Boat*, the maximum slider is set to 158%.

The image is finished, so go now and try out this technique on one of your own favorite images.

Sanctuary in Morning Light

Using Filters for a Realist-Style Oil Treatment

Photographs from the shoot. The photograph in the upper-right corner has dramatic lighting, graceful curves and rhythm. After the foreground values are adjusted, it will be a good candidate for a realist-style oil look.

The graceful curves in the foreground of *Sanctuary in Morning Light* lead the viewer's eye into the composition, and the repetition of the foreground shapes add rhythm and interest. Dappled light on the lawn and trees evokes an Impressionist feeling.

Sanctuary in Morning Light was inspired by my favorite French realist painter Gustave Courbet and the beauty of an early morning hike in La Jolla, California. For the chosen photo, I used a Canon EOS 20D camera set to Aperture Priority mode, with these settings: aperture f/11, shutter speed 1/250 and ISO 200. These settings produced a photograph that was underexposed in the shadows, which is corrected using an Adjustment Layer in this technique.

In this project we will look at two Photoshop filters in detail and use them to build a realist oil look with textural details. In conventional oil painting, I often begin by blocking in broad areas of color and value by using large brushes. You can achieve a similar look by using the Dry Brush filter to build broader patches of color for a look similar to a conventional palette knife or a dry flat brush. You can then use the Spatter filter for texture and detail.

To get inspired before shooting, look at the landscape paintings of Gustave Courbet, such as *The Grotto of the Loue* and *The Cliffs of Etretat*. Courbet favored dramatic scenes and sensuous shapes, such as the rounded foliage shapes and sweeping vista in the photo above. He applied paint using palette knives and brushes.

Plan your shoot for the golden hours of the very early morning or late afternoon to take advantage of the intense color and long shadows. Now, let's get to work!

The original photograph of La Jolla Cove.

The photograph is enhanced with brighter color.

1 **Finessing a composition by adding saturation.** The original photograph used in this project measures 2544 x 1696 pixels. If your file is larger or smaller, it may be necessary in Steps 2, 3 and 4 to proportionately increase or decrease the settings in the Spatter and Dry Brush filter dialogs.

The photo above was saved in TIF format and is opened directly into Photoshop to begin the project. If you shot your images in Camera Raw, use the Photoshop Camera Raw dialog to process your image. For information about using the dialog, turn to the Camera Raw sidebar on page 12 in Chapter 1.

For this project, a rectangular composition with an asymmetrical balance is used. The soft curves and diagonals in the foreground foliage lead the viewer's eye up into the focal point of the composition with the bright sunlight on the grass. The grassy area near the center of the image, lit by the sunlight, and the backlighting on the lacy trees in the upper-right help the circular flow of the composition.

Before beginning the filtering process, the colors are subtly brightened. The brighter colors add to the modern, painted look to come. The most flexible way to add saturation to the colors in your image is to use an Adjustment Layer. In the Layers palette, click the Adjustment Layer button, and choose Hue/Saturation from the pop-up menu. In the dialog, move the Saturation slider to the right (try 40%) to increase Saturation to your taste. The preview will update on your image. After clicking OK to accept the adjustment, combine the Adjustment Layer with the image by choosing Merge Down from the pop-up menu on the right side of the Layers palette (or by typing Ctrl-E/⌘-E.) So that you don't accidentally replace your original photo, choose File >Save As, and save a new version of the file, giving it a descriptive name.

The Dry Brush filter simplifies the image into chunky patches of "paint," as shown in this detail.

In this detail you can see how a coarse Spatter setting breaks up the image and adds texture.

2 **Making a layer and simplifying detail.** For a flexible work flow, first put a copy of the photo onto a layer. Click the Background layer in the Layers palette, and press Ctrl-J/⌘-J. A new layer, named Layer 1 will appear. Rename this first layer Dry Brush to reflect the filter setting, or give it another name of your choice.

Now you're ready to apply the filter. The first filter application, Dry Brush, will transform the photograph into simpler patches of color. With the new layer active, choose Filter > Artistic > Dry Brush. Your image will appear in the Preview window, and it will be transformed dynamically as you adjust the settings. By default, the Dry Brush filter simplifies photographic detail in the image by transforming it into chunky patches of paint, similar to those painted with a dry flat brush or a palette knife. For this layer, the settings are as follows: Brush Size: 5, Brush Detail: 7 and Texture: 1. The illustration above shows the result. Click the eye icon to the left of the first new layer name to temporarily hide it while you work on Step 3.

3 **Adding a new layer with textured "paint."** To continue working with a nondestructive workflow, place a new copy of the original photo onto a new layer. Drag this new layer above the Dry Brush layer. The next filter application will break up the photo and add texture.

With the new layer active, choose Filter > Brush Strokes > Spatter. To achieve a coarse, textured effect similar to the illustration above, set the Spray Radius slider at 20 and Smoothness to 6.

The Spatter filter applied to the image, using a Smoothness setting of 6 and two different Spray Radius settings: The left image uses a low Spray Radius setting of 5, whereas the image at right uses a Spray Radius of 20 for a coarser result.

A high Smoothness setting removes overall photographic detail, as shown in this detail.

The Coarse Spatter layer without the mask applied (left) and areas of the layer hidden by the mask to expose the Dry Brush imagery (right).

4 **Making a new layer and building up "paint."** In preparation for the next step, hide the Spatter Coarse layer. Now that your image is broken up into dabs of paint (on the first layer) and textured paint (on the second layer), add a new layer on which you have smooth details. Rename this layer Spatter Smooth to reflect the filter setting, or give it another name of your choice.

Now, you're ready to apply the filter. With the new layer active, choose Filter > Brush Strokes > Spatter. Your image will appear in the Preview window, and it will be transformed dynamically as you adjust the settings. For this layer, use only the Smoothness setting in the Spatter filter dialog to simplify the overall photographic detail. Try using a Smoothness setting of 15 and set the Spray Radius at 0. The illustration above shows the result. When you are pleased with the image in the Preview window, click OK.

Position the filtered layers to best suit your image; my layers are top to bottom: Spatter Coarse, Dry Brush and Spatter Smooth.

5 **Blending the layered imagery with layer masks.** Now that you have the filtered layers set up, you can add a mask to a layer and hand paint it to hide areas of the layer and reveal imagery on the underlying layers. A layer mask is a valuable tool for combining imagery on multiple layers into one image.

Carefully analyze your image and decide which areas of your Spatter Coarse layer that you want to hide. Open the eye icons to show all of your layers. Target the Spatter Coarse layer and add a layer mask by clicking the Add Layer Mask button on the Layers palette. Choose the Brush tool in the Tools palette, and in the Options Bar, choose the Soft 65-pixel brush tip. By default, a layer mask is white and shows all of the imagery on the layer. To make sure the default black-and-white colors are chosen in the Tools palette, click the tiny Foreground and Background Colors swatch or press the D key. Click on the layer mask and to display an outline border around it. Using the Brush tool, paint on the Spatter Coarse layer mask. In this example, the mask is painted to reveal the underlying

The image before the Dry Brush mask was painted (left) and areas of the layer masked to expose the underlying Spatter Smooth layer (right).

In this detail of the final image, you can see imagery from the Spatter Smooth layer, for instance, the brighter highlights on the trees and lawn.

highlight areas of the cliffs and the foreground foliage on the Dry Brush layer. To reveal areas of the Spatter Smooth layer (under the Dry Brush layer), the layer masks on both of the top layers are painted to reveal imagery below.

Which areas of the underlying Smooth layer in your image do you want to reveal? To reveal portions of this

Flexible editing with layer masks. For the most flexible work flow, use a layer mask to hide a portion of a layer rather than removing the area using an Eraser. To add a layer mask to a layer in Photoshop, select the layer and then click the Add Layer Mask button on the Layers palette. A mask filled with white appears to the right of the layer thumbnail. To hide a portion of the layer, paint with black on the mask; to reveal, paint with white. Painting 100% black on a layer mask completely hides that area of a layer, and lower percentages of black creates transparency. Layer masks work similarly in Painter.

layer, add a mask to your Dry Brush layer and paint on it to hide areas, as you did with the Spatter Coarse layer. Target the Dry Brush layer and add a layer mask. Click on the layer mask and then paint using the Brush tool with black color.

For my image, areas of the Spatter Coarse and Dry Brush layers are masked to reveal smooth details from the Spatter Smooth layer below, for instance, the glowing backlighting in the tree foliage and bright highlights on the lawn. The fence railing areas and the highlights on the cliffs are also masked. To remove some of the black paint on a mask, switch to white color and paint over the area. Good work! You have learned how to use filters to create a realistic oil look.

The final Layers palette showing the layer order and the Spatter Coarse layer mask targeted.

The Herald

Creating a Bold, Graphic Woodcut Look

Photographs from the shoot at Heidelberg Castle. The photograph in the upper-right has a good center of interest and is a good candidate for applying the Woodcut effect.

The bold, graphic look of the woodcut, a method of relief printing, has been admired for centuries. The woodcut process allows solid areas of color to be transferred from the block to the substrate, and depending on the amount of ink that is used and the amount of pressure that is applied while burnishing, interesting textured effects can also be achieved.

Using the Woodcut effect in Painter, you can simplify the colors and values in the photograph into linear elements and flat areas of color. As you'll discover in this project, creating a woodcut from a photograph involves selecting a suitable image, removing texture and detail, adding color and bringing a certain degree of detail back into the image.

The photo selected for this project comes from a photo shoot during my stay in Germany. I visited Heidelberg, where I enjoyed an exciting photographic journey in the town and the surrounding countryside. Some of the buildings within the historic castle are more than 600 years old. The historic Gothic and Renaissance period architecture, with the rich textures on the aged masonry, served as a great inspiration.

I planned a photo shoot at the castle for late afternoon to take advantage of the warm, golden light and longer shadows. I was hiking and traveling light, so I did not use a tripod on this shoot. Because I hand-held my camera, I used a quick shutter speed (1/200 sec and faster) to assure my images would be in focus. A faster shutter speed requires a larger aperture which may create a shallow depth of field, so I metered the light and bracketed during the shoot.

The photograph that I chose for this technique features a sculpted figure from the Renaissance period facade at Heidelberg Castle. I chose it, for the woodcut, because it had a strong center of interest and was without large areas of fine detail, such as tiny leaves. My camera settings for the chosen photo were ISO 100; f-stop: f/4; Focal length: 24 mm and shutter speed: 1/225 second.

In addition to this bold, graphic woodcut look, the Woodcut effect is also useful for adding textured details to images as shown in Step 7 on page 74 and for a sculpted look as described on page 76.

Now, let's begin with the project!

The original photograph.

Cropping the image around the arch.

The image needs tonal adjustments.

1 **Cropping in Photoshop.** The original uncropped image in this project measured 1680 x 2240 pixels. If your file is larger, it will be necessary in Steps 3 and 5 to proportionately increase the settings in Painter's Woodcut dialog.

Open your image in Photoshop. For a bolder, less cluttered design that would work better as a woodcut, you can further simplify the composition by cropping the image. In this image, the arch and the statue ornament are good areas for focus.

If your image needs cropping, choose the Crop tool in the Toolbox. Set the tool to its defaults by clicking the Clear button in the Options bar. Now, drag with the Crop tool to create a marquee around the area that you want to retain. When you are satisfied with the composition, double-click inside the marquee (or press the Enter or Return key) to accept the crop.

2 **Adjusting the tonal range.** You might notice in the cropped image above that the photograph needs more contrast and a broader tonal range. The Levels Adjustment Layer in Photoshop is a useful tool for making the tones less harsh.

To adjust the tones, click the Create New Fill or Adjustment Layer button on the Layers palette and choose Levels from the pop-up

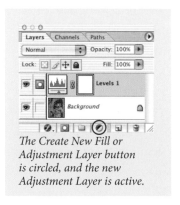
The Create New Fill or Adjustment Layer button is circled, and the new Adjustment Layer is active.

The image with tonal adjustment applied.

Detail of the adjusted image.

menu. In the Levels dialog, you will notice a histogram. If the Black Input and White Input sliders (circled) fall outside the edges of the histogram, drag them up to the edges of the black areas, which contain the image information. When you are satisfied with the preview of your image, apply the Adjustment Layer by merging it with the background (Ctrl-E/⌘-E). Choose File > Save As and save the file in PSD format.

3 Setting up layers in Painter.
Now that your image cropped and looking the way that you want, you'll switch over to Painter to create the Woodcut effect. This project describes creating a woodcut with black and color elements. In Painter, you can create a woodcut directly

on the background layer (called the Canvas, here), but the woodcut process is more flexible and easier to control when the black elements are on a separate layer from the color elements. This will allow you to edit each layer individually. Create two layers, which are copies of the photo on the image Canvas. (The two layers are simply copies of the image on the Canvas layer.) To create the first layer, choose Select > All, press the Alt/Option key, and then choose Select > Float. To create a layer for the second plate, choose Layers > Duplicate Layer. Now, you should have two layers in the Layers palette, that are exact copies of the original image.

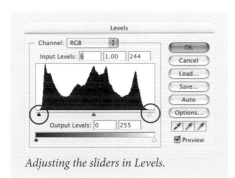

Adjusting the sliders in Levels.

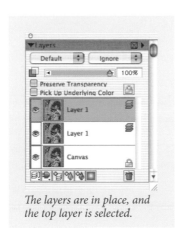

The layers are in place, and the top layer is selected.

The Woodcut dialog with settings for the Black Plate woodcut layer. The Black Edge is decreased slightly to retain detail.

Detail of the Black Plate woodcut layer with the layer viewed in Default Composite Method, showing the opaque white areas.

4 **Building the black wood block.** To begin making the black woodcut layer, make the uppermost Layer 1 active by clicking its name in the Layers palette. It's a good idea to rename your layer (Black Plate is used for this project). To access the Woodcut dialog, choose Effects > Surface Control > Woodcut. When the dialog appears, enable Output Black and disable Output Color. (The options for Output Color will now be grayed out.) For more detailed edges, adjust the Black Edge slider to the left. (This project

The top layer is renamed, and the black woodcut is applied.

uses approximately 37.29.) Also, try reducing the Erosion time from 4 to 2. This helps retain detail in the face of the statue.

When you've arrived at Woodcut settings that you like, you can save them for use on other illustrations. To save a preset, click the Save button near the top of the Woodcut dialog and when the Save

Preset dialog appears, name your Preset and click OK. The new Preset will appear in the pop-up menu at the top of the Woodcut dialog. Click OK to apply the Woodcut effect.

At the top of the Layers palette, set the Composite Method for the Black Plate layer to Multiply so that the white areas on the layer will appear transparent and the colored image on the underlying layer can be seen.

The Output Black settings. To learn how the Output Black sliders work, open an image, choose Effects > Surface Control > Woodcut and then select the Output Black check box. Using the Black Edge, you can control the detail of the black edges. A higher value builds simpler edges around elements, and lower values create complex detail. Erosion Time controls the erosion on the black edge (higher values produce a simpler result), whereas the Erosion Edge controls the smoothing of the black edges. (Higher values will make the black edges rounder.) To adjust the amount of black in the image, adjust the Heaviness.

Cleaning up areas of the black woodcut layer, shown in this close-up view. The black layer is viewed in Multiply Composite Method.

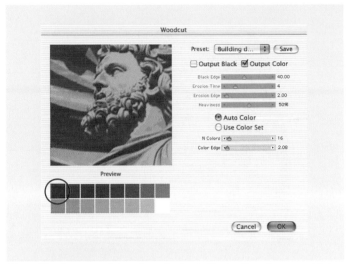

The red border around the selected color indicates the color you wish to use on the woodcut.

5 **Cleaning up the black layer.** The settings that worked well for the detail in the statue left black texture on the masonry arch. Removing the black texture from the archway would focus more attention on the statue.

If your black layer needs some touch-up work, choose the Smooth Ink Pen variant of Pens and then choose white in the Colors palette. Paint white over these areas. The Smooth Ink Pen paints with a crisp edge, which complements the appearance of the woodcut. The illustration above shows the in-progress woodcut image with the underlying color layer visibility turned on.

The Output Color controls. To use the Color Output settings, open an image, choose Effects > Surface Control > Woodcut, and select the Output Color check box. The Auto Color option uses the colors from the original image to build the colors for the woodcut. The Use Color Set button allows you to choose an existing color set. When using Auto Color use the N Colors slider to adjust the number of colors. To adjust the thickness of a color edge, click a color swatch and move the Color Edge slider.

6 **Building the color layer.** Now, you are ready to build your color woodcut layer. Turn off the visibility of the Black Plate layer temporarily by toggling its eye icon in the Layers palette. Next, click the underlying layer (the second copy you made in Step 3). Rename this layer Color Plate. Now choose Effects > Surface Control > Woodcut. This time, when the dialog appears, deselect the Output Black check box. The options for Output Black will now be grayed out. In the lower portion of the window, accept the default number of colors (16) and make the edges between the colors crisper by adjusting the Color Edge slider slightly to the left (a setting of 2 is good for this project).

When the edges are as you like them, you can change the colors by clicking on a color swatch from the selections at the bottom of the Woodcut dialog and then choosing a color in the Colors palette. (If the Colors palette is not open, choose Window > Color Palettes > Show Colors to open it.) The color in this project is "warmed" up by changing the colors to rusty browns. The highlight areas on the statue's face are also lightened for a more dramatic highlighting effect.

The in-progress woodcut showing the Black Plate layer cleaned up and the first woodcut color applied.

The in-progress woodcut showing the brighter, warmer colors applied to the image.

To select a color in the Woodcut dialog, click on it. You will see a thin red outline appear around the color. Now that it's selected, you can choose a new color in the Colors palette, and the swatch will change to the new color. To see other areas of your image in the Preview window of the Woodcut dialog, drag with the grabber hand pointer to move around the image preview. When you're satisfied with the colors, click OK to accept.

Click or drag in the Hue Ring to choose a new color.

7 **Adding more texture.** You might be satisfied with your woodcut at this point. However, this image, called out for subtle masonry texture. The texture to be added needs to be a subtle, translucent-nature solution, so it won't distract from the line work and flat color shapes. To add subtle masonry texture to your image, add a second black Woodcut layer. Target the Canvas and then choose Select > All. Press the Alt/Option key and then choose Select > Float to put a copy of the Canvas on a layer. Drag this layer to the top of the Layers palette list. Now, choose Effects > Surface Control > Woodcut to open the Woodcut dialog. In the Woodcut dialog, disable Output Color and enable Output Black. For a more detailed texture overall in your image, move the Black Edge slider to a setting of about 30. When you are pleased with the image in the Preview window, click OK to accept.

The texture layer in place with its opacity set to 100%. The Composite Method is set to Multiply to make the white areas appear transparent.

In this detail of the final image, you can see the masonry texture blended with the image. This was accomplished by reducing the opacity to 40%.

Now, to make the white areas in the layer appear to be transparent, set the Composite Method for the Layer to Multiply in the Layers palette. Your image may appear too busy with the texture layer at 100% opacity. So that the texture will become a subtle, supporting element, reduce the opacity of this new black layer to your taste. The opacity of the texture layer is reduced to 40% for the statue image.

The final Layers palette showing the additional texture layer with opacity set to 40%.

Congratulations, you've completed the project! You learned how to choose an appropriate image to achieve the best results using the Woodcut filter and how to adjust its tonal range with Photoshop. Using Painter's Woodcut effect in a creative way that employs layers, you applied unique settings and custom colors to your image. Now take a break to admire your work or move on to the sidebar on the next page, which demonstrates an alternative woodcut look.

Sculpting a Woodcut

In this variation of the image shown on page 60, I created an elegant, sculpted look, in contrast to the main project technique, which produces a result with linear elements and flatter color areas.

The cropped and adjusted photograph is ready for the Woodcut effect to be applied.

The in-progress image with new golden colors. The black plate is hidden.

1 Building the woodcut. Choose a photo with strong contrast and open it in Painter. (For this variation, the adjusted photograph from Step 2 on page 70 is used.) Copy the image Canvas to two layers for the woodcut, as you did in Step 4 on page 72.

Make the uppermost Layer 1 active and then choose Effects > Surface Control > Woodcut. When the Woodcut dialog appears, select the Output Black check box and then deselect the Output Color check box. For more detail, adjust the Black Edge slider to the left, as you did in Step 4 on page 72 (approximately 36.50 for this project.) To help retain detail, its a good idea to reduce the Erosion Time from 4 to 2. Leave other sliders at their defaults. Click OK. Set this layer's Composite Method to Multiply. Before you begin making

the color plate, toggle the visibility for the Black Plate layer off.

Now, set up the color layer. Target the underlying layer, and open the Woodcut dialog. Deselect the Output Black check box and select the Output Color check box. For crisper edges, reduce the Color Edge to about 2. Leave N Colors at the default. Now, click on the lightest color in the Woodcut dialog, and in the

Setting up the black plate for smooth edges.

Colors palette, choose a different hue but keep the value the same as the original. You can use the HSV readout in the Colors palette to check the Hue and Value as you work. To choose a new hue, click in the Hue Ring. Click on the next color swatch and edit its color to coordinate with the first. I set each of the colors to progressive values from bright gold to a rich brown.

Adjusting the range of colors for the woodcut.

The gold woodcut image with the black layer visible and set to Multiply.

The black is replaced by brown, creating a more graduated sculpted look, as shown here in the detail of the final image.

2 **Building a more sculpted look.**
Now that the black and color woodcut layers are in place, you can replace the black color and create an image with smoother transitions.

For this variation, integrate the imagery on the black layer with your image by changing its color from black to a rich, dark brown so there will not be a stark contrast. The dark brown in this image gives it a smoother, natural look that is less graphic. To select the black areas,

The selection highlights the black areas in the image so that you can replace them with color. The Auto Select dialog, ready to select the black on the layer.

choose Select > Auto Select > Using Image Luminance.

Now that the black is selected, choose a color that you want to use to replace the black. Next, choose Effects > Fill and then fill the marqueed areas with your new current color. (To make sure that the new color will complement your image,

Using the Dropper tool to sample a dark brown from the color plate layer.

sample a color from the color layer and then adjust its value to darken it.) After the area is filled, deselect the selection by choosing Select > None.

To complete the image, change the Composite Method for this upper layer to Saturation using the pop-up menu on the Layers palette. If you desire, experiment with different Composite Methods because Screen, Overlay and Soft Light can also produce intriguing results while preserving much of the color.

In this sidebar you learned how to further customize your woodcut images by editing the color of the black plate and by using different Composite Methods. Now, you can take a break or move on to the next technique.

**Subduing a Busy Background
and Adding Painterly Brushwork**

Photoshop **80**

Brushing in Sharp Focus

Photoshop and Painter **88**

3

EMPHASIZING THE SUBJECT

D o you have a photograph that has good content, but the background is distracting? This chapter shows how to improve composition design and focus more attention on your subject, using features in Photoshop and Painter to select the background and soften it. After finessing the composition, painterly brush effects are used over the image background and subject.

Subduing a Busy Background and Adding Painterly Brushwork shows how to improve the composition in a casual portrait and create a painting. A mask is built for the background, then the Lens Blur filter is used to soften the focus. Painterly brushwork and a border are added using the Art History Brush and Smudge tool in Photoshop.

Brushing in Sharp Focus demonstrates the process of adjusting the contrast and color in a casual portrait and then simplifying photographic detail with Smart Blur. Using a pressure-sensitive tablet and expressive Blenders brushes, the colors are smudged and pulled, to paint a border. Then sharper focus is brushed in and detail is restored on the subjects. Three creative variations for emphasizing the subject in Photoshop follow.

Jovial Street Musician

Subduing a Busy Background and Adding Painterly Brushwork

Photographs from the shoot in Strasbourg. The photograph in the upper-right has an intriguing circular composition, and its busy background makes it a good candidate for this project.

When doing a walk-around shoot in Strasbourg, France, I discovered a quaint outdoor restaurant with a lively and charming accordion player. The plaza was crowded, so I had to shoot photos quickly, composing intuitively and spontaneously.

I had only one lens with me, in this case, a 17–40mm f/4 L on my Canon 5D. The f/4 aperture did not allow for an extremely shallow depth of field that would let me easily focus on a portrait subject and softly blur the background.

The accordion player is a perfect subject for a casual portrait; he could have been a subject in a Franz Hals painting. Hals was a seventeenth century Dutch painter known for expressive portraits of people in their everyday lives. He often painted jovial, almost cartoonist expressions of personalities, using deft, nearly *ala prima* brushwork.

The busy image of the musician will be improved when the background is less distracting, so that the viewer can easily focus more attention on the musician.

To simplify the chosen image, I used the Lens Blur filter in Photoshop, a powerful feature that allowed me to build multiple planes of focus in my composition, and treat elements in the background as abstract shapes. After adding the blur, I used the Art History Brush, incorporating an artistic brush tip and stroke style to paint over the photograph, and then added an irregular border to complete the image.

After you download your photos, choose the best candidates from the shoot. To check the focus of your images, it's a good idea to view then in Camera Raw at 100%.

The photograph before the adjustments were made in the Camera Raw dialog. The Rotate Image 90° Clockwise button is circled.

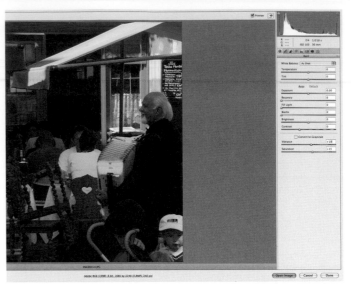

The Camera Raw dialog shows the image rotated, and with increased vibrance and saturation.

1 **Making adjustments in the Camera Raw dialog.**
Now that you have chosen a photo from the shoot, use the Camera Raw dialog to make adjustments prior to working in Photoshop. See the Camera Raw sidebar on page 12 for more information about using the dialog. The image for this project is adjusted to achieve bright, saturated colors by increasing the Vibrance to +10 and the Saturation to +15. The image is then turned into a vertical format by clicking the Rotate Image 90° Clockwise button at the top of the dialog.

When you are satisfied with your image, open the image in Photoshop. The image for this projects measures

 Preserve your original by opening a copy in Camera Raw. Never modify an original photo; instead open a copy. Press the Alt/Option key to temporarily convert the Open Image button in the Camera Raw dialog to Open Copy. Always remember to archive the original photos and working files on removable media. Should an accident happen with your computer, you'll be glad that you did!

2240 x 1680 pixels. It's important to preserve the original photo by choosing File > Save As, and then giving the working image a new descriptive name.

Opening JPG files in Camera Raw. As you can see, the Camera Raw dialog offers a wealth of pre-processing tools for your photos. Some digital cameras capture photos in only JPG format. You can set the Adobe Photoshop > Preferences > File Handling dialog in Photoshop CS3 and later to open JPG files using Camera Raw. Select the Prefer Camera Raw for JPG Files check box.

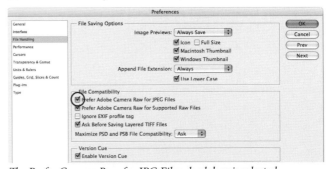

The Prefer Camera Raw for JPG Files check box is selected.

The adjusted image of the musician shows the brighter colors.

Using a large, soft brush tip and black color to begin painting the mask, which isolates the musician from the background.

2 **Putting the image on a layer.** For a flexible, non-destructive workflow, put a copy of the image on to a layer. Click on the Background layer and press Ctrl-J/⌘-J, and a new layer labeled Layer 1 appears in the Layers palette. To keep your file organized, it's a good idea to give the layer a descriptive name. To rename the layer, click the layer name and when a cursor appears, type the new name. For this project, the first layer was named Musician Focus to reflect the use of the layer to come.

The renamed layer in the Layers palette. The Create a New Layer button is circled.

3 **Making a mask for the musician.** To simulate a shallow depth of field, a selective Lens Blur filter will be applied to the layer in Step 4, and only the musician will remain in focus. To prepare for the blur, a silhouette mask is needed to isolate the musician from the busy scene. My favorite method for an organic subject like the accordion

The Quick Mask mode is active in the Toolbox, and the Brush tool is chosen.

player is to use the Quick Mask feature to paint a mask and then save it as a channel. Quick Mask provides a transparent orange overlay that makes it easy to see the image underneath as you paint the mask. When the Quick Mask is complete, it will be turned into a selection and then saved in the Channels palette as a silhouette mask. Choose the Brush tool in the Toolbox, and a large soft Brush Preset Picker. (I used the 65-pixel and 100-pixel brush

A small soft-edged brush is used to finesse the edges of the Quick Mask. This illustration shows the completed Quick Mask.

The Lens Blur dialog with the settings for the silhouette. The More Accurate button is enabled to generate the final version of the image.

tips to paint larger areas and small, soft 10–20 pixel brush tips to finesse the edges.) Make sure that the colors are set to the default black (foreground color) and white (background color) for an opaque mask. Shades of gray will yield a semitransparent mask. Now click the Quick Mask button near the bottom of the Toolbox. Use the Brush tool to paint the mask, using black to add to the mask and white to remove the mask. When the Quick Mask is completed, click the Quick Mask button to convert it to a selection, and then choose Select > Save Selection to save it as a mask channel in the Channels palette. In the Save Selection dialog, select Save as New Selection, and then name it Silhouette. If the Channels palette is not open, choose Window > Show Channels.

4 **Adding selective focus with Lens Blur.** The Lens Blur filter lets you achieve the look of a shallow depth of field—and different planes of focus can be incorporated into one image. You can use selections, layer masks and alpha channels as depth maps. The black areas of a channel will yield sharper focus, and the white areas will have more blur, as if they are in the distance. To apply Lens Blur to the active layer, choose Filters > Blur > Lens Blur. For quicker previews when experimenting with the settings, click the Faster option. Next, under the Depth Map menu, choose the channel you made in Step 2. The Blur Focal Distance slider controls the depth of the pixels in focus (try 56). To add more blur, adjust the Radius slider (try 20.) Because the blurred areas become smooth, you may want to adjust the Noise Amount slider (for a subtle look, try 3.) Save your image after this Step, using a descriptive name. This project uses *Musician Lens Blur.psd*.

The working image with Lens Blur applied. You can see the subtle plane of focus on the musician and the subtle noise.

In this detail you can see the oily Art History brushwork. Large Spatter brushes are used on the canopy and the other background elements.

5 Adding brushwork with the Art History brush.

More attention is focused on the subject, and the image is now less busy, but I wanted a painterly look. With your pressure-sensitive tablet and stylus and the Art History brush, you can easily apply expressive strokes.

Begin by choosing the Art History Brush in the Toolbox. The Art History Brush uses a snapshot or history

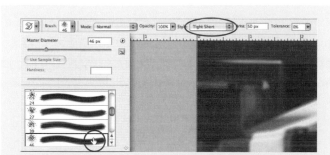

Choosing the Spatter 46 brush preset from the Brush Preset menu. The Style pop-up menu is set to Tight Short.

state as source material, in combination with a Brush Preset and Style, along with other choices in the Options bar. Choose a Brush Preset from the pop-up menu on the Options bar. (This project uses the Spatter preset in various sizes.) Then choose a Style. (Tight Short is used here.)

The Musician Focus Copy layer is active and ready.

For utmost flexibility, copy the blurred layer by pressing Ctrl-J/⌘-J. Applying brushwork to the layer copy allows you to start over, if needed, or

Smaller, detailed brushstrokes are painted on the musician, and larger, looser brushwork is used on the supporting elements and background.

The full working image. You can see the simplified shapes and looser brushwork, combined with the tighter expressive strokes on the subject.

use a layer mask to hide areas of the painting if you want to show portions of the blurred layer underneath.

Next, open the History palette by choosing Window > History, and from the pop-up menu on the palette, choose New Snapshot. In the From pop-up menu, choose Current Layer as the source for your snapshot. The blurred imagery you created will lend itself well to the Art History Brush. Using your stylus, gently stroke

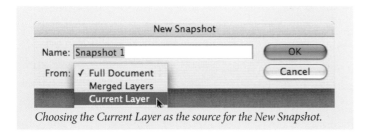

Choosing the Current Layer as the source for the New Snapshot.

along the direction of the forms. Use a larger brush size for the background imagery and for supporting elements that need less detail. (Try the Spatter 46-pixel brush tip.) Switch to a smaller brush—a 10–20 pixel brush tip works well for the main subject and the details.

The completed final image shows the intriguing circular composition, with the viewer's eye entering at the bottom right and traveling up to the left and then around to the musician. The playful brushwork adds movement, texture and interest to the composition. Choose File > Save As and name the file with a descriptive name. (The image for this project uses *Musician Paint.psd.*)

Painting short, dubbed strokes with the Art History Brush along the edge of the image border.

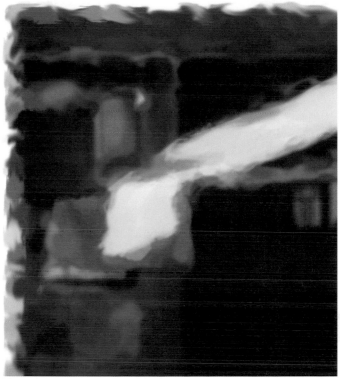

Using the Smudge tool to smooth the textured Art History Brush strokes along the border.

6 Adding a painted border. To enhance the painterly look, use the Art History Brush to paint an irregular border with interesting brushwork.

To begin the border, choose Image > Canvas Size, and in the Canvas extension color pop-up menu, choose White. Add equally to the width and height of your image by selecting the Relative check box. (Two inches were added for this project.) Save a new version of the file using File > Save As. (This project uses *Musician Paint Border.psd.*)

Next, take a new Snapshot of current layer, as you did in

Set the anchor at center in Canvas Size.

Step 5. Choose the Art History Brush, a medium-sized tip (try the Spatter 46-pixel), and the Tight Short Style used in Step 5, and then paint short strokes from the image out toward the border, along the edges as shown in the left illustration above.

After brushing the irregular edge, use a small, soft-tipped Smudge tool and your stylus to soften the strokes to blend them with the brushwork. The Smudge tool smears and pulls existing color. Choose the Smudge tool in the Toolbox, make sure that Finger Painting is disabled in the Options bar, and gently brush over the Art History Brush strokes that you painted along the edges, until you are satisfied with the result. The entire completed image can be seen on page 80. Congratulations! You've completed this project. The next technique uses Painter to create a soft look with sharp focus on the subject.

Summer Afternoon Play

Brushing in Sharp Focus

Here are a selection of photographs from the shoot. The subjects and lighting in the photograph in the upper-right make it a good candidate for a photo-painting in Painter.

The composition, color and lighting in *Summer Afternoon Play* were inspired by the Impressionist and Realist styles, most notably the work of favorite Spanish master Joaquin Sorolla y Bastida. Sorolla painted portraits, beach scenes and landscapes, and captured the striking golden sunlight of Spain.

Up in Laguna Beach at a surfing event, I shot candid portraits during breaks in the surfing action. As you can see, the image in the upper-right is a good candidate for an impressionist image because of its lively subjects, the compelling backlighting and highlights, good color and lovely water reflections.

The original image needed warming up, a bit more color saturation and contrast. You can achieve these enhancements using Camera Raw before opening the image in Photoshop and then saving it for working in Painter. After opening the image in Painter and making a clone, the overall clone image is softened using the Smart Blur. After these adjustments, I used my Wacom tablet and pen and the expressive Blenders brushes in Painter to pull and move the colors and to paint the irregular border for the image. Finally, I brushed in sharper focus and restored detail to the center of

interest which, in the case of this image, is the little girl's face.

To get inspired before shooting, look at the compositions in the beach scenes and portraits of these favorite master artists: *Walk on the Beach* and *Beach at Valencia* by Joaquin Sorolla, and *The Beach at Trouville* and *Camille at the Beach at Trouville* by Claude Monet. Plan your shoot for early morning or late afternoon to take advantage of the more colorful long shadows. Now let's get started!

The photograph before the Camera Raw adjustments are applied.

The photograph with the contrast and color adjusted in Camera Raw.

1 **Making adjustments to your photo.** Now that you have chosen a photo from the shoot, you can use the Camera Raw dialog in Photoshop to adjust the color and contrast prior to working in Painter. See the Camera Raw sidebar on page 12 for more information about using the dialog.

The image for this project is adjusted to achieve brighter, warmer colors and more contrast. Also, the photo is warmed by setting the Temperature slider at +8 and the Tint slider at –1. Brighter colors are achieved by increasing the Vibrance to +15 and the Saturation to +15. Contrast is increased by adjusting the slider to +25.

When you are satisfied with your image, press Alt/Option and click Open to open a copy of the image in Photoshop. The image for this project measures 2544 x 1696 pixels. It's important to preserve your original photo by choosing File > Save As, and giving the working image a new descriptive name.

Color and tonal adjustments in Painter.
In Painter, you can make color adjustments using several useful features, including the Effects > Tonal Control > Adjust Colors and Correct Colors dialogs. However, the Underpainting palette (Window > Show Underpainting) offers more intuitive controls for artists. You can preview color and tonal adjustments on your image in real time as you adjust the sliders. The adjustments are "live" and are applied to the image when the Apply button is clicked. The Underpainting palette also offers controls for applying Smart Blur, Edge Effects and more.

Adjusting the Contrast and Saturation sliders in the Underpainting palette.

This example shows the 100-pixel border applied to the image.

You can see the Smart Blur applied to the clone in this detail.

2 **Preparing the image and blurring a clone.** Navigate to the image that you adjusted in Photoshop, and open it in Painter. Add a white border to the image by choosing Canvas > Canvas Size and then adding 100 pixels to each of the fields. You can see the image with the border added above. The white border is used later in the process when painting an irregular edge around the image. Save a new version of the file in Photoshop format (This image is titled *Girls Painter Border.psd*.)

Next, make a clone of the image with the border. The blur effect will be applied to this clone. When you choose File > Clone, a copy of the image is created, with a link to the source file that allows you to restore imagery from the source file. All of the images in Steps 2–4 are the same size so that cloning can be used with these multiple files in later steps. In preparation for the softening, choose File > Save As and name the clone a descriptive name. (This project uses *Girls Painter Blur.psd*.) The Smart Blur feature on the Underpainting palette offers an intuitive method for softening photographic detail. Open the Underpainting palette by choosing Window > Show Underpainting. With the clone image active, move the Smart

Blur slider to the right. For my 2240 x 1680 pixel image I used 75%. Click the Apply button to accept the Smart Blur. For this image, I did not make other adjustments in the Underpainting palette. To learn more about the Underpainting palette features, see page 90. Make sure to save the file before moving on to Step 3.

 Using Smart Blur. In Painter you can use the Smart Blur slider on the Underpainting palette to quickly simplify fine photographic detail. Smart Blur softens the low-contrast areas while preserving edges in the high-contrast areas. The effect is "live" and adjustable until you click the Apply button to accept the setting. Here are two examples.

The Smart Blur effect is applied to the image, using a moderate setting of 25% (left) and the maximum setting of 100% (right).

In the white water and the water reflections, you can see the brushstrokes applied with the Just Add Water and Oily Bristle variants of Blenders.

The subtle, loose brushwork applied with the Smooth Blender Stump variant of Blenders can be seen on the girl's T-shirt.

3 **Applying loose brushwork to the image and border.** Painter offers a wealth of natural media brushes that work especially well with a pressure-sensitive tablet. Take a good look at your subject and decide how the movement of your strokes will go. In this case, I brushed along with the motion of the water. If you have solid forms in the background of your image, loosely paint over the forms, letting your brushstrokes follow the shape and direction of the forms. For this image, I began by loosely brushing over the background water and waves using medium-to-large-sized Blender brushes (20–60 pixels) to paint over the shapes. Choose the Oily Blender variant of Blenders in the Brush Selector Bar. The Oily Bristle brush will smear and move existing color, and add subtle bristle marks, without applying new color. The Soft Blender Stump and Just Add Water variants of Blenders are also excellent choices for smearing color, applying brushwork and achieving a smooth surface similar to conventional watercolor on smooth paper.

To paint the irregular border, use short, dabbing strokes to pull and smear color from the image into the white border, as shown in the illustration above.

For the figures, I let my brushstrokes follow the direction of the forms, paying careful attention to preserve the beautiful light on the folds of the girl's T-shirt, and the backlight on the edges of the figures.

Check to make sure that no pixels are left from the original photograph. Zoom in to 200% using the Magnifier tool chosen from the Toolbox. Switch to the Grabber tool, and pan around your image. If you want to touch up the brushwork, switch back to the Brush tool and Blenders brush category and then use your stylus to paint over the area. When you have painted loose brushwork over your image, save a new version of the file. I named my file *Girls Painter Paint 1.psd*. In preparation for the next step, save a new version of your file. (This project uses *Girls Painter Paint 2.psd*.)

In this detail, you can see the painted highlights on the girls' hair. Detail needs to be added back into the girl's face.

Brushing focus and detail back into the girl's face, using the Soft Cloner variant of Cloners, chosen from the Restoration palette.

4 Brushing in sharp focus and painting details. At this stage, the entire image is now painted with loose brushwork. Take a good look at your image. Where would it benefit from having more detail or sharper focus?

In this case, I wanted to brush sharper focus into the little girl's face, so I used the Soft Cloner variant of Cloners to restore imagery from the adjusted photograph saved in Step 1. Open the Restoration palette by choosing Window > Show Restoration. To quickly choose the Soft Edge Cloner brush, click its button in the Restoration palette. (Clicking the button chooses the Soft Cloner variant of Cloners in the Brush Selector Bar.)

The Soft Edge Cloner brush can easily be chosen by clicking its button in the Restoration palette.

Make sure the following images are open, as you will need to use them as clone source files in this step to refine your image:

Image adjusted in Camera Raw in Step 1, image blurred in Step 2, and earlier painted stage from Step 3. Now choose a clone source, by choosing File > Clone Source and then choosing your image from Step 1. Now that you have the clone source selected, use the Soft Cloner to brush in sharp focus and to subtly restore details in the center of interest. To change the brush size as you work, use the Size slider in the Property Bar. Remember not to restore too much photographic detail, or your image will look more like a photo than a painting. If you restore too much, you can switch the clone source by choosing File > Clone Source, choosing the blurred clone, and then restoring some of the blurred imagery. If you want to add more brush detail, you can switch back to the Blenders category and choose a small Just Add Water Blender brush or Oily Bristle brush to finesse details.

Good work! You explored the Smart Blur feature in Painter, Blenders brushes and how to restore focus. Now you can take a break or continue to the next project.

Nondestructive Dodging and Burning

In a traditional darkroom, using a mask or small piece of paper to block light from a print is known as dodging. The area of the print will appear lighter, as it is exposed to less light. Burning is exposing an area to more light, causing it to be darker. Here you will use a layer and the Dodge and Burn tools in Photoshop to nondestructively brighten and darken areas of a photo.

The original photo of Joy, Brady, Brooke and baby Morgan. As you can see, Brady's face is in shadow and would benefit from dodging.

1 Choosing a photo. In the image above, the boy in the foreground is in shadow. The image would be improved if his face were subtly lightened. Also, the other subjects' faces would benefit from being subtly lightened. A few areas in the foreground would be less distracting if they were darkened. In this project, we will selectively brighten and darken areas without altering the photograph.

2 Setting up a dodge and burn layer. Choose a photo and open it in Photoshop. If the Layers palette is not visible, open it by choosing Window > Show Layers. To set up a layer for dodging and burning, hold down the Alt/Option key and click the Add a New Layer button on the Layers palette. The New Layer dialog will appear. Set the Mode pop-up menu to Overlay and enable the Fill with Overlay-neutral color (50% gray).

3 Using the Dodge and Burn tools on the layer. You will use white paint to "dodge" and black paint to "burn" on the new layer created in Step 2. In Overlay mode, the gray-filled layer appears as "clear," allowing you to see the underlying image. Painting with white on the layer will

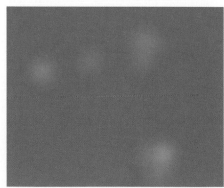

Dodging on the Overlay layer using white and a soft 300-pixel brush is shown in this detail.

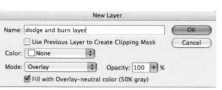

Setting up the New Layer dialog.

The edited photograph with faces subtly lightened using the Dodge tool and the foreground distractions darkened with the Burn tool.

lighten the underlying image, and painting with black will darken the underlying image. Press the D key to return the foreground and background colors to black and white, and then press the X key to reverse them, making the foreground color white.

To dodge, or brighten an area, choose the Dodge tool in the Tools palette and choose a large, soft brush

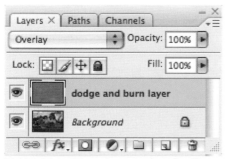

The Dodge and Burn layer is selected in the Layers palette and is set to Overlay mode.

tip from the Brush Preset Picker in the Options bar. Set the Exposure at 3–10 percent so you can build up color slowly. (I used a soft 300–400 pixel brush tip at 3–5 percent Opacity on my 3504 x 2336 pixel image.)

Before you begin dodging, make sure that the Dodge and Burn layer is chosen in the Layers palette, and then paint lightly to brighten the area slowly. You will see the effect on your image. (I lightened the right side of Brady's face and cheek, and his forehead. Then I subtly brightened the other faces.)

To burn or darken an area, exchange the foreground color from white to black by pressing the X key. Choose the Burn tool (it's nested with the Dodge and Sponge in the

Tools palette) and paint soft black strokes in areas that you want to darken. In my image, the highlights on the blanket in the foreground were distracting, so I darkened them. I also subtly darkened Brady's lower arm and the shoulder of his shirt.

Good work!! You've learned how to enhance your images with nondestructive dodging and burning.

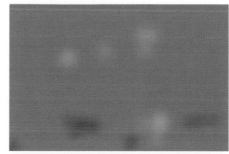

Burning on the Overlay layer using black and a soft 300-pixel brush.

Enhancing the Subject Using Saturation

By adjusting the background color, you can focus more attention on your subject. Bryn and her father, Michael, are candidly photographed in front of the hills and ocean on a cool winter morning. To focus more attention on the subjects, try desaturating the background.

A Hue/Saturation Adjustment Layer is used to desaturate the background and focus more attention on the subjects.

1 **Opening a photo and putting the subject on a layer.** Open a photo in Photoshop. To prepare for desaturating the background, make a silhouette selection around the subjects in your image using the selection tools in Photoshop. In the case of this image, I used the Magnetic Lasso and Lasso tools to make a selection. To make the edge of the selection seamless, give it a small feather by choosing Select > Modify >

The active selection border around the subjects

Feather (I used a 2-pixel feather on my 2544 x 1696 image.) With the selection active, press Ctrl/⌘-J to put your feathered selection on a layer. Prior to applying the Adjustment Layer, copy the Background layer by dragging it over the Create a New Layer button on the Layers palette.

The Background Copy layer is selected in the Layers palette.

2 **Applying an Adjustment Layer.** Using an Adjustment Layer allows you the flexibility to try out different settings and view them on your image. Target the Background layer, click the Create New Fill or Adjustment Layer button on the Layers palette, and choose Hue/Saturation from the pop-up menu. In the dialog, move the Saturation slider to the left to desaturate. (Try –60.)

Detail of the final image with the subtly desaturated background.

Sepia-Toning a Background

To emphasize a subject and warm up the background, you can use a variation of the desaturation technique to apply a sepia-tone effect to the background of your image. The sepia-tone adds a warmer feeling to my photo that was shot on a cool, overcast morning.

A Hue/Saturation Adjustment Layer is used to desaturate the background and apply a warm, subtle sepia tint.

1 **Opening a photo and putting the subject on a layer.** Choose a photo and open it in Photoshop. Use the Lasso or other selection tools to select your subject as you did on page 96. Then choose Select > Modify > Feather to give it a soft edge so it will blend seamlessly with the background. (Once again, I used a 2-pixel feather on my 2544 x 1696 image.) With the subject selected, press Ctrl-J/⌘-J to put your feathered selection on a layer. Prior to applying the Adjustment Layer, copy the Background layer by dragging it over the Create a New Layer button on the Layers palette. In the case of this technique, making your adjustments to a Background layer copy gives you more flexibility.

2 **Applying a sepia-tone with an Adjustment Layer.** Clip the Adjustment Layer to the Background copy layer so the result will apply only to it. Click on the Background Copy layer to select it, press the Alt/Option key and click the Create Adjustment Layer button. In the pop-up menu, choose Hue/Saturation. To use the previous layer to create a

The Hue/Saturation Adjustment Layer is clipped to the Background copy layer.

clipping mask, select this check box and click OK. In the Hue/Saturation dialog, select the Colorize check box in the lower-right corner. By default, the Hue slider jumps to 0 (a reddish-brown) and the Saturation jumps to −25. My image needed a subtle look, so I reduced the Saturation to −5.

Good work! You have learned new ways to emphasize your subject.

Detail of the final image with the warmer sepia-toned background.

Taming the Art History Brush

Photoshop **100**

Creating a Dry Media Textured Look with Pastels

Photoshop and Painter **110**

Painting a Textured Black-and-White Study

Photoshop and Painter **118**

4

ADDING TEXTURE TO PHOTOGRAPHS

This chapter shows how to enhance photographs with textured brushwork and filtered effects, using the features in Photoshop and Painter.

Taming the Art History Brush shows how to use the Camera Raw dialog to bring back detail needed for painting and editing the image to improve its composition. Then the Art History Brush is used in combination with brush styles and several brush presets to create a textured, painted look.

Creating a Dry Media Textured Look with Pastels begins with processing the image in Photoshop Camera Raw, and then retouching it. Then Surface Control effects are used in Painter to build a textured surface. A custom cloning brush is built and the photograph is cloned into the textured background. Blenders brushes and Pastels are used to brush over the image and to paint an irregular border.

Painting a Textured Black-and-White Study shows how to use the Camera Raw dialog to convert a color photo to black-and-white, adjust tones and crop the image. For the appearance of a charcoal drawing, a custom Charcoal brush is built and used to paint over the image. A Surface Control effect is applied to build three-dimensional texture and then more brushstrokes are painted using the Blenders and Charcoal brushes.

Children of Tuileries

Taming the Art History Brush

Children sailing boats in Paris's Jardin des Tuileries has been a familiar sight for many decades. Each day provides a great photographic opportunity; only the faces change from day to day.

Aperture and Shutter Priority modes allow the photographer to shoot relatively carefree, trusting the equipment to carry part of the burden of obtaining usable results. Unfortunately, knowing this is of no help when one *thinks* one is shooting with Aperture or Shutter Priority mode turned on, but discovers upon later examination that the camera was left in manual mode. A reshoot is the first thing that comes to mind in this situation, but this wasn't an option after capturing a set of images of children sailing toy boats in Paris's Jardin des Tuileries on the very last day of vacation.

The sun was bright, the kids were quick, and sporadic clouds appearing overhead constantly changed the lighting. In theory, I chose Aperture Priority mode over Shutter Priority because I knew the shutter speed

would already be fast, and I wanted control of the depth of field.

Shooting with my 80–400mm telephoto lens, I chose a low f-stop setting of f/5.6 to capture a relatively narrow depth of field, blurring the unattractive and busy background. The first two shots were properly exposed due to a manual setting I had previously set in another part of the garden, but when a cloud passed by, the brilliant sunlight overexposed subsequent photos.

The product of the shoot was a series of photographs with very little apparent data in the highlight range. The shutter was open just over twice as long as I'd wanted, but Camera Raw was able to bring back enough lost detail to provide an excellent candidate for hand painting.

This particular image was selected for the Art History Brush

tool because the tool is simply phenomenal for rendering water and clouds. Unique and varied results are relatively easy to achieve so that personal touches and highly stylized results are possible. If two people use the same photograph the results can be worlds apart.

Photoshop's Art History Brush is notorious for its reputation of being difficult to control. Whenever I break out the Art History Brush, it is with low- to medium-frequency (not too busy) images and a willingness to lose a certain degree of detail throughout the image. Great results are far more difficult to obtain using high-frequency (very busy) photos, which can take on a filtered and excessively manipulated appearance.

This unaltered version of the original Camera Raw file shows how the highlight detail was seemingly lost.

The highlights were recovered by a reduction using the Exposure slider on Camera Raw's Basic tab.

1 Opening the Camera Raw file. Camera Raw files are capable of rendering more detail than first glance suggests because there is much more information available in an unprocessed Camera Raw file than in a clipped, 24-bit image (see page 12 for a more detailed explanation.) Although it is possible to recover subtle detail across the entire tonal range, Camera Raw's ability to reveal highlight details is particularly effective because it works from what the camera actually "sees" and records, which is considerably more than what is eventually translated into an image.

Open the Camera Raw file (File > Open) to reveal the Camera Raw interface with the picture in the "as shot" state. The first step is to adjust the Exposure slider. In this case, I chose a setting of –.65. Although the "lost" information starts reappearing, the exposure adjustment affects the image globally, with shadows and midtones becoming darker.

Next, set the Vibrance slider to 85% to saturate the image. Vibrance differs from saturation in that moving the Vibrance slider saturates unsaturated color to a greater degree than already saturated areas and magically avoids destroying skin tones.

A close look along the edge of the sails reveals a red/cyan fringe along the edges of color fields. It is not a problem in the middle, but gradually becomes more pronounced the farther from center you look. This is called chromatic aberration and is caused by the light waves being refracted through the curved glass within the lens. While chromatic aberration can occur with any lens, telephoto and wide-angle lenses are especially affected, with lower grade lenses more problematic than high-end, professional (expensive!) lenses. For more information on chromatic aberration see pages 171–172.

The Lens Corrections panel of Camera Raw corrects many instances of chromatic aberration, but not every type of chromatic aberration can be corrected. Click the Lens Corrections button and set the Red/Cyan slider to +28; then select Defringe All Edges from the pop-up menu.

The image is ready for opening, so click Open Image. It will open in Photoshop, where you should immediately save the file by choosing File > Save, or pressing Ctrl-S/⌘-S before continuing. This first save does not overwrite your Camera Raw file and you'll have to come up with a descriptive name. A reasonable name for this file might be *KidsandFountainFirstOpened.psd*.

Some occurrences of chromatic aberration can be fixed on the Lens Corrections panel.

The main cropping consideration is the triangular convergence of the children, their sticks, and the objects of their attention.

2 **Cropping and editing the starting image.** The focus of the picture is the childish excitement displayed by the motion and expression of the children as they watch and redirect their boats. The garbage bag on the left and the woman sitting on a white plastic chair are distractions and will be painted out, so the crop is made as though they are not even there.

Choose the Crop tool and then enter 2025 px in the Width box and 1530 px for the Height. (Be sure to include the "px!") In the Resolution box, enter 150. Click and drag to crop the image, noting how the proportions are constrained by the 2025 x 1530 ratio. Consider how the image would look with the woman replaced by the gray sidewalk and green bushes. When you're ready to clip out the unwanted area of the photo, press Enter.

Save the image using File > Save As, and assign a new name to define this file as the one used to produce your art. For example, this working file might be appropriately named *Children of Tuileries Master.psd.*

When first approaching any photo editing task, a plan of attack is critical. In this image the two areas to change cover a significant amount of area, and a lot of time could be spent perfecting every edit. Because the Art History

The best of multiple versions. You may encounter an instance where changes to one area of an image conflict with what you want to do elsewhere. The answer is to open your Camera Raw file twice and then use Photoshop to merge the two images. Easy, right? Actually, it's not quite as simple as that, if you want to keep both Camera Raw settings. When you open a file using Camera Raw, a second file is created called an .xmp file. It is placed in the same folder as your original Camera Raw file, and when the file is loaded, the settings in the .xmp file are also loaded. If you open the file a second time and make changes, the previous settings are overwritten when the new .xmp file is automatically saved. The easiest way to open a Camera Raw file multiple times with different settings is to make a prior duplicate of the original file for each time you open it. Edit multiple files once instead of one file multiple times.

The garbage bag was easy to remove using the Clone tool, especially because the alteration can be so rough.

Eliminating the garbage bag first supplied an area that could be copied, pasted and merged to cover a major portion of the sitting woman.

Brush blends edges, it is unnecessary to make your changes appear perfectly seamless. Areas that would normally stand out will look fine once you paint over them.

It's obvious the woman will be more work to remove than the garbage bag. Although it is tempting to start there, the advantage to removing the garbage bag first is that the entire area can be copied and pasted over much of the woman, at least from the grass line and above.

To edit the image prior to using the Art History Brush you'll use the Clone Stamp tool, Brushes, and a few layers. Start by duplicating the Background layer by choosing Layer > Duplicate Layer or dragging its name in the Layers palette onto the New Layer button. Lock the Background layer by selecting it and clicking the Lock button at the top of the Layers palette.

Select the background copy, unlock it and then select the Clone Stamp tool. Click the Brush Preset Picker on the Options bar and select the Hard Round 19 brush. Adjust the brush size by setting the Master Diameter slider to 25 and the Hardness to 50%. Before leaving the Options bar, choose Sample All Layers from the Sample pop-up menu.

To use the Clone Stamp tool you must first define the area to be cloned by Alt-clicking /Option-clicking in the

area you want to copy. Now as you paint, your stroke will clone the area indicated by the crosshair, moving in relationship to your direction. To avoid the appearance of obvious pattern repetition, be sure to move the source point of the Cloning brush every so often and change the brush size.

The completed area of where the bag used to be is now an excellent area to copy and paste over the woman in the right side of the image (see above). Use the Lasso tool (L) to select a liberal amount of image. Press Ctrl-C/⌘-C to copy the selection, then paste the selection onto a new layer by pushing Ctrl-V/⌘-V. Choose the Move tool (V) and position the cloned area over the woman.

Choose Layer > Layer Mask > Reveal All to apply a layer mask. Select a new brush by selecting the Brush tool (B) and choose the Soft Round 200 brush. Click on the Brush Preset Picker and reduce the Master Diameter

 Choosing when to edit. Sometimes it's useful to edit your image prior to cropping. You may want to work with areas that will get cropped out, so use them before getting rid of that data permanently.

The copied area is broken up using a combination of the Clone tool and the Brush tool.

The edits are done and the image is ready for the Art History Brush. Some of the picture has been cropped .

to 150. With black as the foreground color, mask out unwanted areas.

Create another new layer (Layer > New Layer), and select the Soft Round 65 brush. Sample a light sidewalk color by clicking on the foreground color. When the Color Picker opens, click on the color you want to sample. (Even easier, with the Brush tool selected you can Alt-Click/ Option-click anywhere in the image to change the foreground color!) Paint over the remnants of the chair and woman. Using the Brush Preset Picker to adjust your brush size, move throughout the image and clean up rough areas.

To complete this layer, return to the Clone Stamp tool and go over areas in the background to break up the cloned area where the woman used to be sitting. Finally, use the Options bar to set the brush's Opacity to 70% and then go over areas that still appear cloned. Again, remember that absolute perfection is unnecessary due to the strokes of the Art History Brush still to come.

Once finished, merge all of your layers by choosing Layer > Flatten Image. Save your file and then choose File > Save As to rename your file once again, replacing the word "Master" with "Working." This ensures you have an original master image to return to should you need it.

3 **Preparing to work with the Art History Brush.**
Understanding the Art History Brush is not difficult in theory, but actually using it can be frustrating in real life. The key to this tool is to not rely on brushes "straight out of the box," but to customize them using Brush controls. Mixing brushes, changing sizes, and blending in your own brushstrokes will all help make your work unique and artistic. On the other hand, simply painting over a photograph with the Art History Brush will make it look processed and uninspired.

Control over the Art History brush is the result of balancing different aspects of the brush's composition. These controls are found in the Brushes palette and on the Options bar. Although the settings for this exercise are specific, exploring different settings will provide hours of entertainment and all sorts of interesting effects.

Prior to painting, load additional brushes by choosing Window > Brushes (F5). Click the Menu button at the top right of the palette. Choose Load Brushes, then navigate to the brushes directory in your Photoshop

The Chalk-Light brush tip is used with both the Brush Tool (left) and the Art History Tool (right). The same tip and settings yield different results.

Similar to the sample to the left, the Charcoal Flat brush tip is used with both the Brush Tool (left) and the Art History Tool (right).

application folder (inside the Presets folder). Ctrl-Alt-click/⌘-Option-click Dry Media Brushes, Wet Media Brushes, and Natural Brushes 2, then press the Load button. Select Append when you're prompted to Append, Cancel or OK the change to the palette. The libraries will be added to your Brushes palette.

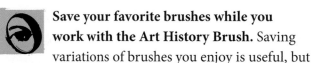 **Save your favorite brushes while you work with the Art History Brush.** Saving variations of brushes you enjoy is useful, but when you make an Art History Brush variant you really like, it's downright bliss. (OK, perhaps that's pushing it…) To save a brush, click the Menu button on the top of the Brushes palette and select New Brush Preset. If you want to save it permanently, do it a second time, but instead of selecting New Brush Preset, choose Save Brushes. This will save your entire open library. Assign the brush a descriptive name so you don't scratch your head a few months down the road wondering what was so impressive that you had to save the brush!

4 **Setting a history state.** The Art History Brush and History Brush work by sampling from a saved point in your progress called a history state. Both tools remain disabled until a history state is created by using the History palette.

The most effective way to establish a history state is to make a snapshot by clicking the Menu button at the top of the History palette. Select New Snapshot, and assign your Snapshot a name. It is very important to choose Merged Layers from the pop-up menu, which is not the default. A new snapshot thumbnail now appears at the top of the History palette, but only becomes a history state by clicking in the empty box in front of its name. An icon of the Art History Brush will display next to the Snapshot, and the tool will become usable.

For insurance that the new, edited Background Layer is kept safe from edits, lock it by clicking the Lock icon on the Layers palette. Create a new empty layer on which to paint by clicking on the New Layer button, and save your document by pressing Ctrl-S/⌘-S. It's time to begin painting.

The Chalk-Light brush results in a lot of texture and loss of detail.

The same area using the Charcoal Flat brush.

5 Laying down your initial brushwork. Choose the Art History Brush tool. Click the Brush Preset Picker and select the Chalk-Light variant. Brush over the entire image. Your strokes should move parallel to any edges in your picture instead of perpendicular. As you work, use the Brush Preset Picker to change the brush size every once in a while. Double-click the name of the layer in the Layers palette and retitle it Chalk-Light to indicate what

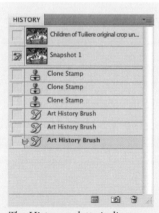
The History palette indicates the step from which the Art History Brush and the History Brush will work.

brush you used on that layer. It's impossible to play "Name That Brush" using the Art History Brush, so recording the brush information on the Layers palette can prove to be a lifesaver if you decide to come back to work on the layer. Don't go overboard trying to finish your entire project on this one layer! Save your file often. It's so depressing to lose good work if the power goes out or the computer freezes.

You're now going to discover how wonderful the Art History Brush is for water reflections, so when you finish brushing the Chalk-Light layer, make another duplicate of the Background layer and click and drag it to the top of the Layers palette. Click on the Brush Preset Picker and select the Charcoal Flat brush.

Repeat the process you followed with the Chalk-Light layer (remember to change the layer's name!), covering the entire canvas. Remember to occasionally change the brush size to make the picture more interesting.

You want to paint the entire canvas, but it is difficult to see whether everything is covered. To make sure the entire image is brushed over, hide the Background layer. You will immediately see what you've missed by the gaping white holes that appear. To see the holes *and* a ghosted copy of the photograph below, double-click on the Background layer on the Layers palette to convert it to a floating layer, then set its Opacity to 20.

When you're satisfied with the appearance of this layer, apply a layer mask to it by clicking on the Add Layer Mask

The layer mask on the Charcoal Flat layer is used sparingly to allow the brushwork on this layer to stand out.

Compare the before (left) and after (right) images after brightening your image in Step 5.

on the Layers palette. You're going to mask portions of this layer sparingly to bring out some of the texture of the Chalk-Light layer. Select the Brush tool (B) and click on the Brush Preset Picker to select the Soft Round 65 brush and set the Hardness to 50%. With black as your foreground color, brush over parts of the image to show the texture of the layer below. Leave the water alone because the Charcoal Flat brush is far superior to the Chalk-Light brush when it comes to the play of the reflections on the surface of the water. Instead, pay attention to the boats, sails and hard edges throughout the image. Use the mask sparingly, as bringing out too much of the underlaying Chalk-Light layer will eventually weaken the piece visually. Remember—save your file every few minutes!

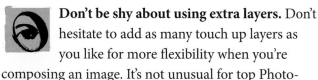 **Don't be shy about using extra layers.** Don't hesitate to add as many touch up layers as you like for more flexibility when you're composing an image. It's not unusual for top Photoshop artists to have as many as thirty to forty layers (or more) active in a document. Just be sure to notate what each layer is for so you don't confuse yourself later on!

6 **Brightening the lower portion.** At this stage of the image's development, the water is already pretty, but it doesn't "pop" with the kinds of colors you get from paints. It kind of just lies there, flat and unremarkable. This step will bring out brilliant hues in the reflections.

Select the Chalk-Light layer and choose Layer > Duplicate Layer. Drag the copy to the top of the layer stack on the Layers palette. Apply a Gaussian Blur filter, setting it to only 3.5. Some hint of the texture, as well as definitive color fields should remain. On the Layers palette, choose Soft Light from the Blend mode pop-up menu.

Apply a layer mask by clicking the Add Layer Mask button on the Layers palette. Click the Brush Preset Picker and choose the Soft Round 200 brush. Mask out everything except the water, boats and the lowest part of the wall along the waterline. Reduce the size of the brush and fine-tune your mask to fit your own tastes. Rename your layer with a description that tells you the layer's function, such as Brightening.

Some images may be simply too bright with this layer set at 100% opacity. On this image the Opacity on the Layers palette was reduced to 85%.

Use the Oil Medium Wet Flow brush variant to build up the facial features and arms, sampling colors already present.

The Large Texture Stroke Brush is excellent for bringing up textures, especially on hard, non-reflective surfaces such as stone, cement, and clay.

7 **Adding the final touch-ups.** The image has shaped up pretty well, but remains a bit sterile, as though a magic set of filters was run over a few layers and called "art." The final touch-ups are what really set apart the image and makes it distinctly your own. To do this, you may use your own favorite brushes or use the ones in this step. This step uses the Brush tool, *not* the Art History Brush.

I strongly recommend that you make a new layer for each brush if you have enough RAM and processing speed. You can also make more than one layer for a brush in order to have more options in stacking your brush effects.

Just like previous steps, whenever you make a new layer, label your layer with a descriptive name so in the future you can know how you achieved your results. On these layers you will sample color often, most easily by Alt-clicking/Option-clicking on the color you want to use while the Brush tool is active.

Make a new layer (Layer > New Layer) and select the Pastel on Charcoal Paper brush. This brush is useful for breaking up the background. Sampling colors, brush over different parts of the plants and tree trunks. Change sizes and use it sparingly, with a light touch. Complete opacity is not particularly desirable, so set the brush's Opacity to

85% on the Options Bar. Doing this instead of reducing the layer's opacity enables you to overlap strokes for greater opacity.

Select the Pastel Medium Tip brush and return the brush Opacity to 100%. This time pay special attention to the children's clothes and skin (don't ignore everything else!), applying strokes full of color at various sizes and places. Add strokes to the sails and every other place you think it is called for. Save your file.

For individual strokes that resemble traditional Oil painting strokes, select the Oil Medium Wet Flow brush. Changing sizes often, sample colors and brush over key areas on the kids' faces, arms, hands, poles, and the straight lines on the sails and masts. In the background, sample darker areas and fill out edges to be more distinct, further reducing the filtered appearance.

The Large Texture Stroke brush variant is the last brush used on this image. Use the brush to extend one color field into another by first sampling a color by Alt-clicking/Option-clicking at your sampling point and begin your stroke from that sampling point. Add your strokes to suit your own style, finishing whenever you like.

Save your file, and this one's done!

Pink Ginger Sky

Creating a Dry Media Textured Look with Pastels

Several of the photographs from the shoot are shown above. The photograph in the upper-right has good contrast, color and a simple composition that make it a fine choice for this project.

The art of pastel painting came into its own in the eighteenth and nineteenth centuries. Pastel works of the Impressionist Edgar Degas are inspirational for their rich texture and exquisite draftsmanship, and the pastel paintings of Georgia O'Keeffe continue to inspire.

When shooting photos on location in Kauai, I focused on close-ups of plants. Looking overhead, I spotted the intriguing diagonals of the leaves and dramatic curving ginger flowers, and loved the composition. I shot several photographs using different exposures and with varied focus. I like the simpler compositions.

To shoot the chosen photograph, I used Manual mode, a shallow depth of field—f/4—so that only the ginger flowers were in focus. I set the shutter speed at 400 and the ISO at 100. The sharp focus on the pink ginger flowers and the soft focus on the leaves lends itself well to a blended pastel painting with crisp details on the focal point.

After settling on the image, closer inspection revealed that it needed retouching. I removed a few specks of dirt on the flowers and a distracting spider web.

Painter has a strong arsenal of textured art materials and effects. In this project, I modified a grainy Pastel brush to clone photographic imagery, while building the grainy, textured look of a natural media pastel.

For this image, I wanted the look of creamy manila charcoal paper, so I used the powerful Apply Surface Texture effect to set up a grainy surface to paint on. After loosely blocking the imagery into the clone file, I modeled forms and painted details.

Before your shoot, get inspired by Georgia O'Keeffe's pastel paintings such as *White Camellia* and *Pink Roses and Larkspur*. Later, when it's time to download your images, view them at 100% to choose the best candidate. Now it's time to begin!

Retouching the image and removing the spider web.

Detail of the retouched image with the spider web and dirt removed.

1 **Adjusting, adding a layer and retouching.** Now that you have chosen a photograph to work with, you can use the Camera Raw dialog in Photoshop to adjust the color and contrast of your image if needed. See the Camera Raw sidebar on page 12 for more information about using the dialog.

When you are satisfied with your image, press Alt/Option and click Open Copy to open a copy of the image in Photoshop. (The image for this project measures 2544 x 1696 pixels.) It's important to preserve your original photo by choosing File > Save As and giving the working image a new, descriptive name.

The original image for this project had good color and contrast, so I did not adjust the image in the Camera Raw dialog. However, the chosen image had a distracting spider web, which needed to be removed.

For a nondestructive workflow, it's best to do the retouching on a copy of the Background layer. Drag the Background layer over the Create a New Layer button on the Layers palette to make a copy of the layer.

To set up for retouching on the layer copy, choose the Clone Stamp tool in the Tools palette. The Clone Stamp

tool retouches by sampling pixels from one area and painting them over another area. In the Property Bar, select the Aligned check box and set the Sample pop-up menu to Current Layer to sample only from the targeted layer. You can use any brush tip with the Clone Stamp tool. Choose a large brush for big, simple areas such as a sky and a small brush for more detailed areas. I used a Soft Round 45-pixel brush tip for the sky and an 8–10 pixel brush tip for the flowers. Now zoom in to the area you want to retouch, using a zoom factor of 100%. To sample with the Clone Stamp tool, Alt-click/Option-click in the area that you want to sample. Then click in the area you want to retouch using the sampled pixels. When retouching with a Wacom tablet and stylus, it's a good idea to make small, careful strokes (without scrubbing) so as not to accidentally smear and create a repeated pattern from the sampled area.

When you are satisfied with your retouching, save your image in Photoshop format, using a descriptive name. (I named my image *Ginger sky retouch.psd*.)

The retouched photograph is shown in this example.

The Quick Clone image canvas with Tracing Paper enabled.

2 **Making a Quick Clone and adding paper color.** Navigate to the image that you edited in Photoshop and open it in Painter.

To prepare for painting your photograph with the brushes, make a Quick Clone of the image by choosing File > Quick Clone. By default the Quick Clone command creates a clone image with the original canvas

removed, Tracing Paper turned on and the Cloners brushes chosen in the Brush Selector Bar.

Now give the image canvas a creamy, manila paper color that will not disappear if you use an Eraser. Choose a very light creamy yellow in the Colors palette and set the paper color by choosing Canvas > Set Paper Color. To reveal the paper color choose Select > All and press Backspace/Delete. The white Canvas will be replaced by the creamy yellow paper color.

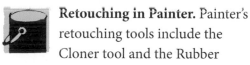 **Retouching in Painter.** Painter's retouching tools include the Cloner tool and the Rubber Stamp tool, nested together in the Toolbox. To access the Rubber Stamp tool, click and hold on the small arrow under the Cloner tool and move to the right. To sample with the Rubber Stamp tool, press the Alt/Option key and click in the image to sample. You will see a crosshair cursor indicating the area sampled. Release the key and then paint careful strokes with the Rubber Stamp tool to repair the area.

The Rubber Stamp is chosen.

A creamy, warm yellow is chosen in the Colors palette.

A detail of the clone image with the creamy, manila paper color applied. Tracing Paper is turned off in this illustration.

The Charcoal Paper texture is applied to the surface. Tracing Paper is turned off in this illustration.

3 Building a textured surface. Next add paper texture to the clone canvas by clicking the Paper Selector button on the Toolbox and choosing Charcoal Paper from the pop-up menu. The Charcoal Paper texture works well for an image that is 2000 x 1500 pixels like the one shown here. Now make a few brushstrokes on the clone image to test the texture. After testing, erase these strokes by choosing Select > All and pressing Backspace/Delete.

Now you're ready to add a textured surface to your image by applying a paper texture to the Canvas. Choose Effects > Surface Control > Apply Surface Texture > Using Paper. For a natural look, it's a good idea to use a subtle Amount setting (try 10–20%). For a matte look, set the

Scaling paper texture. If your image is large and you want coarser texture, scale up the texture in the Papers palette. To open the Papers palette, choose Window > Library Palettes > Show Papers. Move the Paper Scale slider in the Papers palette to the right to increase the scale.

Shine slider at 0% and leave the other settings at their defaults. When you're happy with the preview, click OK. Save this version of the image using a descriptive name. I named my image *Ginger Sky texture 1.psd*. Now that your canvas is textured, you are ready to paint!

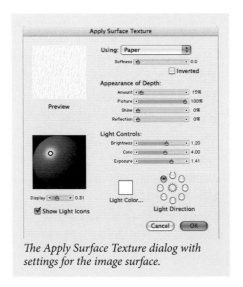

The Apply Surface Texture dialog with settings for the image surface.

Using the Square Hard Pastel 40 brush as a cloner to loosely brush the photo imagery into the textured canvas.

In this example, most of the compositional elements are loosely brushed in with the Square Hard Pastel 40 brush.

4 Using a custom Pastel brush cloner on a layer. In this step, you will block elements of the photo into the image using a custom cloner version of the Square Hard Pastel variant of Pastels. Choose the Square Hard Pastel 40 brush from the Pastels category in the Brush Selector Bar. Turn the brush into a cloner by enabling the Clone Color option (the Rubber Stamp) on the Colors palette. The Clone Color option allows you to paint with imagery from the clone source. Save the custom brush by choosing Save Variant from the pop-up menu on the Brush Selector Bar. When the dialog appears, name the brush and click OK. (I named my brush *Square Pastel Cloner.*) Now restore the original brush to its default settings by choosing Restore Default Variant from the Brush Selector

The Clone Color button is enabled.

Bar menu. After restoring the original, choose the Square Pastel Cloner.

For a more flexible, nondestructive workflow, add a new layer to your image for your brushwork. Working on a layer allows you to leave the surface texture on the canvas intact as you paint. In the Layers palette, select the Pick Up Underlying Color check box so you can pull color up from the paper surface below.

Use Tracing Paper as a general guide and loosely begin to brush the photographic imagery onto the layer. To see how your brushwork will actually appear, you can toggle Tracing Paper on and off as you work by pressing Ctrl-T/⌘-T. Using the custom Pastel cloner, continue to brush the imagery into the file. For a natural look, vary the size of the strokes by adjusting the Size slider in the Property Bar. I used a 70-pixel brush to layer in areas of the sky and leaves.

If you want an irregular border, you can leave some textured paper showing along the edges as I did, shown in the above image.

In this detail, a smaller brush is used to bring a few details into focus.

The Grainy Water variant of Blenders is used to smooth areas.

5 Bringing areas into focus with the custom pastel.
Brushing the imagery into the file with a grainy brush helps the image look more painterly and less photographic. You can retain much of the loose brushwork and add details only in areas where you want to focus on the subject. Now that the basic shapes and colors are laid in, you can use the custom Square Pastel Cloner brush to begin to clone subtle details from the source file into your working image. The Square Pastel Cloner brush picks up the paper grain, and the square brush tip keeps you from getting too "tight." Leaving the image a little "rough" will make it appear more natural. At this stage, concentrate on modeling the forms. Allow your strokes to follow the direction of the forms, especially in the center of interest. I like the grainy texture of the Square Hard Pastel brush, so I used a smaller version of this brush when modeling the flowers and leaves. To bring the edges of the flowers into focus, I varied the size of the brush from between 8–15 pixels.

6 Blending areas while preserving texture. Painter has several exciting Blenders brushes that allow you to blend while retaining texture, such as the Grainy Water, Grainy Blender, Flat Grainy Stump and Smudge variants of Blenders. To focus more attention on the flowers, I made long, careful strokes over the leaves using the Flat Grainy Stump. I also used a small Grainy Water brush when sculpting the rounded forms on the ginger flowers. In areas where the texture was overpowering, I smoothed it slightly, brushing lightly over the areas with a large Grainy Water brush. This brushwork can be seen in the leaves on the right and the bottom of the close-up illustration above.

Refining the border to balance the composition.

Painting crisper details along the edges of a few of the flowers.

7 Adding to the border, blending and scumbling. Now that many of the forms in your painting are modeled, it's a good time to assess the border. In the case of this image, I felt that the original asymmetrical border shape was too distracting from the composition, so I used the custom Square Pastel Cloner to add to the border and make it more even. Choose the custom Square Pastel Cloner and increase its size to about 70 pixels using the Size slider in the Property Bar. Carefully brush out from your image to the edge. Make sure that you leave some paper showing along the edge of your image.

When your border is laid in, switch to the Grainy Water 30 variant of Blenders and subtly smooth the texture along the edges. When the border is as you like it, choose the custom Square Pastel Cloner and brush lightly over areas of your image where you want to add a little more texture. This technique is called *scumbling*, a traditional pastel technique that adds texture and allows colors to blend optically.

8 Blending and adding crisp details. Take a good look at your image. Are there areas that need finessing? When the modeling is as you like it, add a few linear details. Size the custom Square Pastel Cloner smaller, (try 10 pixels) and paint along the edges of forms in your central subject. I touched up the edges of a few of the ginger flowers. You can also touch up areas using sampled color from your image. Choose the Round Hard Pastel 25 variant of Pastels in the Brush Selector Bar and the Dropper tool in the Toolbox. Click with the Dropper tool to sample color from your image. Switch back to the Round Hard Pastel 25 brush and paint. To sample on the fly while painting, press the Alt/Option key to access the Dropper, and sample the color. Release the Alt/Option key to return to the Brush tool. In my image, I refined the edges of the flowers and one small leaf near the flowers. You can see the entire final image on page 110.

Congratulations! You have used Painter to create a pastel study from your photograph.

Torch Ginger Study

Painting a Textured Black-and-White Study

Here are six photos from the shoot. The photograph in the upper-right has dramatic backlighting and a good tonal range, which make it an ideal choice for a black-and-white study.

Appreciated by artists since the fifteenth century, charcoal is one of the oldest drawing mediums.

The charcoal and pastel studies of artist Georgia O'Keeffe continue to inspire me. For this project, I focused on close-ups of the magnificent torch ginger plants near Makana on Kauai. I shot several photographs with simple compositions using different angles and exposures.

For the chosen photograph, I used Manual mode and ISO 100. To achieve a shallow depth of field, I set the aperture to f/5.6, with the shutter speed at 250. The sharp focus on the ginger and the soft focus on the background lends itself well to a black-and-white charcoal study.

After the shoot, I downloaded my images and viewed each of them in Camera Raw to check the focus and exposure. For the chosen photograph, I converted it to grayscale and adjusted the tonal range to accommodate a black-and-white image. To achieve a more intimate close-up and stronger diagonals, I cropped the photograph into a horizontal format. Then I retouched a few small white specks on the image.

In this project, I modified a Charcoal brush to clone the photographic imagery, while achieving the appearance of a blended charcoal drawing over textured paper. To enhance the texture in the image, I used the Apply Surface Texture effect to bring

out the texture of the brushwork and to apply a Charcoal Paper texture to the entire image. So the effect would not look filtered, I then painted back into the image with the Blenders and Charcoal brushes and painted the border.

Before your shoot, look at the charcoal works of Georgia O'Keeffe, particularly *Banana Flower No. 1*. When you download your images, view them at 100% to choose the best candidate. Now you're ready to begin!

Making adjustments and converting to grayscale in the dialog.

Detail prior to retouching. The white specks are to the right of the flower.

1 **Adjusting and cropping.** After choosing your image, open it in Camera Raw and view it at 100%. Adjust the color and contrast, and crop it if necessary. See the Camera Raw sidebar on page 12 for more information about using the dialog.

For this black-and-white study project, it's best to have good contrast and a broad tonal range. Select the Convert to Grayscale check box to convert the image to black and white; then adjust the Brightness and Contrast to your taste (I set Brightness at +10 and Contrast at +20). For a closer view of the subject and a horizontal format, I used the Crop tool in the dialog. When your image is as you like it, press Alt/Option and click Open Copy to open a copy of your image in Photoshop. (The image for this project measures 2336 x 3504 pixels.)

When the adjustments are complete, preserve your original photo by choosing File > Save As and giving the working image a new descriptive name. I named my image *Torch Ginger.psd.*

2 **Retouching in Painter.** There were a few distracting white specks on my image, so I retouched them with the Rubber Stamp tool in Painter.

Navigate to the image that you edited in Step 1, and open it in Painter. For the utmost flexibility, retouch on a copy of the Canvas. To create a copy of the Canvas, choose Select > All, press the Alt/Option key and then choose Select > Float.

Now choose the Rubber Stamp tool in the Toolbox. To sample with the Rubber Stamp tool, Alt-click/Option-click in the area that you want to sample. Then click on the area you want to retouch. For more information about retouching with the Rubber Stamp tool, see page 112. When the retouching is complete, preserve the edited photo from Step 1 by choosing File > Save As, and giving the working image a new descriptive name. (I named my image *Torch Ginger Retouch.psd.*)

 Try Smart Blur. If your image has too much busy photographic detail, consider using the Smart Blur option on the Underpainting palette. See page 91 to learn more about Smart Blur.

Using the custom Soft Charcoal Cloner to paint the background glows.

Blending and modeling on the flower using the Round Blender Brush.

3 Cloning, painting and blending with brushes. To prepare for painting, clone the retouched image by choosing File > Clone. Choose File > Save As and resave the clone with a descriptive name. (I named my image *Torch Ginger Paint 1.psd.*)

Now choose the Charcoal Paper texture from the Paper Selector in the Toolbox and the Soft Charcoal variant of Charcoal from the Brush Selector Bar. To use the brush to paint with color from the retouched photo, change the brush into a cloner by turning on the Clone Color option (the Rubber Stamp) on the Colors palette. Clone Color allows you to paint with colors from the active clone

The Clone Color button is enabled.

source. Save your custom Soft Charcoal Cloner, into the current brush category, by choosing Save Variant from the Brush Selector Bar menu. In the dialog, name the Soft Charcoal Cloner, and then click OK. After saving your new brush, it's a good idea to restore the original brush to its default settings by choosing it in the Brush Selector Bar and then choosing Restore Default Variant from the Brush Selector Bar menu. After restoring the original, choose the custom Soft Charcoal Cloner from the Variant menu.

Next, for the most flexible workflow, add a new layer for your brushwork. Select the Pick Up Underlying Color check box in the Layers palette so you can pull color up from the image below. Keep in mind that to achieve a natural look, you should vary the size of the brushstrokes. I used a 50–60 pixel brush to lay in areas of the broader leaves, an 80-pixel brush for the background and 10–20 pixel brushes for the flowers. First, work over your image with the Soft Charcoal Cloner, carefully smoothing over any photographic details. Let your brushstrokes follow the forms. After working over your image with the Soft Charcoal Cloner, add brush bristle texture by blending areas with the Round Blender Brush variant of Blenders. In the image above, you can see the bristle marks along the edge of the flowers. The Round Blender Brush is also used to model and sculpt the curved forms and highlights and shadows on the flowers. Save your image.

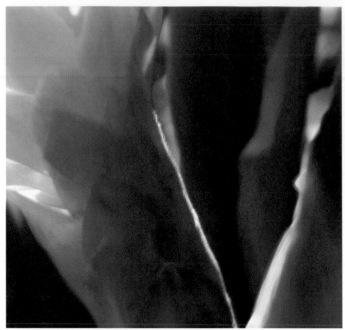

In this detail, a small Charcoal brush is used to paint a few highlight details along the edge of the leaf and flower.

In this detail, the brush marks are enhanced by the Apply Surface Texture effect using Image Luminance.

4 **Painting details on the center of interest.** Now that you have painted over the entire image, you can add a few carefully placed freehand brushstrokes with a grainier brush. Pause and take a good look at your image.

Highlights are brightened by sampling a bright white from the image with the Dropper tool and then using a small default Charcoal brush to paint over the area. Choose the Dropper tool in the Toolbox and click on your image to sample color. The Charcoal brush is more sensitive to paper texture, whereas the Soft Charcoal brush is smoother and picks up less texture. I like the combination of the grainy texture of the Charcoal in combination with the Soft Charcoal. To paint along the edges of the flowers, I varied the size of the brushes from 10–20 pixels. At this point, I also sampled color from the image and used the Soft Charcoal brush to paint a few areas to subtly darken a few shadowed areas. Choose File > Save As > and save your image using a new, descriptive name.

5 **Adding texture effects.** Now you're ready to add textured effects to your image. In this step, you will use two applications of Apply Surface Texture to bring out brushwork and add paper texture. Choose Effects > Surface Control > Apply Surface Texture > Using Image Luminance. For a subtle look, I suggest using a subtle Amount setting (try 5–15%). For a matte look, set the Shine slider at 0%. The light source in my image is from the left and back, so I chose the 11 o'clock light direction button. Leave the other settings at their defaults. When you're happy with the preview, click OK.

Now for the second application. Choose Effects > Surface Control > Apply Surface Texture, this time, Using Paper. Again, for a subtle look, use a subtle Amount setting (try 5–15%) set the Shine slider at 0% and leave the other settings at their defaults. The light source in this image is from the left and back, so I again chose the 11 o' clock light direction button. Choose File > Save As and save this version of the image using a new, descriptive name.

In this example, you can see the subtle paper effect applied in Step 5. The Round Blender Brush is used to paint over some of the textured areas.

After additional Canvas Size is added, the subtle border edge is painted with the Round Blender Brush.

6 **Selectively blending and painting details.** Before adding more brushwork, take a good look at your image. Are there areas that need finessing? Prepare for blending smaller areas by sizing the Round Blender Brush smaller (about 5–10 pixels) and brush lightly to smooth a few areas of texture along the edges of the forms. In the image above, a few crisp edges on the flower are smoothed. You can also touch up areas using sampled color from your image. Choose the Charcoal variant of Charcoal in the Brush Selector Bar and the Dropper tool in the Toolbox. Click with the Dropper tool to sample color from your image. Switch back to the Charcoal brush and size it down to about 8–10 pixels. In this image, the highlights are brightened, and the lightest highlight edges are refined. To sample on the fly while painting, press the Alt/Option key to access the Dropper and sample the color. Release the Alt/Option key to return to the Brush tool.

7 **Adding the border.** After you finesse the forms in your painting, it's a good time to consider the border. To begin, click on the Canvas in the Layers palette. Add more Canvas by choosing Canvas > Canvas Size. In the dialog add 100 pixels to each of the four sides and click OK.

Fifteenth-century artists blended charcoal studies with brushes made of bird feathers. For the image above, I used a Round Blender Brush to add a subtle border edge and bristle mark textures. Choose the Round Blender Brush 20. Pull color from the image out into the white area with your stylus and carefully brush along the edge of the entire border. The subtle and slightly wavy border on the image adds a natural look. You can see the entire final image on page 118.

Congratulations! You have explored painting over your photograph with the Charcoal brushes and Blenders in Painter. Now you can take a break or move on to the next project.

**Soft, Diffused Painting with
Digital Watercolor and Blenders**

Photoshop and Painter **126**

**Extraordinary Watercolors from
Ordinary Pictures**

Photoshop **136**

5

Emulating the Look of Watercolor

This chapter shows how to simulate the look of conventional watercolor, using painting tools and other features in Photoshop and Painter. The projects will give you ideas for taking photographs that will work well with transparent watercolor techniques.

Soft, Diffused Painting with Digital Watercolor and Blenders teaches how to create a realist-style watercolor seascape. For a high-key reference suitable for a watercolor look, the tones in the photograph are lightened. Traditional watercolor practices such as sketching with a brush, and transparent glazing are used as inspiration for this Digital Watercolor technique. Transparent Digital Watercolor brushwork is painted on layers. After the paint is dried, then Blenders brushes are used to smooth areas.

Extraordinary Watercolors from Ordinary Pictures shows how to create a pleasing water-color portrait using Photoshop. The Pattern Stamp, Pattern features, and brush presets combined with the Wet Edges brush option are used to build the look of translucent watercolor washes on layers. To complete the image, texture is added using a scan of watercolor paper that is blended with the watercolor brushwork.

Carpenteria Shore

Chapter 5: Emulating the Look of Watercolor

Soft, Diffused Painting with Digital Watercolor and Blenders

Several photos from the shoot. The image in the upper-right has good color. The extreme wide angle of view and the intriguing diagonals give the perspective a good sense of depth.

With *Carpenteria Shore*, a realist-style painting with a dramatic atmosphere, this project demonstrates using Digital Watercolor brushes in Painter. Digital Watercolor is a transparent medium that is versatile and easy to use. Numerous conventional watercolor techniques can be replicated using Digital Watercolor. For this seascape, a soft, diffused look is desired. When printed on Arches cold pressed paper, the watercolor look is amazingly realistic.

As my husband, Steve, and I traveled through Carpenteria, California, a storm was approaching, and the sky offered dramatic clouds and lighting. I focused on the rapidly changing atmosphere and the dynamic shapes along the shore using a Sony Cybershot DSC-F505V camera with a Carl Zeiss zoom lens. In some cases, I captured more than one shot of a scene using different exposure settings. For the chosen photo, I used Aperture Priority mode, an aperture of f/2.8, and for an extreme wide angle view, a 7mm focal length. I set the shutter speed at 1/600 and ISO at 100.

Back at the studio, I adjusted the tones and color to build a reference that would lend itself to watercolor painting. Later, after the sketching and basic overall washes are established, the wet Digital Watercolor is dried. Then, using a process inspired by the traditional watercolor process of *glazing*, more transparent washes are painted to build atmosphere and give dimension to the forms. The wet paint is dried again, and the Blenders brushes are used to finesse forms and details. Final texture and detail is added with Digital Watercolor using the Salt brush.

For inspiration look at the paintings of the master realist Winslow Homer, such as *Northeaster*. When possible, it is helpful to view the actual conventional watercolor paintings. Now let's get to work!

The photograph with colors and tones enhanced.

Using the Distort feature to change the shape of the foreground rocks.

1 **Opening the digital original.** The original photo for this project measures 1279 x 960 pixels. The photograph was captured in JPG format, and opened directly in the Camera Raw dialog and viewed at 100% to start the project. (See page 82 for information about opening JPG files directly in Camera Raw.) Open your image and determine whether the color and tones need adjustment. To brighten the colors and balance the saturation of the color, the Saturation is increased to +15 and Vibrance is increased. For more dramatic lighting, Contrast is increased subtly to +10. Please note: Step 2 demonstrates using controls in Painter's Underpainting palette to give the photo reference a brighter, higher key palette for watercolor. The higher key palette can also be accomplished by making more dramatic changes to the Saturation, Vibrance, Brightness and Contrast controls in the Camera Raw dialog. See the Camera Raw sidebar on page 12 in Chapter 1 for detailed information about using the dialog.

When you are satisfied with the edits on your image, press Alt/Option and click Open Copy to open a copy

of the image in Photoshop. Preserve your original photo and the edited photo by saving a new version for retouching. Choose File > Save As, and then give your working image a new name.

Take a good look at your image at 100% magnification. Does your photo need retouching? This photograph has beautiful color and detail, but the composition could be improved by giving the foreground more room to breathe. A wider format allows room for more water and sky. Two inches of Canvas Size is added to the right side of the composition, and then the water and sky is extended into the area. The rocks in the foreground are

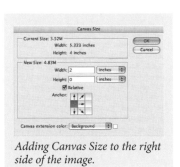

Adding Canvas Size to the right side of the image.

subtly distorted to help lead the viewer's eye into the composition. Set the Background Color to white in the Tools palette. To add Canvas Size to your image, choose Image > Canvas Size. In the dialog, select the Relative

The wider, retouched image has more graceful curves in the foreground.

The photograph with color and tones enhanced for Digital Watercolor.

check box, enter a number in the Width field, choose the Anchor field that suits your taste and then click OK to accept. White canvas is added to the right side of the image. You can clone imagery to cover the white area. In the case of this image imagery is selected and copied, pasted back into the image, and then the Clone Stamp tool is used to sample content from one area and paint it into another, to vary the content for a natural appearance.

The foreground rocks were distorted to create a more pleasing curve. If you have an element in your photo that you want to distort, select it with the Lasso tool and float a copy of the area to a layer by pressing Ctrl-J/⌘-J. With the new layer selected, choose Edit > Transform > Distort. Drag a corner handle to stretch the bounding box. When you are satisfied with the new shape, press the Enter key to accept the transformation. Drop the layer to the Background by choosing Flatten Image from the pop-up menu on the right side of the Layers palette. When you've finished retouching your photo, choose File > Save As and save your edited image in Photoshop format, with a descriptive name.

2 Building a higher key reference for watercolor. This step demonstrates using Painter to make adjustments to a copy of the adjusted photograph that will create a brighter, higher key reference for painting with Digital Watercolor. (If you want to use the photo reference with more natural color from Step 1, you can skip this step.)

When working in conventional watercolor, I like to use a glazing process in which transparent washes of color are painted and then more washes of color are added to build up tonal and color variations. A similar process can be achieved in Digital Watercolor when working from a photograph. For a transparent watercolor look, it is often best to use a light or high key reference photograph.

Now open Painter. In Painter, choose File > Open, and navigate to the edited image that you saved in Photoshop. To preserve the retouched version, perform this step on a clone copy. Choose File > Clone, and save the clone using a descriptive name. Open the Underpainting palette by choosing Window > Show Underpainting. Take a good look at your photograph and imagine it as a watercolor painting. Would you like to brighten the colors, or adjust

The enhanced photograph with Smart Blur applied shows less high frequency detail.

Brushstrokes painted over the photo, from top: Broad Water Brush, Coarse Mop Brush, Dry Brush, Round Water Blender and Simple Water.

the tones? In the case of the project photo, the Saturation and the Brightness are increased.

To simplify the detail in the reference, the Smart Blur feature is used. (The simplification process can also be achieved in Photoshop, as shown in "Simplifying a Photograph to Achieve a Hand-Rendered Result" on page 54.) In the Underpainting palette, experiment with the Smart Blur slider, based on the size of your file and the level of detail that you want to retain. This approach calls for an image with less detail, so the project uses a moderate amount of Smart Blur (try 40%), because of the look desired and the diffused brushes that are employed. Save the blurred file in Painter's native format, RIF. See page 91 for more information about the Smart Blur feature.

In preparation for the steps that follow, choose a paper texture. Click the Paper Selector in the Toolbox and make sure that Basic Paper is chosen. Basic Paper is reminiscent of conventional Cold Press watercolor paper. It is an organic texture and works well with Digital Watercolor, Blenders and other media such as Pencils and Pastels.

3 Exploring the Digital Watercolor brushes. To experience the feel of the Digital Watercolor brushes and observe the transparency of the washes, use your stylus to paint brushstrokes over the photograph. Choose the Digital Watercolor category in the Brush Selector Bar, choose the Broad Water variant and then choose a color in the Colors palette. To experience the feel of the brush, paint a horizontal, curved stroke using your stylus and varied pressure. Continue exploring the Digital Watercolor brushes. When you are done trying out the brushes, undo the brushwork by choosing File > Revert.

 Digital Watercolor and Watercolor. Painter features two kinds of watercolor media, Digital Watercolor and Watercolor. This project focuses on Digital Watercolor. Watercolor brushes require using a special Watercolor layer, on which wet transparent washes of color can mix, drip and run down the page. Rich textures are possible with Watercolor. For additional information about Watercolor layers, see page 203.

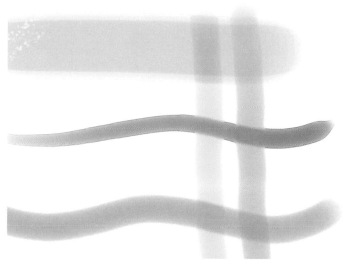

Wet Digital Watercolor paint interaction over Basic Paper texture. Horizontal strokes: Broad Water Brush (with Salt speckles), Simple Water, Soft Diffused Brush. Vertical strokes: Soft Diffused Brush over wet paint.

Painting the brush sketch with a Broad Water Brush and Round Water Blender. Tracing Paper is turned on in this illustration.

Further explore Digital Watercolor by opening a new file (File > New) at a size of 1500 x 1000 pixels. Paint using the brushes listed above, observing the transparency and interaction of wet strokes over existing wet paint.

 Painting with Digital Watercolor. The versatile Digital Watercolor medium in Painter allows the easy application of washes of wet transparent color using a wide variety of exciting brushes, for instance, Broad Water Brush, Coarse Mop Brush, Dry Brush, Round Water Blender and Simple Water brush. The medium is more forgiving than conventional watercolor and even offers a Spatter Water brush, Wet Erasers and Salt. You can apply Digital Watercolor paint to the Canvas or to default layers. Important controls for customizing Digital Watercolor brushes are located in the context-sensitive Property Bar. Grain affects how much paper grain is revealed in the strokes. Diffusion gives the soft edges to strokes, and Wet Fringe pools color along the stroke edges.

4 Sketching and painting the first washes. The first stage of the painting is a loose brush sketch and some areas of wash, painted with the Broad Water Brush, Simple Water and the Round Water Blender. In this project, painting is done on a clone copy of the reference photograph. The clone has an empty, or white Canvas. Select the reference image and choose File > Quick Clone. A clone copy appears with a blank Canvas, Tracing Paper turned on and the Cloners brushes selected in the Brush Selector Bar. In the Brush Selector Bar, switch to the Digital Watercolor category and choose the Simple Water brush. Using the Opacity slider in the Property Bar, reduce the Opacity to about 10%. For the sketch, choose a light color that will blend with the composition. You can choose a color in the Colors palette or sample color from the reference photo using the Dropper tool in the Toolbox.

Study your photograph carefully before you begin sketching and painting the first washes. Where is the light shining from? Take careful note of the light direction and the location of highlights, midtones and shadows.

Sketching the rocks and hills with the Simple Water brush over Basic Paper texture.

Painting light washes to suggest the background hills using a Broad Water Brush.

In this photograph shot in the morning, the clouds are lit from above and slightly from the left. Make note of the strongest lines in your composition. In the case of this image, these lines would be the leading lines from the foreground to midground and the gentle sloping lines of the hills that run into the horizon.

When you are pleased with the sketch, begin laying in the first washes using light tints. It's often best to work from background to foreground, with the background painted with less detail and less contrast. The Broad Water Brush is ideal for painting smooth areas of transparent color and for laying in the gentle forms of the coastal hills in the background. The Round Water Blender variant applies a small amount of color and blends new color with existing wet paint. In the Colors palette,

The Clone Color check box is selected in this illustration.

choose a color that harmonizes with your image (or you can paint with color from the reference photo by selecting the Clone Color check box on the Colors palette). To begin the sky, light colored washes are painted using a low opacity Soft Diffused Brush and a Round Water Blender brush. To suggest the sunlit areas on the clouds, leave the areas of "white paper." When you are satisfied with the first washes on the background hills and sky, save a new version of the file.

The first washes on the sky are painted using a Soft Diffused Brush and Round Water Blender. Use varied pressure on your stylus while pulling curved, horizontal strokes to suggest clouds in the sky.

Imagery from the reference is cloned into the working image to begin painting the foreground rocks and the water.

Using the Grainy Water variant of Blenders to model and blend the cloned in rock imagery, simplify it and give it a watercolor look.

5 Painting the foreground and water. The rocks in the foreground are complex shapes. When working from a photo reference that is complex like this one, it is often easier to clone some of the photo imagery directly into the painting and then blend areas with a Blenders brush—for a wet-into-wet look—later following up with more Digital Watercolor. To clone imagery into your painting, choose the Soft Cloner variant of Cloners in the Brush Selector Bar. To build up color gradually, reduce the Opacity of the Soft Cloner (try 10%) in the Property Bar. Here the imagery is cloned directly onto the Canvas. To clone imagery for a large area—for instance, the water—use a large Soft Cloner brush (try 60–70 pixels). Use a light touch on your stylus and change the size of the brush as you work over the various forms. For a traditional watercolor look, leave the brightest highlight areas as unpainted "white paper." Save the file.

The cloned imagery will be a base for loose brushwork using Blenders brushes to blend, smudge and pull paint. Choose the Grainy Water variant of Blenders in the Brush Selector Bar. The Grainy Water brush is sensitive to the paper texture chosen in the Paper Selector. Now view your image at 100%. Using the Grainy Water brush and your stylus, gently brush over the foreground imagery that you cloned, making sure to follow the direction of the forms. Pay careful attention to the most important shapes and to the highlights and shadows on the forms. Where possible, leave the white paper showing for highlights, as is done here for the sea foam next to the rocks. If you paint over an area you wanted to leave as white, you can always touch it up later with a small Eraser.

Carefully brushing over the rock forms using the Grainy Water. Leave less detail in the background areas and more detail in the foreground.

The in-progress image with the blended strokes on the foreground rock forms and water.

Using the Round Water Blender variant of Digital Watercolor to apply transparent washes of deeper color to the background cliffs and hills.

6 Applying deeper colored washes. With the rocky foreground painted, now it is time to add more color to the background hills and sky. The addition of deeper color in these areas will help to balance out the foreground. This process uses a new layer. To add a layer to your image, click the New Layer button on the bottom of the Layers palette. Select the Pick Up Underlying Color check box for the layer in the Layers palette. When you paint on a layer with Digital Watercolor, the layer automatically changes to Gel Composite Method, a transparent method that darkens as it builds up color.

Zoom out and take a good look at your image. Would the composition be improved by adding darker or lighter colors to the background? In the above right image, gray-purple washes are painted on the background hills using a low opacity Broad Water Brush. The Broad Water Brush applies transparent washes of smooth color with subtle pooling color along the edges of the strokes. Resize the brush if needed, using the Size slider in the Property Bar.

To apply deeper colored washes with soft edges to the clouds, try the Round Water Blender brush or the

Flat Water Blender brush. For the softer-edged strokes, in the Property Bar, increase the Diffusion from 6 to 10. To build up color on the clouds gradually, decrease the Opacity to 10% using the Opacity slider in the Property Bar. (You can sample color from the image using the Dropper tool or paint with color from the clone source, as you did in Step 5) For the wispy clouds, paint light

 Painting, drying and glazing. The glazing process in conventional watercolor involves laying down washes, letting the paint dry and then applying new color over the top of the dried color. With this process details can be painted without the new paint blending with or smudging the wet paint. To dry Digital Watercolor washes, choose Dry Digital Watercolor from the Layers menu or from the pop-up menu on the Layers palette. Now that the paint is dry, you can use a Digital Watercolor brush to apply a transparent glaze over the top. Glazing is an important technique to use when modeling forms in watercolor.

Blending the transparent washes of richer color on the clouds with a low opacity Round Water Blender.

Finessing the foreground water using the Round Water Blender, the Salt brush and the Wet Eraser.

tints using expressive, curved strokes. When the color and tones are as you like them, you can soften the Digital Watercolor imagery on the layer using the Diffuse Digital Watercolor feature chosen from the Layers palette menu.

For this painting, paint is dried, and the Grainy Water and Just Add Water variants of Blenders are used to further blend the brushwork on the soft cloud shapes. You can dry the imagery on the layer by selecting the layer and then choosing Layers > Dry Digital Watercolor. When the sky is complete, drop the layer to the Canvas by choosing Layers > Drop.

Softening Digital Watercolor. You can soften the look of wet Digital Watercolor brushwork using the Diffuse Digital Watercolor feature. Choose Diffuse Digital Watercolor from the Layers menu, or from the pop-up menu on the Layers palette. Applying the Diffuse Digital Watercolor command multiple times will continue to diffuse the stroke edges and the transitions between the colors.

7 **Finessing the foreground rocks and water.** Step back and take a good look at your image. Does the composition have balance and flow? Adding deeper colors to the sky in this image helped add interest and balance the composition, which has a strong foreground. The rocks and the foreground water are subdued to focus attention on the intriguing rocky shore. The final water and shore details are painted on the Canvas. Choose the Round Water Blender (Digital Watercolor) and size it smaller (try 7–10 pixels). Sample color from the image using the Dropper tool and darken or lighten as needed using the Colors palette. Then using the Round Water Blender, add subtle dimension to the water swirls and submerged rocks. The Salt brush is used to add texture to the sea foam. To lighten or remove wet paint, try the Gentle Wet Eraser or the Wet Eraser. Finally, the Digital Watercolor is dried and a brushed, smudged border is added to complete the image. (See page 92 for an example of a soft edge treatment.) The completed painting can be seen on page 126. Good work! In this project, you have explored using Digital Watercolor, Blenders and cloning.

Thoughts Hidden in Blue

Extraordinary Watercolors from Ordinary Pictures

My son was taking a break from important kid things when I grabbed my camera and caught him sitting still for a minute.

The biggest artistic influence in my own life is one of the more talented contemporary southwestern watercolorists, and my own father, Donal C. Jolley. Growing up in a home filled with wonderful art created by decades of trades with other fine artist friends left an appreciation for the skill, hard work and dedication required to be a successful artist.

A pencil in my father's hand was a magical thing when I was a boy. Try as I might, even using the same pencil, my own attempts to create anything as lively as his creations did not produce nearly the same results. The closest I could come was to trace his lines, and even that appeared awkward to me.

Fortunately, the pencil genes were passed on to me, and as I grew, so did the quality of my own work. It became my turn to make a pencil

"magical." Ultimately a keen interest in graphic arts turned into a profession, and then Adobe Photoshop came along. Creating interesting work came easily, but a way that satisfied my desire to create a Photoshop "watercolor" without stereotypical Photoshop fingerprints was one of the more elusive techniques.

This exercise does not rely upon filters, but instead uses a customized Pattern Brush, a regular Spatter Brush and layers with layer masks. Designed to be a springboard to your own experimentation, this process scratches the surface of what can be done. With custom brushes, scanned textures and brushwork on layer masks, you can extend the basics on the next few pages and take your work even further.

I find that prior to starting, taking the time to take a close look at a few

well-done watercolors by such artists as Charles Demuth, Edward Hopper and the contemporary master Steve Hanks helps me to stay on-target (and humble) with simulating the medium. I look at how each artist uses paper white, washes, spatter and salt so that I work more intuitively.

To take this New Year's Day 2006 snapshot of my son, my Canon Rebel XT with a 70–200mm lens was set on Shutter Priority at 1/60th second and ISO at 100. With an overcast day the aperture was forced to the lowest available, f/4.5, creating a narrow depth of field. Focusing on his facial features and zooming in eliminated details that detracted from the composition.

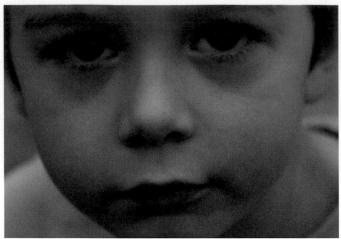

The original exposure is dark. Underexposed gray value pollutes every hue, so the goal is to remove the pollutant tints in Camera Raw.

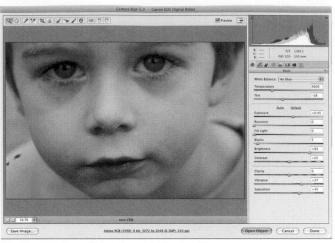

The Camera Raw dialog shows the basic adjustments.

1 **Opening the Camera Raw file.** There are several reasons why watercolor is notoriously difficult to reproduce in print. Limited color gamuts of traditional and digital printing are only part of the problem, with oranges, greens and blues being especially hard to match to the original. Reaching those bright colors are a challenge.

The goal of opening the Camera Raw file is to eliminate tints of unwanted color that pollute other colors, leaving them drab and muted. The tinting is due to underexposure, dirtying everything with a consistent gray tone. Increasing the exposure by setting the Exposure slider to +.45 changes the shadows, midtones and highlights as this tint is removed. Move the Brightness slider to +93 to brighten the highlight through mid-tone ranges without affecting the shadows further.

The White Balance for this shot was left as it was. By moving the Vibrance slider to +37, the already saturated colors became more saturated. A global saturation boost was added by moving the Saturation slider to +30. Click Open Image and immediately save your document, assigning any name that describes your work.

2 **Cropping and making a Stamp Pattern.** The initial cropping is pleasing, nicely framed and colored. To work in a high resolution to maximize detail, the image was resized to 3000 pixels wide by choosing the Image > Image Size command. The Resample Image and Constrain Proportions boxes should both be checked. Because the camera's sensor is built at a 3:2 ratio, the depth becomes 2000 pixels exactly. With a target output resolution of 300 dpi, the image is 10 inches wide. High-quality prints made at 200% increments will render excellent results at 20 and 40 inches wide, and good results at even 80 inches wide.

A Pattern Brush variation is arguably the best tool in the Photoshop arsenal for watercolor emulation. Pattern Brushes use a source pattern from which to draw color and form. When the image is at the desired size, the entire canvas is designated as a new pattern by choosing Edit > Define Pattern. A dialog prompts you to name the pattern. Name the pattern something related to your work. This pattern will become part of your own custom Pattern Library and can be used not only in this image, but also in others.

Cropped and sized, the white layer with reduced opacity allows you to see the original as you paint.

Experiment on the test layer to get the feel of the Pattern Brush settings. Note both the large areas of continuous strokes and individual strokes.

3 Adding paper and paint layers and testing brushes.
Just as a watercolorist paints on fresh, white paper, the Photoshop watercolorist needs a fresh, white layer on which to work. Make a new layer by choosing Layer > New > Layer or by using the New Layer button at the bottom of the Layers palette. Fill the new layer with white by pressing Shift-F5 and selecting White from the pop-up menu. Click OK to fill the new layer with white, hiding the background layer below. On the Layers palette move the Opacity slider to between 85–90%, enough to see the basic shapes and color fields from the background layer.

Lock your new layer by clicking on the Lock icon at the top of the Layers palette and make another new layer. This layer will eventually be the first layer of your painting, but first is used to make and test your watercolor brush, and to practice controlling the brush.

Select the Pattern Stamp tool from the Tools palette. Click on the Preset Pattern Picker on the Options Bar and scroll down to your newly created pattern. Click on it to establish this as your source pattern. Choose Window > Brushes to reveal the Brushes palette. Only two brushes are necessary to create *Thoughts Hidden in Blue*, one for painting and the other for the salt effect.

Click the arrow icon at the top right of the Brushes palette and choose Dry Media Brushes. Click Append when prompted; Photoshop's Dry Brush library is added to your list of available brushes. Select Pastel Medium Tip 29 and click in the box in front of Wet Edges. If you are using a pressure-sensitive tablet, be sure to click on the Shape Dynamics box, which allows pressure sensitivity to determine the brush tip size.

The brush preview at the bottom of the palette shows that this brush has just a bit of texture, with slightly uneven edges. The edges and ends are important to the stroke. A perfectly smooth edge is unrealistic on watercolor stock because of the nature of cold press paper, so avoid selecting brushes with perfectly smooth ends and edges.

Use the Master Diameter slider to enlarge your brush to 120 and begin painting individual elements onto your test layer. Go over the skin, experimenting with how the strokes work together. Before tackling the eyes and lips, scale down the brush tip to 60 pixels.

Block out large areas on this practice layer as well as small strokes, trying large and medium brush sizes. The more familiar you are with the brush before you begin,

Watercolors build up as wet layers are allowed to dry, then covered by new strokes.

The Pattern Brush builds until near full opacity of the solid cyan, yellow and magenta patterns is achieved.

the more satisfaction you'll have creating your art, and the better your work will appear upon completion.

Two characteristics of traditional watercolors easily emulated by hand are white edges, and wet or dry layers. White paper often separates one field of color from the next when an artist paints. Although this natural aspect is so much a part of watercolor painting, filters have a difficult time producing the irregular separations of a hand-painted original across an entire piece. As you paint along with this project, you'll naturally re-create this filter-free effect, enhancing the "watercolor" appearance.

It is *very* important to realize that the watercolor "look" requires several layers, not just one. One layer on its own will appear rather plain and uninspired. Wet and dry layers are emulated by controlling both brushstrokes and layers. When Photoshop draws a stroke with Wet Edges enabled, it is semitransparent with build up around the edge of the stroke. As long as pressure is maintained, the stroke's edge remains active and large areas can be covered. Each stroke behaves as a traditional wet layer that drys immediately when pressure is released.

The semitransparency of the strokes is an important difference between the traditional media and Photoshop. Traditional watercolor is transparent, and all layers are visible. Photoshop's semitransparent strokes build up opacity, eventually becoming fully opaque and hiding everything below. To re-create the effects in this project, multiple layers are created for strokes covering the same area. Placing these strokes on different layers instead of placing all of them on one layer allows more flexibility to build interesting effects such as brush detail, multiple washes and the salt effects on page 142.

One very noticeable difference between a watercolor painting on cold press paper and digital emulation is the lack of visual texture. Paper plays an immense role in how pigment is absorbed and distributed, and its physical dimension literally adds a sense of depth. Don't worry about that right now. Texture will be added in two ways— through the watercolor effects in the project and either a digital texture applied or output on watercolor stock. It is worth knowing it now, however, so that you can consider your approach while you work and paint accordingly.

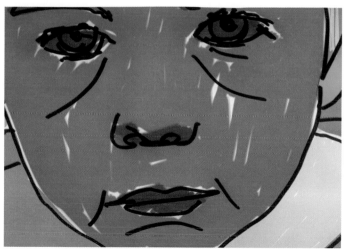

Each color represents a unique "wet layer" area. When brushing over these areas, one continuous stroke is often required.

The first areas to tackle are the medium-sized color shapes. Avoid a lot of overlap on the layer by keeping the pressure on your stroke.

4 **Making a metaphoric roadmap to follow.** Now that you've become a bit more familiar with the brush and how edges come together, choose Edit > Select > All; then press the Delete key to clear your practice layer. Examine the photograph with the intent of dividing the image into working areas.

For *Thoughts Hidden in Blue,* the different grouped areas are pictured above. The five areas to handle separate from each other are the eyes, the inner nostrils and mouth, the hair and ears, the neck, the gold shirt and brown background, and the rest of the facial skin. Each grouping has distinct shapes and colors and are logical items to handle separately. *(Note: There is no need to actually create a map like the example above!)*

Unlike traditional watercolor media, the sequence in which each group is painted is not nearly as important as the groupings themselves. Using traditional media you apply large washes over areas such as sea or sky, gradually building up from simple washes toward more specific details. It's a completely subjective decision where you start, but at the beginning, it's wise to select medium-sized areas, such as the shirt and background, to get going.

5 **Starting with medium-sized coverage areas.** An advantage of beginning with medium-sized coverage areas is that small strokes and detail are easier and more effectively placed in the last stages, while large areas are difficult to cover. When large areas are covered, you can't let up on the stroke until the entire area is painted, so knowing exactly where you want to paint is helpful.

In this image, the brilliant orange sweatshirt presents an attractive place to start work due to its location and size. Double-click on the test layer's name on the Layers palette, and retitle it Sweater/Background. On the

 Look before you paint! As you plan the area to cover with your stroke, be sure none of it is hidden behind any palettes and that there is ample room for your hand and arm to reach comfortably to every section. It's quite frustrating to be well into covering a large area with a long and complex stroke only to find a critical area covered! Once you let up on the stroke, the edge is completed, and overlap becomes a problem.

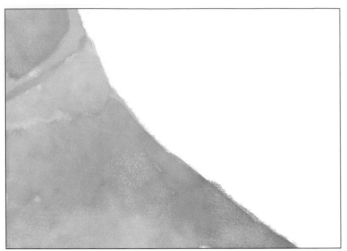

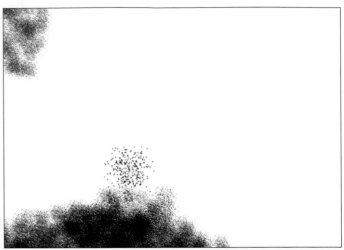

Two layers of the sweater and the background combined make believable watercolor blends and edges. The Salt effect can be easily seen.

This is the grayscale layer mask applied to the Sweater/Background 2 layer, resulting in the salt effects shown in the picture to the left.

Options Bar, use the Master Diameter slider to make the brush 70 pixels wide. (You should still be using the Pastel Medium Tip 29 brush from Step 3.)

Start with the orange in the lower-left, keeping pressure applied with the stylus until the shirt is completely covered. Paint the opposite side to complete the sweater; then move to the background. Paint the background exactly like you did the orange sweater, again avoiding multiple strokes and overlaps. As you paint, try to minimize edge overlap and try to butt color fields one to another. When small white lines separate one stroke from the next, leave them! They are common in watercolor painting, and their irregular size and placement is something you can not duplicate using filters.

The stroke will appear lighter than the original pattern due to the natural reduced opacity of the brush. As more strokes are placed over each other, opacity is built up. At first it appears that the brush is set to Multiply mode because where strokes overlap, they darken. This isn't due to a Multiply setting, but because the brush is grayscale. The strokes are actually on Normal mode, and the overlapping strokes will only get to 100% opacity of the original pattern.

When the area is covered to your satisfaction, make a new layer using Layer > New > Layer. Name the new layer Sweater/Background 2. Paint over the same areas on this new layer, again keeping the stylus pressure applied until your stroke is completely done. The edges don't have to trap perfectly, and with each overlaying layer it becomes less important to keep the pressure down during the entire stroke as the increased opacity hides edges and overlaps.

When you are finished with the second layer painting, apply a layer mask by choosing Layer > Layer Mask > Reveal All. With the layer mask targeted, select black as the foreground color and select the Brush tool by pressing the B key. Press F5 to open the Brushes palette, select the Spatter 59 brush tip, and scale the brush to 90 pixels on the Master Diameter slider. Click on the Brush Tip Shape control near the top left of the Brushes palette and change the Spacing slider to 85%.

Paint on the layer mask either with short dabs or more irregular, yet defined shapes to create traditional salt-like or wet-in-wet wash effects. Experiment with your own custom brushes and textures on your layer masks.

Save your image before you continue.

The first Face layer is made from one long, continuous stroke with the Pattern Stamp brush.

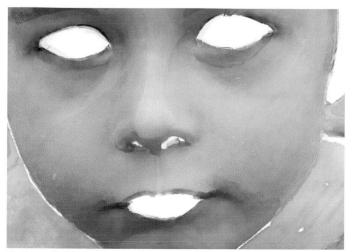

At the end of Step 6 the facial features have yet to be started.

6 Painting larger areas. Larger areas of coverage are trickier than smaller areas due to brush control. It is difficult, but you must keep your strokes going for as long as possible. If you lose grip on the stylus, or run out of mousepad space, you'll have to undo the entire stroke and start over. This is particularly frustrating near the end of a well-done job of blending! Make sure you have enough room before you start and that you can see the entire area you plan to cover, including areas covered by palettes.

In *Thoughts Hidden in Blue,* the skin tones of the face and neck make up these more difficult layers. Make a new layer by choosing Layer > New > Layer, and name it Face. Select the Pattern Stamp tool again. The same Pattern Stamp brush you previously used returns when returning to a tool. Scale the brush to 120 pixels using the Master Diameter slider on the Brushes palette.

Start on a cheek, away from the edge of the face, and then work your way around the face until all of the skin is painted, applying pressure throughout the entire stroke. Use circular motions instead of straight strokes to bring out more depth.

The result of this one, long stroke is a layer that appears paler and weaker than the original picture. To build up

the tone, choose Layer > Duplicate Layer and leave the name Face copy. Leaving these two layers visible, make another new layer by choosing Layer > New > Layer.

Name the layer Skin and Neck and then paint over the face yet again. This time it is not important to keep the pressure on the stroke for the entire time because the third layer has enough built-up coverage that new brushwork doesn't stand out so easily.

Thus far, the neck remains unpainted. Add a new stroke to cover the neck on this layer, including it in the stroke to build up the left cheek so as to be seamless.

Add a layer mask by choosing Layer > Layer Mask > Reveal All. Select the Brush tool by pressing the B key. Select the Spatter 59 brush, adjusting it exactly as you did in Step 5. Create your watercolor effects by painting with black on the layer mask.

Repeat this on the Face copy layer, so that it also receives a layer mask and brushwork. Waiting until the Skin and Neck layer is completed before coming back to add this layer mask makes the brushwork on the mask more subtle and well-placed. Save your image!

The Features One layer with the skin layers turned off shows how one layer of color on the eyes, ears, nose, mouth and neck appears.

The "Features Two" layer, now with all layers turned on, is used to darken and add detail to the facial features.

7 Painting the eyes, nose and mouth. Details are usually the last thing to add when finishing any work of art, and painting a Photoshop watercolor is no exception. The two layers of this step include the finishing details, with a lot of small, overlapping strokes on both.

Once again add a new layer by choosing Layer > New > Layer. Double-click on the layer's name in the Layers palette, renaming it Features One. Immediately make a second new layer, naming it Features Two. Add layer masks to each of these layers by individually selecting each one and choosing Layer > Layer Mask > Reveal All.

Select the Features One layer, choose the Pattern Stamp tool once again and reduce the Pastel Medium Tip brush size to 45. Rough in the lips, leaving irregular white highlights to show reflections. Move to the eyes, first filling in the whites, then pupils, and then the iris, again leaving traces of white for the reflections. After working in the nostrils, increase the brush size back to 120 to fill in the hair and ears. Finish the painting on this layer by laying down a second pass of color over the neck.

When the neck is complete, select the Features Two layer and reduce the brush size to 30. Again, go over each

area, this time leaving off the neck. The pupils should be built up to black and the iris made up of overlapping strokes resembling spokes on a bicycle wheel.

Select the individual layer masks and choose the Brush tool by pressing the B key. With the Spatter brush still active, again mask out areas to bring out the salt and wash effects, just as you've done in the previous two steps.

The final task, if you choose not to go on to Step 8, is to return 100% opacity to the white layer above the original background. On the Layers palette, select and unlock the layer, and then slide the Opacity back to 100%.

Save your image.

At this point, you can decide whether to add texture or leave it as it is. If the work is to be output on a textured watercolor stock, Step 8 may not be necessary, or you might reduce the opacity of the texture layer. The paper itself will show texture, and printing a texture onto a texture may render strange results. If the stock has little or no texture, move on to Step 8.

The grayscale scan of a painted piece of watercolor stock needs to have its entire range compressed to fit between 60–92% gray.

Applied on Overlay mode, the watercolor scan adds natural watercolor texture and imperfections to the piece.

8 **Finishing with texture.** Texture is an impressive, lifelike addition to the appearance of a Photoshop watercolor. You'll need actual watercolor stock and a brush full of blue, green or dark brown watercolor paint.

Tape down the piece of watercolor paper using masking tape on all sides. When it's tightly fixed to the table, get the entire face of the paper wet using a paper towel and a glass of water. Before it dries, paint it as evenly as possible with the watercolor paint. It only has to be dark enough to bring out the roughness and natural imperfections in the paper, and one wet layer is enough. Brush out distinct bleeds or dark areas until the entire surface appears nearly uniform.

After the paper dries, place it in your scanner bed. If the paper is not flat to the glass, place a book or stack of paper on it until it lies completely flat.

Scan the surface using Grayscale mode at 100% using a resolution of 300 dpi. Open the scan in Photoshop then choose Image > Adjustments > Curves to bring up the Curves dialog. Because your scan is different from anyone else's, there isn't any one setting to make this layer perfect. Using both ends of the Curves line, reduce the contrast of the layer one end at a time until the lightest area hovers close to 60% gray and the darkest is no more than a very occasional 92% gray pixel. The majority of the darker pixels will fall somewhere between 72% and 80% gray. To check your pixel shade, choose Window > Color. Click on the arrow button at the top right corner of the Color palette and select the Grayscale Slider option. Select the Eyedropper tool and sample individual pixels. The percentage will appear on the color slider. When you're happy with the scan, save it to the same folder as your painting.

Select the entire textured area by choosing Select > All and then return to your watercolor emulation. Click on the top layer in the Layers palette and choose Edit > Paste to place the texture over every other layer. Scale the texture to fit by choosing Edit > Transform > Free Transform. Press and hold the Shift key to constrain the proportions. When you're satisfied with the placement press Enter/Return to complete the resizing.

On the Layers palette, set the layer mode to Overlay, reduce the opacity to 50% and save. You are done!

Using Real Bristle Brushes for a Quick Acrylic Study

Photoshop and Painter **148**

Using Chiaroscuro Lighting in an Oil Painting

Photoshop and Painter **156**

Turning Noise into Beautiful Digital Oils

Photoshop **168**

Using the Artists' Oils for an Expressive, Old Masters Style

Photoshop and Painter **180**

146

6

ACHIEVING ACRYLIC
AND OIL-PAINTED LOOKS

In this chapter, you'll see recommendations for taking photographs that are appropriate for applying painterly techniques. In the projects, you'll learn how to combine your photographs with acrylic and oil-paint brushstrokes and effects, using the features in Photoshop and Painter.

Using Real Bristle Brushes for a Quick Acrylic Study begins with shooting a seascape with a wide angle lens and preparing the photo for painting. After the photo is retouched in Photoshop, it is opened in Painter and cloned. Then an underpainting is made and the Real Bristle Brushes are used in combination with a Wacom tablet to paint a dramatic seascape.

Using Chiaroscuro Lighting in an Oil Painting teaches how to shoot and retouch a photograph that will be used as reference for a dramatically lit painting. The Artists' Oils brushes are used on layers to paint the portrait, including modeling the forms and painting the head and hair. As a final step, the contrast is adjusted for more drama and the brushwork is finessed.

Turning Noise into Beautiful Digital Oils is a Photoshop project that shows how to use the texture in photographic noise in combination with the Wet Media brush presets to build a digital oil painting, and Wet Media brushstrokes of different sizes are applied to layers. A variation with more ideas for incorporating film grain, texture and digital noise into your painting projects follows.

Using the Artists' Oils for an Expressive, Old Masters Style is an advanced project that uses Photoshop in combination with the Artists' Oils Brushes in Painter to create a expressive painting. The values and color are adjusted and the image is cropped. The project then turns to Painter for incorporating custom brushes, using multiple clone sources for reference, applying loose brushwork and modeling of the forms.

Moon Over Lennox

Using Real Bristle Brushes for a Quick Acrylic Study

Six of the photos from the shoot. The image in the upper-right has interesting horizontals and a dynamic perspective that gives it a good sense of depth.

Known for its versatility, conventional acrylic paint is great to use for quick studies with large brushes. The paint dries quickly and can be extended with water or mediums, slowing its drying time and facilitating blending. The Real Bristle Brushes in Painter are ideal to use when creating acrylic looks. With *Moon Over Lennox*, this project demonstrates loose, expressive brushwork on a simple landscape with an amazing sky. The Real Bristle Brushes in Painter can be used for both acrylic and oils looks.

For this photo shoot of the sky and sea in Australia, I focused on capturing the color and perspective of the clouds using my Canon 18–55mm zoom lens on the Canon 20D. I was intrigued with the moon and colorful lighting on the puffy cumulus clouds after a rain. I shot several photographs using a variety of compositions.

For the chosen photograph, I used Aperture Priority mode, with an aperture of f/9, and a 35 mm focal length, for a wide angle view and good depth of field. I set the shutter speed at 1/400 and the ISO at 200. The wide depth of field would yield good detail and reference for painting the clouds.

When I opened the photograph in the Camera Raw dialog, I saw that it would benefit from subtle color and tonal adjustments. Enlarging the moon slightly would add drama.

For inspiration before your shoot, look at skies in the landscapes of the English master John Constable, including such works as *Brighton Beach* and *Willows by the Stream*. For a warmer palette, look at the landscapes of Spanish master Joaquin Sorolla y Bastida. Now let's get to work!

The photograph with colors and tones enhanced.

The retouched image with the larger moon.

1 **Opening the digital original and making edits.** For this project, the original photo measures 3504 x 2336 pixels. This photograph was captured in Camera Raw, and opened directly in the Camera Raw dialog and viewed at 100%.

Open your image in the Camera Raw dialog and decide if the tones and colors need adjustment. In the case of this image, the Vibrance is increased to +20 to balance the saturation of the color, and to enhance the blues in the sky and sunrise color in the clouds. Saturation is also increased to +10. To rescue details the narrow band of foreground foliage, Fill Light is increased to +30. See the Camera Raw sidebar on page 12 in Chapter 1 for detailed information.

When you are satisfied with the edits on your image, press Alt/Option and click Open Copy to open a copy of the image in Photoshop. Preserve your original photo by saving a new version. Choose File > Save As, and then give your working image a new, descriptive name.

Does your photo need retouching? This photograph did not have any unwanted artifacts that needed to be removed, but for drama and compositional interest, the size of the moon is increased.

The retouching can be done in Photoshop (used here) or Painter. Drag the Background layer over the Create a New Layer icon on the Layers palette to make a copy the Background layer for retouching. To edit and increase the size of an area, make a selection around the area you want to enlarge. The Elliptical Marquee tool is used to select the moon. To constrain the selection to a perfect circle, hold down the Shift key when dragging. For a transparent edge on the selection that will help it merge with the existing sky, choose Select > Modify > Feather and enter a number in the field (try 20). Now that the area is selected and feathered, choose Edit > Free Transform. Four handles will appear on the corners of the selection marquee. To scale the area proportionately, press the Shift key as you drag a corner handle.

When you've completed retouching the photo, choose File > Save As and save your edited image in Photoshop format, with a descriptive name. (I named my image *Lennox clouds retouch.psd*.)

The photo, before using Smart Blur, shows more fine detail in the water (left); after applying, the image has a smoother appearance (right).

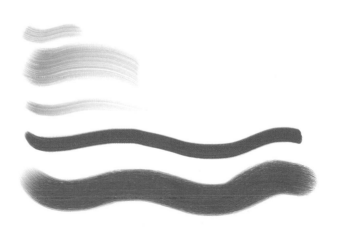

A sampling of Real Bristle brushstrokes, from top to bottom: Real Fan Short, Real Fan Soft, Real Flat, Real Flat Opaque and Real Round.

2 Making a clone and simplifying. Open Painter, choose File > Open and navigate to the edited image that you saved in Photoshop. To preserve the retouched version, you'll perform this step on a clone copy. Choose File > Clone and save the clone using a descriptive name. To simplify the photographic detail, this project uses the Smart Blur feature. Open the Underpainting palette by choosing Window > Show Underpainting. In the Underpainting palette, experiment with the Smart Blur slider, based on the level of detail that you want to keep. This image uses a small amount of Smart Blur (15%) because a bit of grain or noise aids in the Real Bristle painting process. The Real Bristle Brushes can pick up a separate color in each brush hair, as you will experience in Step 3. Save the blurred file in Painter's native format, RIF. For more information about using the Smart Blur feature, see page 91.

3 Getting acquainted with Real Bristle Brushes. The Real Bristle Brushes are unique bristle brushes that are sensitive to the pressure, tilt and bearing of the stylus, allowing very natural-looking brushstrokes. Varying the pressure and the angle of the brush causes the bristles to splay and twist, just like a conventional brush. In the example above, several Real Bristle Brushes are shown that apply new, colored paint. The Real Bristle category also features several Blenders that are very useful for working over photos. These Blenders smear pixels, without applying new color.

 Setting up Brush Tracking in Painter. Before you begin to paint, set up Brush Tracking so you can customize how Painter interprets the input of your stylus, including parameters such as pressure and speed. Choose Edit > Preferences > Brush Tracking or choose Corel Painter > Preferences > Brush Tracking. Make a brushstroke in the preview window.

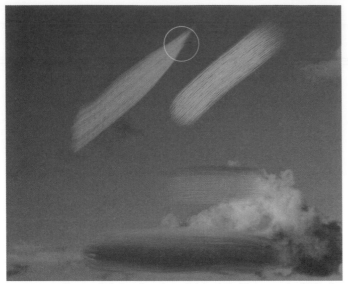

Practice strokes: Real Flat and Real Round (top) and bottom: Real Blender Round and Real Blender Flat. The Enhanced Brush Ghost is enabled.

Analyzing the lighting in the photo with Smart Blur applied. The lighting comes from above and from the upper-left.

Because the Real Bristle Brushes can interpret every subtle movement of the stylus, they are sensitive to Brush Tracking. Make sure to set up the Brush Tracking before you begin to paint.

Choose the Real Bristle Brushes category in the Brush Selector Bar. The Real Blender Flat and Real Blender Round variants smear existing pixels without adding new color and are ideal for laying in the first brushwork.

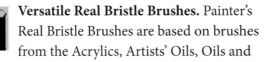 **Versatile Real Bristle Brushes.** Painter's Real Bristle Brushes are based on brushes from the Acrylics, Artists' Oils, Oils and Watercolor categories. As you paint, the Real Bristle Brushes are sensitive to subtle nuances of your hand and stylus. The Enhanced Brush Ghost gives visual feedback on the tilt, bearing and rotation of the stylus if your tablet is equipped with these features. Choose Edit or Corel Painter > Preferences > General, and make sure that Enable Brush Ghosting and Enhanced Brush Ghost are turned on.

Make some practice strokes on your photo using both of these brushes. Now try making practice strokes with the Real Round and Real Flat brushes. These last two brushes apply new color, based on the color chosen in the Colors palette. When you have finished practicing, undo the strokes by choose File > Revert.

The first stage of the painting is the loose understudy, built by smearing the pixels on the photograph—and

Using a large 50-pixel Real Blender Flat brush to smear the pixels on the cloud.

Building depth in the clouds by painting brushstrokes of various sizes with the Real Blender Flat and Real Blender Round brushes.

To achieve a feeling of movement in the sky, expressive horizontal strokes are used to suggest shadows on the clouds in the lower areas of the sky.

loosely painting over the entire photographic image. In this project, painting is done on a copy of the Canvas layer. To put a copy of the Canvas on a layer, choose Select > All and then press the Alt/Option key and choose Select > Float. With the layer selected, select the Pick Up Underlying Color check box on the Layers palette.

Before you begin painting the clouds, study your photograph carefully. Which direction does the light shine from? Where are the highlights, midtones and shadows? In this photograph, the clouds are lit from above and slightly from the left side. The loose brushwork on the sky and clouds is painted using the Real Blender Flat brush, varying the size of the brush while working over broad or fine areas. (Try 25–50 pixels.) If the size of your file is much smaller or larger, you'll want to proportionately adjust the sizes of your brushes in Steps 3–4.

To paint the shadow under a cloud, the stylus and brush are pulled horizontally to suggest the shadow. The repetition of horizontal strokes in the clouds also gives the sky a feeling of exciting, dynamic movement. If you want to add additional color, you can sample color from

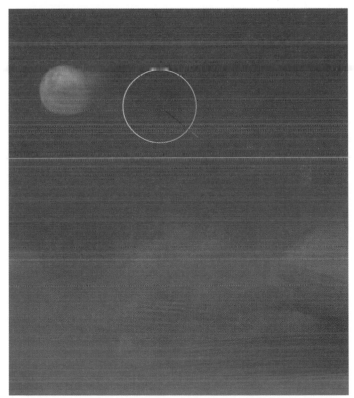

Painting short, horizontal strokes over the blue sky. The Enhanced Brush Ghost shows the size, tilt, bearing and rotation of the brush and stylus.

The highlights are painted with shorter curved strokes.

The completed loose understudy painted with various sizes of the Real Blender Flat, Real Blender Round and Real Blender Tapered brushes.

the image using the Dropper tool and mix it using the Mixer palette or choose a color in the Colors palette. For information about using the Mixer, see page 224 in Chapter 8. Then apply the new color using the Real Oils Short, Real Flat or Real Round brushes. The Real Oils Short is an ideal brush for blocking in large areas of color quickly.

Colors sampled from the image, applied to the Mixer palette and blended to create color variations.

Take another careful look at the highlights in your image and look for any suggestion of movement that will inspire the direction of your strokes. In this image, the midtone and highlight areas of the puffy cumulus clouds are painted using shorter, curved strokes to model the airy forms. When you are pleased with the understudy, save a new version of the file.

4 **Finessing and refining while keeping it loose.** Now zoom into your image and look for the wilder, more random brushwork in the understudy. Where would your painting benefit from subtle finessing and touch-up? It's important to keep a loose feeling with this project and not to make your painting too polished or rendered. The beauty of the Real Bristle Brushes is that they paint so naturally. A few wild, expressive accents add character and excitement to your painting.

Next add a new layer for the refined brushwork. Click the New Layer button on the Layers palette, and when the new layer appears, select the Pick Up Underlying Color check box. As you finesse the forms and brushwork, switch back and forth between the Real Blender Flat and Real Blender Round brushes, changing the size of the brushes as you work. For more dramatic thick-to-thin brushstrokes, try the Real Blender Tapered brush. The details on the moon and the highlights on the clouds are painted with small Real Round and Real Flat Opaque brushes (7–10 pixels). The Real Flat Opaque is an expressive brush that applies more opaque paint. A small Real Round brush (10–12

Adding more subtle detail to the clouds and sky while retaining the loose feeling.

Painting brighter color on the broken waves in the foreground and loose strokes under the clouds.

pixels) is used to paint brighter color on the breaking waves in the foreground. As details are finessed, brushwork is kept loose, and elements are suggested rather than rendered. The completed color study can be seen on page 148.

Next try adding touches of new color sampled from another area of your image or from the Mixer palette, applying paint with the Real Flat or Real Round brushes. For interesting bristle textures, try the Real Fan Short or the Real Fan Soft brushes. For a tapered bristle brush that paints with a wet, oily feel, try the Real Tapered Bristle brush.

Good work! In this project you explored painting with the amazing Real Bristle Brushes in Painter, using layers and the Pick Up Underlying Color feature.

The Paint 2 layer is chosen and the Pick Up Underlying Color check box is turned on.

Using a small Real Tapered Round brush to paint highlights on the moon and clouds.

Rachel

Using Chiaroscuro Lighting in an Oil Painting

The photo shoot was done with Rembrandt-inspired lighting and an oil painting in mind. The photograph in the upper-corner has a strong, dynamic composition and good lighting.

Chiaroscuro—dramatic light and shadow—is most often used with portrait and still life subjects. For this painting of *Rachel*, the lighting is simplified by using only one light source from above. Then the subject is painted with three planes in mind, the plane facing the light, the middle-tone plane and the forms away from the light, or the shadow plane. The light against the mostly dark composition gives the subject a strong three-dimensional quality.

The candid, live action shoot required capturing numerous photos to achieve the desired portrait. It was not practical to use a tripod in the dark room because of the need to move around in the crowd. To capture the chosen photograph, I used a Canon f/1.4 fixed focal length lens on the Canon 5D, a shutter speed of 1/100 and a very high ISO of 1600.

The Artists' Oils medium in Painter allows you to fill a canvas with oil and dip your brush into a photograph and smear pixels as if they were wet oily paint. This project uses the Pick Up Underlying Color feature in Painter, which allows you to pull color from underlying layers onto new layers. The studio lighting in the image is left warm, and a limited palette of warm browns, reds and golds are used. Before completing the image, a final contrast adjustment is made using a dynamic layer and a layer mask, and then final details are painted with expressive strokes.

Before beginning the project, check out the work of master artists Michelangelo Caravaggio, Leonardo da Vinci, and Rembrandt van Rijn. In this technique you'll set up a portrait or still life with an angled overhead light source and then use the Artists' Oils brushes on layers to build an oil painting.

Before the tonal adjustments, the photo has blown-out highlights.

The adjusted image with some highlight detail restored in the face.

1 **Opening the digital original and recovering detail.**
The original photograph used in this technique measures 2336 x 3504 pixels. If your file is much smaller or larger, you may need to proportionately adjust the sizes of the brushes in Steps 2 through 9.

Make sure to preview your image at 100% in the Camera Raw dialog to check for focus, highlight and shadow detail, and any noise problems. The candid photograph above was shot under a spotlight in a dark studio. The dramatic look is exciting, but to use it as a reference for a painting, it's helpful to recover detail in the highlights and shadows. To begin, the photo was captured in Camera Raw and opened directly in the Camera Raw dialog. For detailed information about using Camera Raw, see page 12 in Chapter 1.

Open your image in Camera Raw and adjust its tones and color if needed. To bring out shadow detail behind the subject, for this image, Fill Light is increased to +5.

Then the Recovery slider is used to restore detail in the highlights (try +15). Brightness is left at +50 (as shot) and Contrast is decreased from +25 to +15. The rich, golden cast of the image is retained for mood.

To further finesse the tones, click on the Tone Curve button and experiment with the sliders to see the effect. This image needs more detail restored in the highlights, so the Highlights slider is reduced to –50 and the Lights slider is reduced to –20. Because the location was dark except for the spotlight, an extremely high ISO 1600 was used. The Canon 5D is capable of shooting at high ISO settings with minimum noise. If you want to minimize the appearance of noise in your image, click on the Detail button and adjust the Noise Reduction sliders. This image uses a Luminance Noise Reduction of +50. Change Sharpening to 0. When the preview of the image is as you like it, press Alt/Option to open a copy of your image, and save the file in PSD format.

Repairing an area on the bass using a soft-tipped Clone Stamp tool.

The retouched photograph.

2 Repairing artifacts. This retouching step can be accomplished in Photoshop (used here) or Painter. Preview your image at 100% and use the Hand tool to pan around and look for image elements that need retouching. For this image, the Clone Stamp tool is used to repair a few artifacts on the bass fiddle and other elements in the background.

For the most flexible workflow, it's a good idea to retouch on a copy of the Background layer. Drag the Background layer over the Create a New Layer icon on the Layers palette to copy it. Choose the Clone Stamp tool in the Toolbox, and in the Options Bar, select the Aligned check box. To sample only from the active layer, set the Sample pop-up menu to Current Layer. Choose a soft brush tip (19–45 pixels is used here) from the Brush Preset Picker. To sample with the Clone Stamp tool, Alt-click/Option-click, click in the area you want to retouch and then paint to replace the damaged area with pixels

from the source area. See page 112 for more information about retouching with the Clone Stamp tool. After retouching, save your image in Photoshop format, using a descriptive name. This image uses *Rachel retouch.psd*.

 Retouching in Painter. Retouching can also be done in Painter. Choose the Rubber Stamp tool in the Toolbox and select either the Soft Mode or Hard Mode in the Property Bar. To sample with the Rubber Stamp tool, Alt-click/Option-click. Release the key, click in the area you want to repair and paint to replace the area. For those who like the feel of a brush, Painter also offers the Cloner tool, which uses the same key combinations to sample imagery, prior to repairing.

Using the Wet Oily Palette Knife to smear test strokes on the cloned photo.

Practice stroking with Oil Palette Knife, Dry Brush and Blender Brush.

3 **Making a clone and trying out brushes.** Begin by opening the retouched photo you saved in Step 2. Now create a clone of the image, by choosing File > Clone. The clone image will be a flattened copy of the retouched image. Choose File > Save As and save the image using a descriptive name in Painter's native format, RIF (this image uses *Rachel paint 01.rif*).

Using the Artists' Oils brushes, you can smear the photographic imagery, similar to oily paint, as if you are dipping your palette knife into the photo and smearing it. Choose the Artists' Oils category in the Brush Selector Bar and the Wet Oily Palette Knife variant. Make strokes on the photo using your stylus, pushing and pulling the pixels like oily paint. The palette knives smear and move existing paint without applying new color, and the brushes apply new colored paint. Try out these palette knives on your photo: the Wet Oily Palette Knife, Oil Palette Knife and Blender Palette Knife. Now use the Dry Brush

and Blender Brush to paint a few strokes on your photo. Note that the leading edge of an Artists' Oils brushstroke changes depending on whether the stylus is held erect or if it is tilted. The effect is subtle. After exploring the brushes, undo the practice strokes by choosing File > Revert. Move on to Step 4 to work on the underpainting.

 **Painting with Artists' Oils.** The Artists' Oils is a rich medium with a remarkable viscous feel similar to conventional oil paint. When you touch an Artists' Oil brush to the canvas, the entire canvas is filled with oil, allowing you to paint expressive strokes until the brush runs out of paint. When you apply a new brushstroke over existing paint, new paint mixes with the underlying paint. For more information about Artists' Oils see page 162. You can also read more about the Artists' Oils in *The Painter X Wow! Book* (Peachpit Press).

The working image with subtle Smart Blur applied to the photo.

Applying loose brushwork to the background behind the subject.

4 Simplifying for an underpainting. The Photo-painting system in Painter has useful tools that can help simplify unwanted photographic detail. For instance, the Smart Blur feature on the Underpainting palette allows you to remove high-frequency photographic detail. Choose Window > Show Underpainting and adjust the Smart Blur Amount slider to your taste. The size of your image will affect the strength of the Smart Blur effect. This image uses 10%, for a subtle effect, as shown in the image above. The effect is "live," and you can continue to experiment with the slider until you click the Apply button to accept. Save the file. For more information about the Smart Blur feature, see page 91.

5 Applying expressive brushwork to a layer. This technique uses a copy of the Background layer and the Pick Up Underlying Color feature on the Layers palette, which allows you to pull color up from the Canvas onto a layer. First, put a copy of the Canvas onto a layer. Choose Select > All. Then Alt-click/Option-click and choose Select > Float. A layer titled Layer 1 will appear. To rename the layer, double-click on its name and enter a new name in the Layer Attributes dialog.

Pick Up Underlying Color is selected and the paint 1 layer is active.

Now the image is ready for brushwork to be applied on the layer. In the Brush Selector Bar, choose the Wet Oily Palette Knife variant of Artists' Oils. Analyze your image,

Painting subtle strokes on the window using the Wet Oily Palette Knife.

Modeling forms on the sleeve using the Oil Palette Knife.

Artists' Oils settings. When you choose an Artists' Oils brush, the context-sensitive Property Bar contains important settings that affect the Artists' Oils: Size, Opacity, Grain (how sensitive the brush is to paper texture), Dirty Mode (allows the brush to pick up color from the canvas as you apply new paint), Viscosity (how the medium flows through the brush, resulting in longer or shorter strokes), Blend (how new brushstrokes blend with existing strokes) and Wetness (how the new paint mixes with the existing paint). These and other settings are also located in the Artists' Oils panel of the Brush Controls (Window > Show Brush Controls > Artists' Oils) and in the Brush Creator (Window > Show Brush Creator). When you have time for a break, try experimenting with some of your own settings.

observing how the light falls on the background shapes and forms. Using your stylus, apply brushstrokes over the background so the strokes loosely follow the contours of the forms. For the windows in this background, subtle diagonal brushstrokes are painted on the shadows. To paint the rectangular window frames, the strokes are pulled vertically and horizontally. Continue painting over the background until the entire area behind your subject is covered with the loose brushwork. Save the file.

Take another look at your image. Notice how the light falls on the clothing, paying careful attention to the direction of the shadows and highlights on the folds. Choose the Oil Palette Knife and use this brush to paint subtle strokes over the forms, letting your brushstrokes follow the contours of the shadows and highlights. Adjust the size of the brush as you work using the Size slider in the Property Bar. (The shadows on the sleeve are painted using a 12-pixel brush.) In these illustrations, the strokes

Using the Oil Palette Knife to paint shadows and highlights.

Loosely painting the planes on the face with the Blender Palette Knife.

are pulled along the direction of the folds on the sweater and pants, painting the shadows first and then the highlights. The highlights at this stage are painted using a smaller 7–10 pixel brush. In areas where the shadows and highlights meet, short, dabbing strokes are used. The process creates a subtle painted texture, which is more

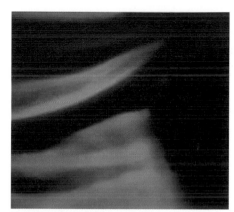

Painting short, dabbing strokes to show the transitions in value on the pants

desirable than attempting to completely blend the highlight areas into the shadow areas. The colors will mix in the eye of the viewer. Try to avoid scrubbing or brushing back and forth over these areas.

6 **Painting the face and hands.** The face is the focal point, and the hands are an important supporting element that often lends expression to a portrait. Take a good look at the face in your image. Notice the planes of the head and how light transitions into shadow on the forms. These elements will benefit from a softer brush that allows more blending. Choose the Blender Palette Knife variant of Artists' Oils in the Brush Selector Bar. Using short, dabbing strokes, paint subtle brushwork to model the forms in the head, paying careful attention to how the light plays over the forms. Again, try not to scrub with the stylus, but leave the small dabbed strokes for the painted feeling at this stage. Final finessing can come later, if you prefer a more blended look on the face.

Now take a good look at the hands. For this project, think simply. Reduce the forms to simple blocks, based on how the light hits the forms. Continue to paint the skin using subtle strokes.

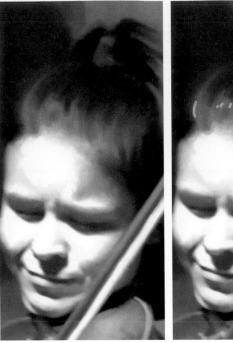

Using the Oil Palette Knife to loosely paint the shapes and forms on the viola, while simplifying the mechanical details.

Painting general shapes on the hair with the Oil Palette Knife (left) and adding a few brighter highlights with a small Tapered Oil brush (right).

7 Simplifying supporting elements. In the original photo, the viola has intricate mechanical detail. Rendering the instrument with full detail would distract from the focal point of the face, so the viola is simplified into painterly shapes.

Sit back and analyze the supporting elements in your image, and visualize them as shapes. Then choose the Oil Palette Knife variant of Artists' Oils and brush over the instrument to blend small details out of the larger areas, letting your brushstrokes follow the forms. For elements such as the strings in this painting, reduce the size of the palette knife and pull your stylus (and brush) loosely along the lines of the strings to generalize them and give them a painted look. Use this small palette knife to paint over other small elements, such as the bow, always keeping in mind that your brushstrokes should follow the direction of the forms. Save the file.

8 Painting the hair and subtle detail. Now it's time to finesse the details in the painting on a new layer. Add a new layer by clicking the New Layer button on the bottom of the Layers palette. In the Layers palette, select the Pick Up Underlying Color check box for the new layer. To keep your Layers palette organized, rename the layer Details.

Now look at the highlights and shadows on the hair and study the movement within the curved shapes. In this technique, the fine detail in the hair is simplified into general shapes, with graceful movement and rhythm. Using a small Oil Palette Knife (about 10–12 pixels), paint curved strokes that follow the direction of the hair. When the basic forms are painted, a few brighter highlights are added that will later be blended into the hair. When you are ready to paint the brightest highlights, choose the Tapered Oils variant of Artists' Oils and size it down to

The highlights in the hair are subtly blended using careful, curved strokes painted with a small Blender Palette Knife.

Using a small Blender Palette Knife, the hands and viola are finessed. A small Blender Brush is used to paint brighter highlights on the shoulder.

about 7 pixels. Choose a color and paint small curved strokes only where you want the brightest highlights. To blend, choose the Blender Palette Knife and size it down to about 7 pixels. Gently stroke along the highlights to soften the edges of the brushstrokes.

Now zoom out and take another look at your image. What other areas would benefit from accents of highlight or possibly a touch of brighter color? In this image, the simple forms on the hands needed a little blending. A small Blender Palette Knife (set to 5 pixels) is used to soften transitions between the highlights, midtones and shadows. The Blender Palette Knife is also used to soften a few of the stronger highlights on the neck of the viola.

To complement the focal point of the face, brighter highlights are painted on the shoulder that holds the viola. For subtly brighter highlights in your image, choose the Blender Brush variant of Artists' Oils. In the

Property Bar, reduce the size of the brush to about 10–12 pixels and then reduce its Opacity to about 50%. Sample color from the image using the Dropper tool, and then brighten it by increasing its value slightly in the Colors palette. Then, using short, curved strokes that follow the forms, gently paint the brighter highlights. If the enhanced highlights are too strong for your taste, you can always soften them using a small Blender Palette Knife, as you did with the hair. A detail of the in-progress image can be seen above.

Your painting is nearly complete. In the next step, you will make a proof print that will help you decide if any final adjustments need to be made.

The working image prior to Brightness/Contrast adjustment shows more detail in the background.

The working image after the Brightness/Contrast adjustment has a less busy background and gives more attention to the subject.

9 Assessing the painting and finessing final details. At this point, consider making a high-resolution proof print of your painting at the size of the final print. The print will allow you to see the entire composition and decide if areas need more contrast, highlights or other enhancements. The composition and the dramatic mood of this image could be improved by adding more contrast. The viola and clothing could be improved by painting loose brushstrokes of accent color and brightening a few of the highlights.

To bring more attention to the subject and add more drama, the background is darkened and more contrast is added using a dynamic layer in Painter. (The dynamic layers in Painter work similarly to Adjustment Layers in Photoshop. For information about Adjustment Layers, see page 64.) Click the Dynamic Plugins button on the bottom of the Layers palette, choose Brightness and Contrast

The layer mask on the converted Brightness/Contrast layer is active.

from the menu and when the dialog appears, and adjust the sliders to your taste. (The dynamic layer has a plug icon to the right of it.) Here, the Contrast is increased and the Brightness is subtly reduced. The dynamic layer provides a "live" preview on your image, and the effect is adjustable. Drag this layer below the Details layer in the Layers palette.

For this image, the increased contrast is pleasing for most of the composition, except for the face and a few other areas. To reveal the underlying imagery on the Paint 1

The highlights on the hands and clothing are finessed with the Oily Bristle variant of Artists' Oils.

Painterly brushwork accents are painted on the viola using the Round Camelhair variant of Oils.

layer, areas of the Brightness and Contrast layer are hidden using a layer mask. Before applying a layer mask to the Dynamic Plugins layer, the dynamic layer must be converted to a default layer. From the pop-up menu on the Layers palette, choose Convert to Default Layer and then click the Create Layer Mask button on the Layers palette. Click on the layer mask thumbnail to activate it. A layer mask filled with white (which reveals all) appears to the right of the layer. Painting black on the layer mask hides a portion of the layer, and painting white reveals imagery on the layer. In order to paint on the layer mask, choose black in the Colors palette and in the Brush Selector Bar, choose the Digital Airbrush variant of Airbrushes. Now apply brushstrokes where you want to hide portions of the layer. Here, the layer mask is painted on the face and hands and on the details on the viola. Before moving on to add details, save the file.

Now activate the Details layer. To enhance the highlights on the viola, color is sampled from the image (using the Dropper tool), lightened in the Colors palette and then applied with the Oily Bristle. Choose the Oily Bristle variant of Artists' Oils and continue touching up the highlights and enhancing the shadows.

You can combine other Painter media with Artists' Oils paint, such as Acrylics, Gouache or Oils for different brushstroke looks. For painterly touches of brighter color, try adding accents using the Round Camelhair variant of the Oils. The Round Camelhair variant changes from thin to thick with pressure and shows the individual hairs of the brush as you paint.

When you have finished adding accents on your image, step back and admire your work. You have learned about using dramatic lighting and painting with the Artists' Oils medium in Painter, using layers and masks.

Night on the Seine

Turning Noise into Beautiful Digital Oils

Night photographs offer great possibilities for images to make into digital oils. The abundance of noise in the shadows can be manipulated during painting for dramatic effects.

A cool, wet July evening found my daughter and me walking along the bridges and walkways along the Seine River in Paris, France. We met new friends and took more than a few pictures before the skies opened up on us, unloading even more cold, wet rain and sending us scurrying back to the hotel.

Shooting with my Nikon D200, aiming down the Seine from atop a bridge, I wasn't sure exactly how I would use the photographs, so I gave myself flexibility by shooting the scene with different exposure and aperture settings.

Nighttime photography is always a bit tricky and capturing a distant panoramic scene with the detail of light refracting off moving water makes it even more so. If I were to shoot to get the perfect exposure for the buildings, the ISO would be set low, with the f-stop somewhere around f/4.5 and the exposure perhaps as long as 10–15 seconds. For my purposes, I needed an exposure fast enough to give some measure of speed to capture the individual waves on the gently flowing river.

The unpleasant solution was to put up with the noise, put the ISO up to 1600, and shoot with an aperture of f/4.5 at 1/10 second.

Back home in Atlanta, Georgia, I transferred all of the images from the trip, and reviewed the river pictures to see what could be done with them. One option stood out: use Photoshop to make an oil painting! And a big one at that.

Some styles of oil painting are suggestive and loose, with the strokes themselves full of life and motion, and this is what I wished to emulate. I was not worried about preserving any tight details, and the noise turned out to be no problem at all, because noise in the image is required for this particular style of emulating oils using Photoshop.

Before we get started, credit must be given to a Photoshop guru, digital pioneer and, from what I've been told by several people, a wonderful human being: Jack Davis. Years ago I ran across an exercise he developed for oil "painting," and it is the best Photoshop oil method I've come across. Although my own processes are found on the following pages, at the core of the method one will find Jack's influence.

The unedited Camera Raw file shows the yellow tones throughout the image.

Detail of the noise before and after changing the Camera Raw Detail sliders shows fewer transitional colors and more distinct edges.

1 **Opening the digital original.** Opening the image in Camera Raw reveals a fair amount of yellow color saturation from the multiple types of artificial lighting and the brown tones of the buildings, bridge and walkways along the river. Although it is technically not the greatest photograph, nothing in the "as-is" shot was necessarily wrong for the work ahead; it is actually rather accurate for the night.

The scene that night did have a yellow cast, although not to the extent the photograph suggests. I liked how the cast appeared in the photograph, providing a ready palette of warm browns and golds. I decided to leave the yellow cast as it was and made no changes on Camera Raw's Basic interface.

This completely Photoshop process requires noise for the oil emulation to work, and this shot has quite a bit with which to work. Unfortunately, it is not the type of noise that will render the best results. The condition of the noise in any image prior to correction will rarely, if ever, be perfect. Your goal is to introduce the right noise quality, not to eliminate all traces, and Camera Raw will take us only part of the way. Zooming in to look at individual pixels reveals the noise to be rather uniform and

free of brightly colored "hot pixels." Pay careful attention to the noise pattern, looking for blotchy patches of yellow. If your image has those distinct patterns you must avoid making them stand out as you make adjustments. You will also need to work more carefully blending your strokes later on.

At this point in the project you want to simplify the image by gathering pixels into more uniform blocks of color to reduce the number of hues in the noise. Open Camera Raw's Detail panel by clicking on the tab with the triangular icon. Set the Sharpening Amount slider to 61, the Radius to 3.0, the Detail to 31 and the Masking to 0.

Just below the sharpening sliders, both noise reduction sliders are used to knock back some of the resident noise. The Luminance slider affects tonal noise, which is the white to black range of the image. Set the Luminance slider to 55. The Color slider affects the noise in the color, not the tones, and in this case is set to 87. These moves bring sharpness to soft edges, breaks up gradations, minimizes errant hot pixels and allows you to better determine your own noise standards in Step 3.

Press Open Image and choose File > Save As, assigning the file a temporary descriptive name.

The barreling in the image is apparent in the vertical lines of these close-ups from opposite sides of the photograph.

This example of chromatic aberration samples the far-left and the far-right of the same photograph taken using a Nikon 80–400mm telephoto lens.

2 **Correcting "barreling" and chromatic aberration.** Even expensive lenses distort images as the light travels through them and they are projected onto the camera's sensor. Photoshop's Lens Correction filter addresses three problems caused by the physics involved: barreling, pincushioning and chromatic aberration. Barreling and pincushioning both warp the image—the former away from the middle and the latter toward the middle. Chromatic aberration resembles misregistered color plates and gradually increases as you move away from center. Not every case of chromatic aberration is fixable due to different physical causes related to light waves and refraction, all of which are outside the scope of this book.

To correct these problems, choose Filter > Distort > Lens Correction. At the bottom of the Lens Correction dialog, make sure the Show Grid box is checked and enter your preferred grid size in the Size box.

The original image suffers from an obvious case of barreling, most noticeable in the vertical definitions of buildings and window frames. To eliminate the barreling, adjust the Remove Distortion slider to –12. In most images, the Remove Distortion slider is all you need, but this image is well suited for additional correction by

Photoshop's Lens Correction filter controls are adjusted prior to cropping the image.

changing the Vertical Perspective. The Vertical Perspective and Horizontal Perspective sliders tilt the entire image as though it were a sheet of paper with one of the edges moved closer to the viewer's eye than its opposite edge. Setting the Vertical Perspective slider to +11 straightens the lines in the upper half of the image just about to perfection.

Chromatic Aberration in this particular image is not troublesome and requires a very minor fix of +3 for the Red/Cyan Fringe and +2 for the Blue/Yellow Fringe.

When you're satisfied with your work, click the OK button at the top of the Lens Correction dialog to accept the changes and then save your image.

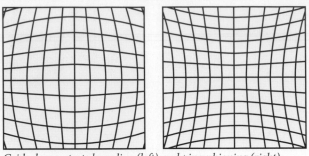

Grids demonstrate barreling (left) and pincushioning (right).

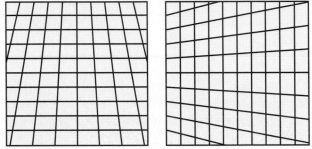

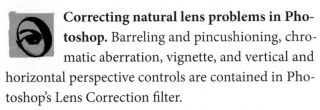

Vertical (left) and horizontal (right) perspective sliders come in handy but are not used as often as the Remove Distortion slider.

Correcting natural lens problems in Photoshop. Barreling and pincushioning, chromatic aberration, vignette, and vertical and horizontal perspective controls are contained in Photoshop's Lens Correction filter.

Barreling, pincushioning and chromatic aberration occur when light waves are distorted as they pass through the curved lenses and are projected onto the camera's sensor. The distortion becomes more pronounced the farther you move away from the center of the image.

One often overlooked Lens Correction option is the Angle control. This tool rotates the image much like Free Transform, but if you're already resampling by using Lens Correction now, save yourself (and your image) a second resampling.

The Remove Distortion and Vertical Perspective sliders combined to produce the bowed appearance near the top, shown here in red.

3 Cropping the image. A large canvas print of *Night on the Seine* is to measure 40.5 x 22.5 inches. To set your canvas dimensions, select the Crop tool. In the Options bar, enter 40.5 inches wide, 22.5 inches tall and 150 dpi. Select one corner of your desired cropping and pull to the opposite corner.

Follow the "rule of thirds" in your crop selection. Looking at the picture to the right one can see the image as I cropped it is roughly divided into three horizontal parts: the sky, the lights and walkways, and the water. The pillar in the bridge falls one-third of the way across from left to right, and the water flows from that point to fill the bottom third. The angles of the darkness at the left and right bring the eye naturally back into the heart of the image. For more information about the "rule of thirds," see page 201.

When you are pleased with your crop, press Enter/Return, and the image will scale to the dimensions you entered at the beginning of this step. Double-click on the background layer in the Layers palette to lift the layer from the canvas and rename the layer "Master Layer."

Cropping too high or too low does not frame the picture well. Look for the best balance for your canvas size.

This area of the image is well suited for testing a wide variety of colors, textures and tones.

Remember not to paint directly onto this layer. A great way to avoid this mistake is to save your image, then resave by choosing File > Save As and assigning the file a new name. When you need a duplicate, you may open the original file and then copy and paste the unblemished image into your working document.

Alternatively, you can select the Master Layer, press the Lock All button on the Layers palette and make and unlock copies as you need them. Either way is fine, and either way you need to complete this step by saving your work.

The final crop follows the "rule of thirds" by dividing the picture into rough thirds, top-to-bottom and side-to-side.

4 **Testing noise options for better results.** Prior to starting an oil emulation, a small test is advisable to see the extent to which the strokes push color. The amount, size and coloring of the noise correlates with how oily and realistic the strokes will appear. Before you settle on your photograph's original noise levels, do some testing to determine what type and quantity of noise produces the results you most prefer.

To do this, use a small portion of the image and apply various noise methods. Select a representative part of your image using the Marquee Selection tool (M). Copy the selection and open a new document. Photoshop opens the New document dialog with the dimensions of the selection in your Clipboard, so simply press Enter/Return and paste the clipped selection directly into the new window by choosing Edit > Paste.

Next choose Image > Canvas Size. Make the canvas 200% wider and deeper by selecting Percent from the pop-up menu and entering 200 in both the Width and Height boxes.

Select the Move tool (V) and move the image into the top-right corner. Paste three more times, moving each image to the other three corners. Use the Layers palette

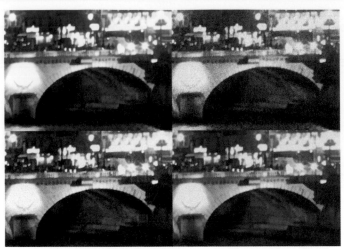

The four quadrants before testing with a brush shows the four different noise settings using the same part of the original image.

Using the same brush on each quadrant shows the results from using the different noise settings.

to select each layer separately as you add noise in different ways to each of the four layers. Be sure to record each setting.

In the test for this exercise, there is no noise added to the top-left quadrant. For the image in the top-right corner, I chose Filter > Noise > Add Noise and set the slider to 15. For the image on the bottom-left, the slider was set to 30. In the final bottom-right corner, I chose Filter > Artistic > Film Grain, set the Grain slider to 4 and both the Highlight area and Intensity sliders to 0. (There are many different ways of introducing noise using Photoshop. For several less-common methods than Filter > Noise > Add Noise filter, turn to page 179.)

Select the Smudge tool and open the Brushes palette by pressing the F5 key. Load the Wet Media Brushes by clicking on the Menu icon at the top-right of the palette and scrolling down to select Wet Media Brushes. When you are prompted to Append, Cancel or OK the addition to your brushes, select Append. The Wet Media Brush library is added to your working brushes library.

Select the Oil Medium to Large Tip brush, and on the Options Bar click the Brush Preset Picker and set the Master Diameter to 75. Select the Sample All Layers check box and confirm that the Strength is set to 100%. Finger Painting should be off.

Finally, make a new transparent layer by clicking the Create a New Layer icon on the bottom of the Layers palette and go to work pushing pixels around. Try to keep your brushwork from flowing into more than one quadrant at a time so the results remain distinctly separate. To get the best side-by-side comparison, try to use the same stroke pressure and direction. Change the size of the brush to see how the stroke is affected. Add new layers whenever one becomes full and take as much time as you need to until you're completely satisfied with your brush(es).

When you find a brush you like, save the variant you created by clicking on the Brush palette's Menu icon. Choose New Brush Preset and assign your new brush a name in the pop-up window. For the balance of this exercise, it is assumed you did not save any custom variants, but if you did, feel free to use them! Save this reference file and return to your original image.

The Undercolor layer is a simple duplicate of the Master layer with the Watercolor filter applied.

The Large Brushwork layer is used to block out large areas. (The opacity of underlying layers has been reduced by 50% for this example.)

5 **Building undercolor, setting the noise and applying the first brushwork.** Duplicate the Master Layer by dragging its name onto the Create a New Layer button icon at the bottom of the Layers palette. Double-click on the new layer's name in the Layers palette and rename it "Undercolor." Choose Filter > Artistic > Watercolor. Set the Brush Detail slider in the filter's control panel to 8. The Shadow Intensity slider needs to be set to 0 so the shadows do not darken and, because there is no need for texture, the Texture slider is set to 1. Press Enter/Return to apply the filter.

Lock this layer by clicking on the Lock All button and hide the layer by clicking on the Eye icon to the left of the layer's name. This layer will remain hidden until the last step.

Duplicate the Master Layer and unlock the new layer *if* you locked it in Step 3. Choose the noise setting you like best from your test and apply it to the new layer. Click on the name of the layer to rename it with the noise setting. This image used the Film Grain settings from Step 4, so the layer is called "Film Grain 4 0 0." After renaming the layer, lock it again to avoid accidentally destroying it as you work. Save the file.

Click on the Undercolor layer and press the Create a New Layer button to make a new layer on which to paint. Name it "Large Brushwork." Select the Smudge tool and click on the Brush Preset Picker. Choose the Oil Medium to Large Tip brush and scale the Master Diameter to 130 pixels.

Begin blocking in larger areas of color, starting with areas with little color variation to get a feel for the size and action of the brush, working with short strokes. Allow the brush to sample and mix color often; then work into smaller shapes, such as the buildings and canal walls. Pull color over the windows and other building details, leaving them for later. On the water surface, use slightly arching strokes and don't try to eliminate the color variations in the strokes. As always, it's critical to save your document often; the results of your brushwork are unique.

 Stay comfortable! It's not unusual to lose track of time and space when you work. Rest your wrist and eyes often and get up to take a break from the screen. Use a variety of views while working: zoom in to paint and zoom out to check your composition.

For the waves, move the brush in a gradually increasing uphill slope. Pull from the bottom toward the top for better reflections.

The Medium Brushwork layer is a transitional layer, with strokes anywhere from 110 pixels wide down to 75 pixels wide.

6 **Adding medium-sized details.** When satisfied with how the initial layer with large strokes appears, it's time to turn off the "Large Brushwork" layer and begin to work with medium-sized details. Bridge definition, tree edges, walkways, smaller walls on buildings, water surfaces and other similar sized elements are the target for the next layer.

Click the Create a New Layer icon and double-click on the new layer's name and call it "Medium Brushwork." Click on the Brush Preset Picker and set the Master Diameter to 85.

Start once again to work your way through the image, confining your work to just those areas that fit your definition of medium-sized detail. As you work, resize the brush as you need to, going no higher than 110 pixels and no smaller than 75 pixels.

Even though a lot of the river has one layer of paint, this is the layer on which the water is truly defined. Work in short strokes that resemble a short, wide slope. Stop at the top of the stroke instead of continuing down the opposite side of the slope. This keeps the same color from being pulled down both sides of the same wave.

The key to painting water is to tell yourself you're not actually painting water, but instead are painting the reflections and interruptions on the water surface. The color of water is made up of both what is reflecting off the surface and what is suspended in the water. In daylight large bodies of water appear blue, but at night even small bodies of water look black, refracting only the natural and artificial lights in the surrounding environment.

With slightly curved movements, make small, horizontal strokes. As areas of colors meet, pull them into each other without trying to blend the two colors into transitional hues.

As you work, occasionally turn on the Large Brushwork layer to check your progress, but turn it off when you're satisfied you've covered enough of the mid-size detail. Save your document regularly as you work because these steps take a lot of time to complete!

When you reach the point where you are happy with what you've done on the layer, turn on the Large Brushwork layer and look for areas that would look better transitioning into each other. Blend those areas until they appear seamless and save your document.

The Small Brushwork and Medium Brushwork layers are combined in this preview, showing the interaction between the two layers.

The brain transforms even loose strokes into recognizable forms.

7 Adding a small details layer. Now the image looks nearly finished, but it still needs small details to really bring it to life. To accomplish this, the small details need to be filled in.

Turn off the Large and Medium Brushwork layers on which you've painted so you can see the noise layer. Click the Create a New Layer button to add another new layer and name it "Small Brushwork." Change the brush size once again by clicking on the Brush Preset Picker and setting the Master Diameter to 65.

There is a lot of small detail to attend to in this picture, so a methodical approach is helpful. Work on items that are alike all at the same time, such as the windows in all of the buildings, then perhaps white lights and then lights of other colors. Work deliberately through the piece with the same looseness in the strokes as in previous layers. Work in some of the smaller reflections on the river, especially the bright areas of green and white. Resist the urge to go to a smaller brush to pick up every tiny little element.

Every once in a while, it is worth turning on all of the layers to check for consistency in how you've applied your strokes. Also look at your work with a CMYK preview by choosing View > Proof Setup > Working CMYK, especially when bright colors are present in the piece. And remember, there is no such thing as saving too often while you work!

Checking your progress. It is often difficult to see what areas have been covered and what haven't. Occasionally you need to hide underlying layers to check for those sneaky areas you might have missed.

The Layers palette at the end of Step 7.

The Clean-ups layer adds dabs of color that bring about a more finished look. This "before" inset just doesn't feel "done."

The same area as the image to the left has been touched up freehand with color sampled from surrounding areas.

8 **Finishing up.** Your piece is nearly complete, but still could be made more exceptional. The last layer adds the small detail that will tie up loose ends and make the piece gallery-ready!

Thus far the only tool utilized has been the Smudge tool, which has pushed existing color around. With a more traditional brush, color can be sampled and applied without mixing with the color below.

Make another new layer by choosing Layer > New Layer, naming it "Clean-ups." Make every layer visible. Select the Brush tool, switching from the Smudge tool. On the Brushes palette, choose the 32 Oil Medium Wet Flow brush.

As you use this final brush, change sizes regularly, and use the Eyedropper tool to sample colors rather than introduce new ones. The quickest way to sample color while using a brush is to press and hold down the Alt/ Option key. The brush temporarily becomes the Eyedropper tool. While the key is held down, click anywhere on your painting to select that particular color as the foreground color. When you're happy with the color selection, release the key and the Brush tool immediately reappears.

Work throughout your image to add additional reflections in the water, little bits of color on the walls or dark sky near the edges of trees, and especially the occasional details along the street level. This is a more intuitive step than the previous steps, so go ahead and experiment! If you don't like what you've done, either undo the stroke by choosing Edit > Undo Brush tool, by using the History palette or even by using the Lasso tool to select what you've done and then pressing the Delete key.

Finally, select the Smudge tool once again and slightly work in some of the ends of the new brushstrokes for a more realistic blending. Voila! Your own *Night on the Seine* is complete!

 Adding depth to your oils. Simulating the paint depth and canvas associated with oil painting is not a difficult process. See Chapter 1 for more information on this technique.

Introducing Noise to Enhance Photoshop Oil Techniques

How often do you hear someone complain they don't have enough noise in their image?

There actually are times when noise is beneficial, but it's hard to get it just as you want using out-of-the-box Photoshop filters. Here are a few methods for introducing noise to get just the effect you're looking for. (And these just scratch the surface!)

1 Make a Lighten Only layer. Copy and paste the image. To lighten the duplicate choose Image > Adjustments > Curves. On the Curves control panel, select the Highlight anchor point on the graph. Enter 255 in the Output box and 210 in the Input box. Apply a layer mask by choosing Layer > Layer Mask > Hide All. Select the layer mask and choose Filter > Pixelate > Mezzotint. Select Fine Dots and press Enter/Return.

2 Make a Darken Only layer. Copy and paste the image. To darken the duplicate choose Image > Adjustments > Curves. On the Curves control panel, select the Highlight anchor point on the graph. Enter 210 in the Output box and 255 in the Input box. Apply a layer mask by choosing Layer > Layer Mask > Hide All. Select the layer mask and choose Filter > Pixelate > Mezzotint. Select Fine Dots and press Enter/Return.

3 Make a Grain layer. Copy and paste the layer. Choose Filter > Texture > Grain. Set the Intensity to 40 and the Contrast to 50, with the Soft mode selected from the Grain Type menu. Set the Blend mode to Lighten on the Layers palette so the image doesn't have the chance to darken.

4 Use the Film Grain filter. Use the original layer and choose Filter > Artistic > Film Grain. Set the Grain to 4, the Highlight to 0 and the Intensity to 10.

5 Take the road most traveled. There's always the tried-and-true Add Noise filter. It can render acceptable results but might also introduce strange colors inside your strokes. Exploring other techniques of adding noise will not only stretch your knowledge, but also will make your work stand out from the crowd.

Danubis Afterglow

Using the Artists' Oils for an Expressive, Old Masters Style

I shot many photographs in the garden on this beautiful fall evening, and several photos of the statue use different exposures. The image in the upper-right has the best lighting for the painting.

With the luscious Artists' Oils medium in Painter, you can use brushes and cloning to create an Old Masters look as I did here for *Danubis Afterglow*.

When traveling in Germany to teach a painting workshop, my husband Steve and I discovered a magnificent royal garden in Schwetzingen. On one lovely evening, the soft sunset lighting on the Danubis statue and the beautiful reflections on the water called out to be painted with oils, and references would be helpful. I shot several photos of the statues and lake using bracketed exposures to make sure that I captured the best lighting on the statues and color in the reflections. The marble statues looked almost iridescent, glowing in the early evening light, as shown in the image in the upper-left.

Because of the low lighting, I used a tripod. I set up my Canon 5D with a 17–40L zoom lens that has a maximum aperture of f/4. To capture a wide-angle shot, I zoomed out to 17mm. Then I chose Aperture Priority mode, a low ISO setting of 100, an aperture of f/4.5 and a shutter speed of 1/60 to shoot the chosen photograph.

When using conventional oil and acrylic paints, I often begin laying in broad areas of color with a large, flat brush. Using the Artists' Oils in Painter, you can achieve a similar result. The Artists' Oils allow you to lay down color easily and blend it with a wet, viscous, oily feeling, that is very similar to working with conventional oil paint.

This technique uses painting on a series of clone files to build the final painting. The Blender Brush variant of Artists' Oils is used as a cloner brush to pull color from the edited original and paint into the working clone painting to create a loose underpainting. Forms are modeled and details are finessed using brushes that blend and pull the paint.

For inspiration before shooting photos and painting, look at the magnificent paintings of John Singer Sargent.

CP

The original image will be improved by cropping and adjusting the color.

The cropped composition with its colors adjusted.

1 **Making adjustments and cropping the image.** In the case of this project, the original uncropped photograph measures 2240 x 1680 pixels. (If the size of your file is much smaller or larger, it may be necessary in Steps 3 through 9 to proportionally adjust the sizes of the brushes used.)

This photograph was captured in Camera Raw and opened directly in the Camera Raw dialog to start the project. You'll find detailed information about using Camera Raw in the sidebar on page 12 in Chapter 1. Open your image in Camera Raw and adjust its tones and color if needed. In the case of this image, the Vibrance is increased to +10 to balance the saturation of the color and give more saturation to the sky and water. Increasing Vibrance adjusts the saturation of the less-saturated colors without over-saturating the highly-saturated colors. To enhance the light on the statue and bring out detail in the background foliage, Fill Light is increased to +15. Fill

Light can restore detail in the midtones and shadow areas while preserving the blacks.

Take a good look at your composition, the subject and the negative space around your subject. Would the composition be improved if some elements were removed or cropped out? In the case of this image, the trees on the left side and top-left edges distract from the beautiful negative space of the water and sky. Cropping the left side of the image and retouching the spray of leaves improves the composition. If your image needs cropping, crop your image as required.

For this image, the Clone Stamp tool was also used to "paint" over the spray of leaves at the top of the photo, replacing them with sampled clouds from the sunset sky. See 159 for information on retouching with the Clone Stamp tool.

When you complete the touch-up on your image, save a new version of the file in Photoshop format. (This image uses *Danube crop adj.psd*.)

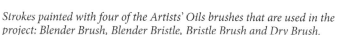

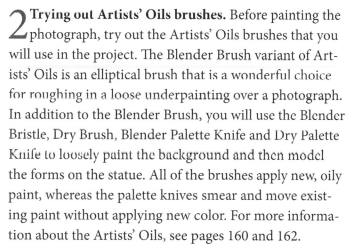

Strokes painted with four of the Artists' Oils brushes that are used in the project: Blender Brush, Blender Bristle, Bristle Brush and Dry Brush.

Strokes painted with the Bristle Brush. The top stroke is smudged with the Blender Palette Knife, the bottom stroke with the Dry Palette Knife.

2 **Trying out Artists' Oils brushes.** Before painting the photograph, try out the Artists' Oils brushes that you will use in the project. The Blender Brush variant of Artists' Oils is an elliptical brush that is a wonderful choice for roughing in a loose underpainting over a photograph. In addition to the Blender Brush, you will use the Blender Bristle, Dry Brush, Blender Palette Knife and Dry Palette Knife to loosely paint the background and then model the forms on the statue. All of the brushes apply new, oily paint, whereas the palette knives smear and move existing paint without applying new color. For more information about the Artists' Oils, see pages 160 and 162.

Create a new 2000 x 1500-pixel file as a test file to try out the brushes. From the Brush Selector Bar, choose the Artists' Oils category and the Blender Brush variant. Make a few strokes with each of the Artists' Oils brushes. Paint new color with each brush and then use another brush to pull color over the top so you can observe the interaction of the paint. Then use the Blender Palette Knife and Dry Palette Knife to smudge and blend the colored paint.

3 **Making a clone and customizing a brush.** In preparation for building a loose underpainting, make a clone of the image from Step 1 by choosing File > Clone. (For more information on cloning in Painter, see page 91). Now save the clone in RIF format with a descriptive name by choosing File > Save As. For efficiency, all painting files for this project are saved in RIF, Painter's native format, which allows faster opening and saving of files and better preservation of Painter's unique natural media characteristics such as Artists' Oils. This image is saved using the name *Danube paint 01.rif.*

Next choose the Blender Brush variant of Artists' Oils and turn the Blender Brush into a cloner by selecting the Clone Color check box in the Colors palette. The Clone Color option allows painting with color from the active clone source. Save your custom brush by choosing Save Variant from the menu on the Brush Selector Bar. For good housekeeping, restore the original Blender Brush to its default settings by choosing Restore Default Variant from the menu on the Brush Selector Bar.

Using the custom Blender Brush Cloner to pull loose horizontal strokes across the sky and clouds. Note to elliptical brush cursor.

Pulling expressive strokes from the foliage into the sky using the Blender Brush Cloner.

4 **Applying loose brushwork to the clone.** In this step, you'll use the custom Artists' Oils brush cloner to paint over a clone of the adjusted and cropped photograph, covering the entire image with loose, expressive brushwork so that no photographic imagery remains. Choose the Blender Brush Cloner and select the *Danube paint 01.rif* file. Take a good look at your image and analyze the forms and shapes in your image. Think about the direction that you will use to pull your brushstrokes. Then, using your stylus, begin painting loose brushstrokes over the sky, trees and water. The sky in this photograph has horizontal bands of clouds, so the brush is pulled across from left to right, as shown in the illustration above. The grass near the water is also composed of horizontal strokes. For the trees, small dabs and curved strokes are used to pull the colors back and forth to blend them. For the edges of the trees, loose, expressive strokes are pulled out into the sky. Continue to paint over your

image, using the Blender Brush Cloner, until no photographic imagery remains. Then, use the Blender Palette Knife to smooth areas (in this image, the sky and water reflections.) Save the file and leave it open.

Smoothing the water reflections and sky using the Blender Palette Knife.

The copy of the photo (second clone source) with increased saturation.

Using the Blender Brush Cloner to selectively add saturated accents.

5 Adding touches of saturated color. Now it's time to add touches of brighter, saturated color to your image. As a source for the more saturated color, this technique uses a second clone source as a basis for the new color. From the Window menu, select the source photo you saved in Step 1 and choose File > Clone. Save the new clone using a descriptive name. (This project uses *Danube statue adj sat.rif.*)

Painter features powerful tools in the Photo Painting system palettes, the Underpainting, Auto-Painting and Restoration palettes. Open the Underpainting palette by choosing Window > Show Underpainting and increase the Saturation slider to

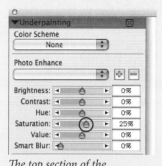

The top section of the Underpainting palette shows the Saturation increased.

your taste. The color will preview on your image. When you are satisfied, click the Apply button. Save the file.

Next activate the working painting file and establish the saturated image as the new clone source by choosing File > Clone Source, and then choosing your saturated image from the menu. (This project uses *Danube statue adj sat.rif* as the clone source.) Take a good look at your painting and decide where you want to add accents of saturated color. Here, touches of more intense lavender color from the saturated clone source are painted on the statue shadows. A few brighter strokes of clone color are added to the sky and along the edges of the trees. Saturated accents are also added to the water. When you have completed adding the saturated accents, save your file with a new descriptive name. (This project uses the name *Danube paint 02.rif.*) Next, you will restore some detail to the statue, and then use Artists' Oils palette knives to model the forms on the subject.

Using the Soft Edge Cloner Brush chosen in the Restoration palette to selectively restore imagery.

Using the Blender Palette Knife variant of Artists' Oils to model forms on the sculpture.

6 **Restoring selected imagery on the statue.** In the Restoration palette, click on the Soft Edge Cloner brush. Set the Clone Source. (This project uses *Danube statue adj sat.rif* from Step 5.) Use the cloner brush to bring back only enough imagery to help you model the forms on the subject. Pick up important details on the face such as the nose and cheekbones, and a few edges such as on the shoulders and hands.

7 **Modeling the forms.** Now that areas of the statue are restored, you can use the Blender Palette Knife (Artists' Oils) to sculpt and model the forms on the statue. Use your stylus to paint longer strokes along the edges of the forms. Use short, dabbing strokes for sculpting volume such as the chest of the larger figure. To blend areas, try brushing back and forth with short strokes. Adjust the size of the brush as you work (try between 6–12 pixels).

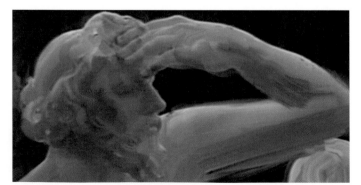

A few details of the head are restored with the Soft Edge Cloner.

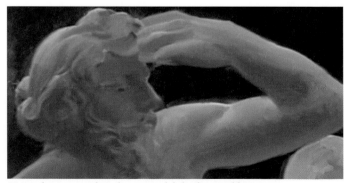

Using short, curved strokes to model the face and hair.

Painting the trees with the Blender Brush Cloner and Dry Brush variants of Artists' Oils.

Softening the brushwork on the trees and clouds using the Blender Palette Knife variant of Artists' Oils.

8 **Painting the background.** Now that areas of the statue are restored, you can use the Blender Brush Cloner and other Artists' Oils brushes to add more brushwork to the background. In this image, short, curved strokes are painted on the trees using the Blender Brush Cloner, using color from the saturated clone source set up in Step 5. (Use either the original clone source or the saturated clone source, whichever suits your taste.) To add new color, choose a color in the Colors palette and use the default Blender Brush or Dry Brush. You can also sample color from the working image by choosing the Dropper tool and clicking on the color you want to sample. Switch back to the Brush tool, choose the default Blender Brush or Dry Brush and paint with short, dabbing strokes. To achieve more varied color on the trees in this project, a few strokes are painted with the Dry Brush.

In this detail, you can see the expressive Dry Brush strokes on the trees.

Using the Blender Brush and sampled color to paint the reflections.

Painting highlight detail onto the shoulder with a small Blender Brush.

Blending the highlight on the shoulder using the Blender Palette Knife.

9 Finessing the finer forms. Now that the subjects and scene are laid in and roughly modeled, step back and take a good look at your painting. Would your image be improved if a few highlights were enhanced? Are there any forms that need finessing to complete the work? As you paint your final details, make sure that you keep a loose painterly feel. Here, a highlight is enhanced on the top of the shoulder. Color is sampled from the image with the Dropper tool and painted with a small Blender Brush (about 5–7 pixels). Then a small Blender Palette Knife is used to blend in the highlight into the form. For subtle brushstrokes, push and pull the paint using your stylus.

Now the final sculpting is completed on the water jar and robe. If needed, you can restore a few edges from the clone source image using the Soft Edge Cloner brush on the Restoration palette. Then switch back to the Artists' Oils category to apply new color with the Blender Bristle. Push and pull paint with the Blender Palette Knife or Dry Palette Knife. For this image, the Dry Palette Knife is used for the larger strokes on the robe. Then a 5–7 pixel Blender Palette Knife is used to tidy up the edges.

Next, the hand resting on the water jar is painted and subtle modeling is added on the foreheads of the figures.

Sculpting the water and robe using a small Blender Bristle, the Dry Palette Knife and a small Blender Palette Knife.

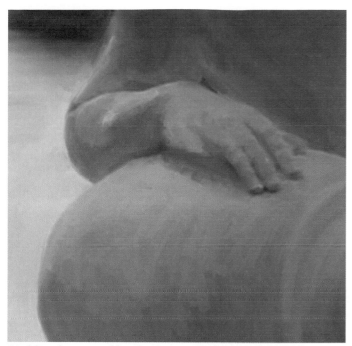
Modeling the arm and hand using a small Blender Palette Knife.

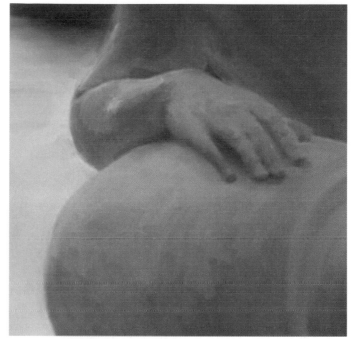
The final modeled forms on the hand and fingers.

Here, lighter color is painted along the back edge of the child's head to suggest luminous translucent marble.

At this stage, take another good look at your painting. If you want more detail in an area, use the Soft Edge Cloner brush on the Restoration palette to restore detail. Then use the Blender Brush, Blender Palette Knife or Dry Palette Knife to blend and smooth paint. On the hand, the fingers can be simplified into cylinders or small rectangular blocks. Paint them with this in mind—they do not need to be tightly finessed for the viewer to recognize them. Keep in mind that you want to retain a loose look, as in the illustration shown in the upper-right. On the profile of the child, a small highlight is painted along the edge of the face using a sampled color and a tiny default Blender Brush, then finessed with a tiny Blender Palette Knife. Detail is also painted on the child's cheek and ear. The eye socket and cheek of the larger figure is refined and blended.

When your painting is complete, save the final working file in RIF format. For safekeeping, or for import into Photoshop, save another version of the file in TIF format. The final painting can be viewed on page 180. Good work! You have completed this oil painting project using the Artists' Oils and custom cloner brushes.

The final modeling on the large figure and child painted with a small Blender Brush and Blender Palette Knife.

**Going Abstract: Bright Colors
and Loose Strokes**

Photoshop   **192**

**Painting an Abstract Mixed
Media Work**

Photoshop and Painter   **198**

7

CREATING ABSTRACT ART
FROM PHOTOGRAPHS

Do you have a photograph that you would like to paint in a simple, yet powerful way? This chapter offers ideas for designing abstract compositions with stylized lines, colors, and shapes, or by adding dynamic movement.

Going Abstract: Bright Colors and Loose Strokes begins by showing how to increase the saturation to achieve stylized color in a photo reference. After loose lines are drawn on layers, new layers are added and painted with flat colors. To complete this contemporary look, brushstroke details are added and then the Hue/Saturation feature is used to adjust colors.

Painting an Abstract Mixed Media Work teaches the process of designing an abstract composition that incorporates dynamic movement and emotion. After the photographic detail is blurred, a custom brush is built. Expressive Real Bristle Brushes and Blenders are used to loosely paint, and then push and pull color to create an underpainting. Finally, a veil of rain is painted with a Watercolor brush.

Blooming Purple

Going Abstract: Bright Colors and Loose Strokes

Spotting a beautiful nursery beside a Chattanooga freeway offered a chance to stretch my legs and capture a lot of colorful images of blooms and bright plants.

Ken Hansen, a long-time friend and professional photographer, passed on to me one of his proven proverbs, "Proper prior planning prevents poor pictures." When you are planning to shoot, the preparations should include figuring out whether you might have a better result by asking for access to a location or borrowing props you don't already have.

Asking permission to take pictures at a colorful neighborhood nursery in Chattanooga, Tennessee, resulted in more than one employee directing me to their favorite flowers, plus a few helpful lessons on how not to kill my plants. There was no particular shot that I was looking for; I was just out to enjoy the pleasure of taking stock pictures of beautiful plants.

As I walked among the rows, I looked for plants and flowers with unusual or brilliant coloring, or unique characteristics. Some were to be used in artwork eventually, so I tried to capture a bit more in each frame to allow me more freedom in cropping at a future date.

I chose the predominately purple and green photograph in the upper-right for its limited palette of secondary colors; plus the sharp, crisp edges make it easier to draw with a stylus—or even a mouse.

Adobe Photoshop was used exclusively for this project, but it can easily be adapted to Painter. Every stroke uses only opaque, hard-edged brushes, making it perhaps the simplest project of this book. The key to this fun, easy technique is drawing with speed—not *too* fast and certainly not too slow. A slack wrist and willingness to go "outside the lines" is critical (one of those valuable things you're never taught in coloring school).

Shooting with a 55–200mm lens allowed me to get relatively close to my subject as well as provided the option of using a wider angle. I preferred having control over the depth of field instead of the shutter speed so that only what I wished to capture was in focus. Setting the camera to Aperture Priority and choosing a small aperture allowed individual flowers to be in sharp focus while leaves and petals close by became blurs of color in the background.

The original photograph was taken for my own personal stock library. Increasing the saturation in areas of rich color will yield limited results.

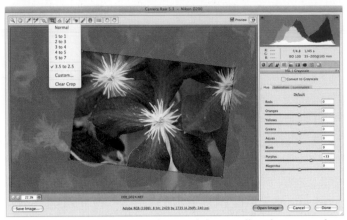

The Camera Raw dialog shows the Hue slider as well as the Crop tool setting. The checked crop option is a custom setting saved earlier.

1 **Opening and cropping the original file.** As it is in every project, the intended result dictates how you open the original Camera Raw file. This project allows exponentially more freedom with the Camera Raw settings than any other project in this book simply because your objective is to sample bright colors and discernible outlines of the shapes within the image. This is one of the few times you can open an image and completely change any or every color you want to change!

The composition of your image is influenced by more than just what's in the picture and how the subject is framed. Changing the colors and contrast can emphasize some objects and colors while others around them may frame the subject better. Increase the Exposure by +1.05 and the Brightness to +45 to bring out dimension in the relatively flat-looking file.

Select the HSL/Grayscale tab to bring up a set of three tabs to control the Hue, Saturation and Luminance. The default and initial tab controls Hue, allowing colors to be changed independently of one another. Set the Purples slider to +33 to make the flower petals richer.

The black arrow on the Crop tool at the top of the dialog indicates additional choices are available. Click and

hold down the Crop tool icon to see the default cropping options in ratio format. Choosing Custom from the list results in a pop-up window where you can input your own width-to-height ratio, in this case 3.5 wide to 2.5 high. When you finish the crop, the resolution of the image will remain unchanged and the image will be opened in a size that can then be scaled within Photoshop.

The Camera Raw dialog makes it very easy to see the crop. The live area remains bright, while the cropped area is heavily grayed out. As with Photoshop's Crop tool, the corners can be rotated by moving the cursor just to the outside of a corner. When the cursor changes to indicate rotation, click and hold while you rotate the crop.

When you are pleased with your crop, open the image by clicking on the Open button. Choose Image > Image Size to scale the photograph. Make certain the Constrain Proportions and Resample Image check boxes are selected, and enter the target width in pixels. Entering a Width of 2100 automatically changes the Height to 1500, maintaining the 3.5 to 2.5 ratio.

Press Enter/Return, and when the computer finishes the task of scaling your image, immediately save your project as a Photoshop (.psd) file with the words *Original*

The image has been cropped and adjusted and is ready for the first layers of Step 2 to be added.

Reduced opacity on the White *layer allows you to easily see the shapes in the image below. A good contrasting color helps the lines stand out.*

Crop in the name. An example of this first save might look like *FlowerAbstractOriginalCrop.psd*. To keep this file as an original reference, resave it one more time by choosing File > Save As. Rename the file, changing the words *Original Crop* to *Working*. This is the file you will use to create your work of art.

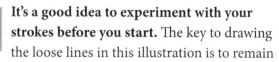

It's a good idea to experiment with your strokes before you start. The key to drawing the loose lines in this illustration is to remain loose while moving your brush quickly so as not to exactly follow the subject's outlines. Vary your stroke pressure to produce lines of varying thickness. Moving too slowly and with even pressure will produce a less animated look. Experiment with your strokes before starting to get used to the brush, making both outlines and fill strokes.

2 **Making new layers and drawing loose lines.** To begin, make a new layer using Layer > New > Layer and fill it with white by choosing Edit > Fill. The Fill dialog has two pop-up menus, one for Contents and the other for Blend modes. For Contents, select White from the pop-up menu, leaving the Blend mode at the default Normal setting. Return to the Layers palette and reduce the Opacity to 85. Double-click on the name of the new layer and change it to the word White.

To start drawing the outlines, a new layer is needed, so choose Layer > New > Layer. Double-click on the default Layer 1 to rename the new layer Linework. Choose the Brush tool (B) and press F5 to reveal the Brushes palette. Select the Hard Round 19 variant. Make sure the Shape Dynamics box is checked, allowing you to draw lines of varying width depending upon the stylus pressure.

An examination of the final product on page 192 shows the importance of loose, fluid brushstrokes to the composition. The edges of the strokes are hard throughout the entire piece, both in the outlines and the fills. The additional lack of any texture in the image shows only one often-resized brush is used.

Purple layers One *and* Two *show the darkest purples. The White layer's opacity is further reduced for better visibility.*

Imagine how it might look posterized as you draw, but don't worry about being exactly perfect! Here, all of the Purple layers are complete.

At this stage, the reduced opacity of the White layer shows the ghosted back image below. Although the final brushstrokes will be white, using white strokes makes it very difficult to see what you're doing. Black is not a great choice, either, but only because there will be a black layer late in the project. Possibly the best choice is orange, as it complements both green and purple, and it is highly visible against both colors. Click on the Foreground Color and select an orange color.

Begin drawing on the Linework layer by loosely tracing the edges throughout the photograph. Follow a comfortable and constant pace as you draw, pacing your strokes so that they are not too fast to follow the edges but not so slow that they become stiff, irregular and jagged. Conserve your strokes to produce just what is needed to define basic shapes. Looking at the image above, orange lines are used not only on the outsides, but also on the fills, with wavy scribbles helping to define individual petals. It isn't necessary to finish this layer at this time, but you must at least outline all of the individual components of the picture. Save your file before moving on.

3 **Painting the fill layers.** The Linework layer will remain the top layer from this point forward, with each new layer being placed below. The White layer will be toggled on and off in order to sample colors, or turned off for the duration of the work if you prefer. Lock the Linework layer by clicking on the Lock icon on the Layers palette and select the White layer as your new target.

Make a new layer by choosing Layer > New > Layer and name the layer Purple One. Resize the Brush tool by clicking on the Brush Preset Picker and adjusting the Master Diameter slider to 30. Toggle off the White layer by clicking on the adjacent eye icon on the Layers palette.

The Brush tool allows you to sample colors on the fly by pressing Alt/Option and then clicking on any color within the image. You can also sample colors by clicking on the Foreground Color and clicking on any color within your image. Either way, the sampled color becomes the new Foreground Color.

Start by sampling the darkest purple you wish to use and rough in the darker parts of the leaves. Depending on your own preference, you may choose to toggle the White layer on and off, or not, or to reduce the layer's

All of the layers and details are completed and the White *layer is returned to 100% opacity.*

The White *layer has been turned to black, and the* Linework *layer to white, both using the Hue/Saturation controls.*

opacity. Remember to keep your strokes loose, and don't feel like you have to follow the old rule of staying in the lines. Sample a couple of other dark purples as well, brushing them on to this layer made for the dark purples. Move throughout the image until you are satisfied and most of the dark areas are covered.

Save your file, sample a lighter purple and make a new layer called Purple Two. Just as before, go throughout the image with the lighter hue, occasionally resampling for variety as before.

Select the White layer again and choose Layer > New > Layer to create a new layer below the first two purples. On this layer, you will sample and paint the lightest purples, sampling often and saving the file when finished.

Select the White layer (again!) and choose Layer > New > Layer to create a layer below the purple layers. Double-click on the name of the layer on the Layers palette and rename it Greens and Browns. Sample the greens and browns in the background and try simplifying the blurred colors. Remember to imagine what you might see if you were to posterize the photograph, using the greens and brown you sample. Save the file before moving on.

4 **Finishing with the details.** Your picture is nearly complete at this point, but key details are missing. Select layer Four and choose use Layer > New > Layer to place a layer between layers Four and Linework. Call your new layer Details. On this new layer will be the flower's stamens as well as occasional dots, lines and small fills.

Sample the light green in the pastilles and loosely fill in these areas. Sample a slightly darker green and add a few strokes just to bring out a little more depth and interest. Once again, examining the final product on page 192 shows how additional purples, dots and squiggles are added throughout the piece, individualizing it and bringing out personality. Be as conservative or as liberal with your strokes as you like.

The last two steps are extraordinarily easy. Turn on the White layer by clicking on the Eye icon on the Layers palette, and return the Opacity slider to 100%. Choose Image > Adjustments > Hue/Saturation and move the Lightness Slider all the way to the left, turning white to black. Select the Linework layer, choose Image > Adjustments > Hue/Saturation, then move the Lightness slider all the way to the right. Save the file and you're done!

Shower at Sunset Point

Painting an Abstract Mixed Media Work

Here are six photos from the shoot. The image in the upper-right has a dynamic composition and good color, which makes it a good candidate for an abstract painting.

With Painter and Photoshop, it is possible to combine media that would be impossible to combine traditionally—and without the mess! This project demonstrates using expressive Real Bristle Brushes that perform like Oils, Blenders, and textured Watercolor brushstrokes to create an abstract composition.

Shower at Sunset Point is inspired by a favorite English master of the romantic era, Joseph M. W. Turner, whose fascination with light as a powerful, dynamic force lead him from romantic realism to romantic abstraction with an expressive use lighting and color.

While working on art and teaching assignments in Oahu, Hawaii,

my husband, Steve, and I stayed with friends on the north shore near Sunset Point. Late one afternoon, extraordinary clouds were approaching, a precursor to evening rain showers. For this shoot, I focused on the quickly evolving cloud shapes using a Canon 5D with a 17–40 zoom lens, choosing a 17mm focal length for a wide-angle view. To capture the chosen photo, I used the Aperture Priority mode, with an aperture of f/11, and a shutter speed of 1/500 with the ISO set at 400.

When we returned home to the studio, I viewed the chosen photograph in the Camera Raw dialog and

made subtle adjustments to its tones and color. When painting the composition, I focused on the dynamic movement and general shapes, using Real Bristle, Oils, Blenders and Watercolor brushes, using Painter.

Before you begin, get inspired by looking at the composition, dynamic movement, light and color in the paintings of William Turner, including *Steamer in a Snowstorm* and *The Burning of the Houses of Parliament.* Now let's get started!

The reference photograph with tones enhanced.

Removing distracting elements from the beach with the Clone Stamp tool.

1 **Opening the digital original and retouching.** The original photograph for this project measures 3546 x 2283 pixels. This photo was captured in Camera Raw and opened directly in the Camera Raw dialog. Open your image and view it at 100% to adjust the tones and color, if needed, and to look for areas that may need retouching. For more dramatic lighting in this image, Contrast is increased subtly to +10. (See the Camera Raw sidebar on page 12 in Chapter 1 for detailed information about using the dialog.)

When you are satisfied with the Camera Raw edits on your image, press Alt/Option and click Open to open a copy of the image in Photoshop. Preserve your original photo by saving a new version in Photoshop format. Choose File > Save As and then give your working image a descriptive name. This project uses the title *Shower at Sunset Point retouch.psd*.

Would your photograph benefit from having distracting elements removed? The photo for this project has beautiful color and composition, with one exception—a dark-colored drainage pipe (partially covered by sand)

in the foreground. If this distracting element is removed, more attention will be focused on the dramatic sky.

The nondestructive retouching can be done in either Photoshop (used here) or Painter. For a nondestructive workflow, consider doing your retouching on a copy of the Background layer: Drag the Background layer over the Create a New layer button on the Layers palette to copy it. Choose the Clone Stamp tool in the Toolbox, and in the Options Bar, select the Aligned check box. To sample only from the active layer, set the Sample pop-up menu to Current Layer. Choose a soft brush tip from the Brush Preset Picker (try 45–60 pixels). To sample with the Clone Stamp tool, Alt-click/Option-click and then click in the area you want to retouch. Release the Alt/Option key and paint with the Clone Stamp tool to replace the desired area with pixels from the source area. The cloned imagery—in this case, the beach sand—is varied for a natural appearance. When your retouching is complete, save the file in Photoshop format with a new, descriptive name.

The retouched photo with lines drawn to dissect the composition.

A detail of the Step 1 image (left) and with Smart Blur added (right).

2 **Analyzing the composition.** Now open Painter, navigate to the retouched photo that you saved in Step 1 and open the file. An awareness of composition design is essential when creating abstract work. In this case, the image is horizontally divided into approximate thirds. The dark cloud formations (rough triangular shapes) move from left to right. In your image, look for angles you can use to suggest dynamic movement. The angle of the beach from lower-left to right is another example. This angle supports the feeling of left-to-right movement of the clouds, plays off the horizon line and leads the viewer's eye into the picture. This composition also employs the "rule of thirds." With the horizon line on the lower third of the image, the sky occupies the upper two thirds. The center of interest includes a dark cloud shape, the slice of sunlight and the veil of rain, near the lower third. The image has an asymmetrical balance of dark and light tones, with the dark triangular shape in the upper-left playing off the bright sunlit areas in the lower-right.

3 **Reducing detail.** To simplify the high frequency detail in the reference photo, the Smart Blur feature is used. (You can achieve a similar simplification result in Photoshop, as shown in "Simplifying a Photograph to Achieve a Hand-Rendered Result" on page 54.)

First, make a clone copy of your photo by choosing File > Clone. Save the clone with a descriptive name. If the Underpainting palette is not visible, open it by choosing Window > Show Underpainting. In the Underpainting palette, use the Smart Blur slider to adjust the level of detail in the clone image. Due to the file size and the low level of detail desired for this abstract project, a Smart Blur of 50% is used. Save the blurred file in Painter's native format, RIF. See page 91 for more detailed information about using the Smart Blur feature.

Using the modified Real Flat Blender to quickly pull pixels as if they are wet paint.

The primary movement in the sky is from left to right. The in-progress roughed-in painting.

4 **Laying in rough strokes and customizing a brush.** In this project, you will work over a clone copy of the blurred photograph using the Real Bristle, Oils brushes, Blenders and Watercolor. If you go too far with the painting process and want to bring back imagery from the blurred photo, you can restore areas easily using cloning. With the blurred photograph active, choose File > Clone, and name the new clone with a descriptive name. Before moving on to working with the brushes, set Brush Tracking by choosing Edit > Preferences>Brush Tracking or Corel Painter > Preferences > Brush Tracking. (See page 151 for more information about Brush Tracking.)

As you saw in "Using Real Bristle Brushes in Painter for a Quick Acrylic Study" on page 148, the Real Bristle Brushes are capable of amazingly realistic brushstrokes. The Real Blender Flat and Real Blender Round variants of the Real Bristle Brushes are very useful for laying in the rough stage of an abstract painting.

To move pixels on your image without laying down new color, make a few changes to the brush. Choose the Real Blender Flat variant of the Real Bristle Brushes in the Brush Selector Bar. In the Property Bar, increase its Size to about 50 pixels. To push and pull pixel imagery, without applying new color, set the Resat slider in the Property Bar to 0%, and for a rougher bristly brush look, increase the Feature slider to 4.0. Save the custom brush by choosing Save Variant from the pop-up menu on the right side of the Brush Selector Bar, and when the dialog appears, enter a descriptive name in the field. (This project uses *Real Blend Flat 0R*.) For good Painter housekeeping, return the original Real Blender Flat to its default settings by choosing Restore Default Brush from the pop-up menu on the rigth side of the Brush Selector Bar.

Using the custom Real Blend Flat 0R, pull directional strokes that complement the movement in your composition, such as the horizontal strokes in the sky. For the foreground in this image, the brush size is reduced to 30 pixels, and slightly angled strokes are pulled. Then the brush is reduced to 20 pixels and short, dabbing strokes are painted to suggest the sandy beach. A smaller brush is used to paint the wavelets surging onto the shore.

Detail of the clouds, with free, expressive strokes painted with the custom Real Blend Flat 0R brush and the default Real Blender Flat.

The rain shower is painted using the Smoothy Runny Bristle 30 variant of Watercolor on a Watercolor layer.

5 **Adding more loose strokes and finesse.** Once the basic movement and shapes are established, sit back, zoom out and take a good look at your image. Would the addition of freer, expressive strokes in the center of interest make your composition more exciting? For *Shower at Sunset Point*, shorter, curved strokes add a lighter, fluffy look to the clouds.

Choose the custom Real Flat Blend 0R brush and with your stylus in hand, begin a stroke and then turn (or roll) the stylus in your hand as you continue to pull the stroke. Try experimenting with squiggly, wavy strokes. At this point, make any other small adjustments your image needs, for instance, brightening highlights or blending areas. In the case of this image, the abstracted line of white water below the horizon is brightened using a small Opaque Round variant of Oils. Textured strokes are added to the beach using the Smeary Bristle Spray variant of Oils. Then, to focus more attention on the sky, areas of the beach are subdued and softened using the Round Blender Brush variant of Blenders.

6 **Suggesting a rain shower.** Now that the image is nearly complete, are there any final details that you'd like to add? Remembering the tropical showers of that afternoon, this image called out for a veil of rain dropping from the darkest cloud. Use the Dropper tool to sample a color from the image. In the case of this image, a medium blue-gray is chosen. Special Watercolor brushes in Painter can be used to suggest rain. Choose the Watercolor category and the Smoothy Runny Bristle 30 variant. Open the Water section of the Brush Controls by choosing Window > Brush Controls > Water. Notice the Wind Direction dial and make sure that it is set to 270°, which allows the paint to drip from top to bottom. When you touch the brush to the Canvas, a new Watercolor Layer appears in the Layers palette. Paint a horizontal stroke just above where you want the rain to fall and then sit back and enjoy watching the paint run and drip, just like wet watercolor paint, or rain.

Congratulations! You have created an abstract composition using the Real Bristle Brushes, Oils, Blenders, and Watercolor brushes and layers.

Simulating Reality Using Compositing, Masking and Color Layers

Photoshop **206**

A Painter's Sense of Composition

Photoshop and Painter **218**

8

COMPOSITION AND COLLAGING

This chapter teaches ideas and processes for assembling compositions using several photographs. Design concepts for photographic collages and paintings featuring multiple elements are described.

Simulating Reality Using Compositing, Masking and Color Layers shows how to design and organize a complex collage work that incorporates many layers, layer masks and clipping groups, and color correction of the layered elements. After the major collage elements are in place, atmosphere is added and bubbles are painted with a custom brush. To complete the work, the brushstrokes and color are finessed.

A Painter's Sense of Composition teaches the process of conceiving a composition using three images: two photographs and a scan of colored pastel paper. The photo elements are scaled and assembled into a layered composite file. Then the photo imagery is cloned into a separate file containing the paper scan. After a color palette is mixed, Chalk, Pastel and Blenders brushes are used to paint textured brushstrokes over the image. The textured Pastel brushes are also used to paint an irregular border for the composition.

Agent Don Gets Wet

Simulating Reality Using Compositing, Masking and Color Layers

The eight images used to make Agent Don Gets Wet *were shot with a first-generation 6-megapixel Canon Rebel and a 10.2-megapixel Nikon D200.*

Assembling different shots of people, action and props can be a delightfully fun — and frustrating— Adobe Photoshop project, resulting in one of the more intricate pieces a digital artist may produce. An image such as the one for this project can easily have dozens of layers when it is finished, each one contributing to the final piece in one way or another.

The key to a nice "super-realistic" piece is planning. It doesn't matter how good your photographs are if the image is poorly laid out or the individual elements don't quite fit due to angle, color or lighting. Although many decisions such as color and placement can be made during the composing stage, you should begin with a good (and flexible) idea of how you want your final image to look.

This project explores effective ways to build your own Photoshop composition using lots of layers, layer masks, groups and clipping groups, as well as mixing global and isolated color correction methods. The twelve pages could easily expand into an epic of repetitious steps and close attention to tiny details (additional shadows, perfect shading, layering bubble sizes and adding schools of fish come to mind), but for the most part there wouldn't be a whole lot of different techniques to introduce. That being said, I encourage you to add your own elements or even paint your final image using other methods we've included in this book.

To create *Agent Don Gets Wet*, I used eight different shots taken over a period of five years. The photos of the fish were shot through glass at the Monterey Bay Aquarium as a drawing reference from which to make cartoon seascapes, so no thought was given to anything other than recording the shapes of the fish. Without a tripod or strong flash, I raised the ISO to 380, dropped the exposure to 1/30 second and set the aperture to f/4.5, then held the camera directly against the glass. (Most of the shots were just *terrible!*)

The other shots were done under better conditions. Each of them was taken on a sunny day, with the camera set on Aperture Priority and the ISO set to 100. The graveyard image was shot at 1/800 second at f/22, and the 1941 Plymouth was shot at f/8 at 1/125 second.

The stunning self-portrait (so that I'd not embarrass anyone besides myself) was shot with a tripod and self-timer, and the camera settings were f/5 at 1/500th second.

The bright color and crisp shadows make this photograph an excellent candidate for digital painting.

These photographs are obviously of poor quality, but when the image is complete, they won't look out of place or inferior.

1 **Opening the digital originals.** The eight images used in the project include JPG and RAW files, so not all of the images are as editable as they would be if they had all been in Adobe Camera Raw format. The fish and the graveyard were shot shortly after the release of Canon's original Digital Rebel and before Camera Raw was commonplace. Though Camera Raw can be used to process JPG files, these JPG files are left as shot.

The other three images are in RAW mode and are also opened without making any adjustments. The exposures are good to begin with, and more specific changes can be made when other elements are there to help make those changes consistent throughout your image. The blue overcast will change how the images appear in a manner that is difficult to predict, so spending time perfecting each individual file right off the bat can end up simply wasting your time. The final colors and tones can be more accurately balanced within a single document instead of eight separate files.

2 **Importing and masking layers.** Although you can do this project in Painter, my preference is Photoshop because it is easier for me to keep track of the many masks involved, plus the process uses filters instead of brushes, with one obvious exception in Step 7.

Choose the size of your picture first. For *Agent Don Gets Wet,* maintaining the original resolution of 2592 x 3872 from the higher resolution images allows the image to be scaled to 24 x 36 without loss of quality for inkjet output or bigger if the picture is to be viewed from a distance.

Start working with what is to become the focal point of your image first, in this case the picture of Secret Agent Don (SAD from here on). On the Layers palette, double-click on the Background layer. This makes the layer float, enabling you to isolate SAD by using a layer mask to get rid of everything in the layer but SAD. To apply a layer mask, first select the layer and then either click on the Add Layer Mask button at the bottom left of the Layers palette or choose Layer > Layer Mask > Reveal All.

Press the B key to make the Brush tool active. Click on the Brush Preset Picker and choose the Hard Round 13 preset. Change the Hardness Slider to 80 to soften the edge of the brush so masked elements throughout the image transition into one another a bit more smoothly.

Each element is roughly trimmed using the Lasso tool before dragging it into the working document, making it easier to work with the layers.

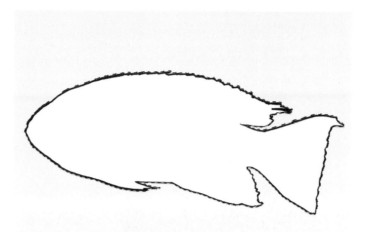

Using a thin, unbroken line to isolate each element makes it easy for the Magic Wand tool to select the rest of the area to be masked (blue).

Make the layer mask your target by clicking on its thumbnail on the Layers palette whenever you start masking. With black as the foreground color, draw a tight outline around SAD to isolate him from the background of the picture. Zoom in as you work, and Alt-click/Option-click on the layer mask's preview to toggle between viewing the layer and the layer mask to make sure there are no white gaps in the outline.

When the subject is entirely outlined and the layer mask is visible you can use the Magic Wand tool to select the remaining area to be masked by pressing the W key and clicking on the mask outside the outline. If there are gaps in the outline, the inside of your mask will also be selected. If that happens, press Ctrl-D/⌘-D to deselect all, carefully examine the layer mask to find and fill each gap, then reselect. When the selection is active, choose Select > Modify > Expand and enter a value of 3 pixels. Change your background color to black and press the Backspace/Delete key, which fills your selection with black to complete the mask.

Save your work by choosing File > Save As and name the file. (This project uses *ADGW1.psd*.) This becomes the working file into which you'll drag the other elements.

Moving the rest of the images into this document is done methodically and without worrying about the layering sequence. To import the images, open each document and move the window so you can view both ADGW1 and the newly opened file. Press the L key to choose the Lasso tool and make a rough selection around the desired element. Press the V key to select the Move tool, click on the image you are bringing into your composition and drag it onto the ADGW1 canvas. After each new layer is dragged into the document, turn off its visibility by clicking on the Eye icon next to the new name.

Once all the pieces are in the single file, put the layers in the correct sequence. To move individual layers, click on the name of the layer and drag it up or down on the Layers palette. After you move each layer, double-click on the name of the layer and rename it. Working from the bottom to the top the layer sequence should be: Graveyard, Lake Bottom, Shark, Car, Two Fish, SAD, Blue Fish, Orange Fish. Save your file!

Now move through the layers one at a time, clicking in the box in front of each layer's name to make it appear. Repeat the masking process used on the SAD layer for the Car, Shark and each Fish layer, saving regularly.

This detail of the final image shows the trees in the background, which wouldn't be found underwater, blending in and appearing "normal."

Merging the background first makes it easier to position elements later.

3 Composing the image. Placing and merging the two images that make up the background is the first priority because it's impossible to see the composition in context until that step is complete.

Turn off the visibility of each layer except Graveyard and Lake Bottom. Typically you don't find grass at the bottom of the ocean, so you'll replace the graveyard's grass with the lake bottom's rocks and dirt. Click on the Lake Bottom layer mask thumbnail and choose Select > All, then choose Select > Inverse or press Ctrl-I/⌘-I. This inverts the white pixels on the layer mask, changing them to black.

Choose Window > Brushes or press F5 and choose the Soft Round 65 brush. Click on Brush Tip

The Layers palette at the start of Step 3, with the layer mask on the Orange Fish layer targeted.

Shape and slide the Hardness setting to 60%; then start painting around the bottom of the tombstones and wall. As you paint, the shoreline image will begin to appear. Finish painting the bottom of the mask so the grass in the graveyard is completely replaced by the barren lakeshore landscape.

Return to the Layers palette and turn on the visibility of the SAD layer by clicking on the empty box in front of the layer's name; then do the same for the Car layer (which should be under the SAD layer).

You're going to scale and position the car now. Choose Edit > Free Transform or press Ctrl-T/⌘-T to use Free Transform to rotate and scale the contents of the layer. Press and hold the Shift key to constrain the proportions, but release it to rotate the subject (unless you wish to constrain the rotation to 45-degree increments). Choose one of the corners and move it either toward or away from the crosshairs in the center of the selection, or just outside the box to switch to rotate mode.

The shadows on the shirt are used as reference to rotate the car. The murky water and bubbles will hide the inconsistencies.

The Adjustment Layer colorizes everything behind the Car *layer.*

Use the lighting on the SAD layer as a reference for positioning to rotate the car until the reflections and shadows appear as correct as they can be. Obviously, there are a few problems matching the direction of the light source in this case, so do the best you can!

Another problem with the picture of the car is the people standing in front of the back wheelwell. Crop them out by simply moving the car to the left when it's upside down.

When you are satisfied with your placement, press the Enter/Return key. Move through each additional layer and repeat the scaling and rotation step to place each item. After each item is placed, save the document. It's disheartening to have everything in position only to lose it from an untimely crash.

4 **Building depth and changing hues.** Under normal circumstances, water is murky with microscopic life and sediment. Things close up are relatively clear, but as you look farther away things become less defined and more uniform and gray, until they can no longer be seen at all. To simulate this effect, you will add layers strategically.

First, bring the blue hue into your image by placing an Adjustment Layer over everything that appears to fall behind the car. Choose the Shark layer on the Layers palette and click on the Adjustment Layer button at the bottom of the Layers palette. Choose Hue/Saturation from the pop-up menu. In the Hue/Saturation panel that opens, click on the Colorize box. Enter 212 for Hue, 60 for Saturation and –30 for Lightness.

With all layers visible, click on the Lake Bottom layer mask thumbnail. Carefully examine the merge between the Lake Bottom layer and the Graveyard layer. Make any needed edits to the layer mask; then Shift-click on both layers' names on the Layer palette. Press Ctrl-E/⌘-E to merge the two layers. The merged layer is busy and noisy, so to simplify it choose Filter > Noise > Dust & Scratches. Set the Radius slider to 4.

The color at the top of the image (circle) was used to get a matching blue color to use for the steps that call for sampling blue.

Water depth is built with two different layers on Normal mode, one at 80% opacity and the other at 55% opacity.

You will begin adding water depth by sampling a blue color. Select the Brush tool, press F5 to open the Brushes palette and select the Soft Round 300 brush. Click on the Foreground Color and when the Color Picker appears, move the cursor into the top of the picture to sample the lightest blue. Choose Edit > Fill or press Shift-F5 to fill the layer with blue, choosing Foreground Color from the pop-up window. Change the layer's Blend mode to Overlay using the pop-up window on the Layers palette.

To build haze in the water, click again on the Foreground Color and move the circle on the Color Picker to a much lighter and more neutral gray-blue color.

On the Layers palette, click on the merged Lake Bottom layer and choose Layer > New > Layer twice to make two new layers. On the first of these layers, leave the Blend mode on Normal, but reduce the opacity by setting the Opacity slider to 80%. Paint on the layer and cover the entire canvas behind the wall and tombstones, making things appear murky. Select the bottom layer, reduce the Opacity to 55 and cover the elements falling in the "middle" distance, such as the wall and the gravestones. Rename the layers 55 Haze and 80 Haze, and save your document.

5 Coloring Agent Don. Agent Don (SAD) is starting to look a bit wet, but the bright blue shirt doesn't help with the composition as much as a different color might. The pants don't look quite the right color either.

Start the process of making SAD appear to fit better in this underwater world by double-checking the mask yet again, refining it if necessary. Once you are satisfied with the mask, hold down Ctrl/⌘ and click on the SAD layer mask thumbnail to make it an active selection. Create a group for SAD by pressing Ctrl-G/⌘-G, then click on the Add Layer Mask button on the Layers palette to turn it into a Clipping Group with its mask in place. Now every layer you place into the group will share this same mask. However, SAD is masked twice—once by the layer mask and again by the Clipping Group's mask. Because you don't want that to happen (see the sidebar on page 214), drag the layer mask thumbnail on the SAD layer to the Trash button at the bottom of the Layers palette. When prompted, click Delete. Double-click on the Clipping Group on the Layers palette and rename it SAD Group.

The subtle blue layer set to Soft Light in the SAD Group makes the pants match the blue in the background a little better.

A simple Adjustment Layer converts the blue shirt to a pleasing yellow color, making the image more interesting.

Most of what you do to colorize SAD will be done within this group, so start by clicking on the SAD layer in the Layers palette. Choose Layer > New > Layer to position a new target layer above SAD. Now you'll change your Foreground Color layer so it contains the same light blue as the top of the water by first clicking the Foreground Color. When the Color Picker dialog appears,

The Layers palette shows both layer masks and SAD's Clipping Group.

move the cursor off the picker onto the top of the image. The cursor transforms to the Eyedropper tool. Click on your desired blue to make it appear on the Color Picker and click Accept. Now fill the layer with your new Foreground Color by choosing Edit > Fill or pressing Shift-F5 and selecting foreground color from the pop-up menu. SAD has disappeared under solid

blue, so bring him back with the blue hue by changing the Blend mode to Soft Light in the pop-up menu on the Layers palette. Reduce the extreme result by dropping the layer's Opacity to 25.

Now SAD blends better with the background, but the blue shirt still needs attention so you will change the color next. First, click on the SAD layer to make it the target layer. Make an Adjustment Layer by clicking on the Adjustment Layer button, the black-and-white circle at the bottom of the Layers palette, and choose Hue/Saturation. A new Adjustment Layer called Hue/Saturation is placed in the group above SAD. Slide the Color Slider to –144, turning the shirt to yellow.

This makes SAD quite a sight. To isolate just the shirt and return SAD to the correct colors, choose the Brush tool and click on the Brush Preset Picker on the Options Bar. Choose the Hard Round 19 brush. Press the D key to return the foreground and background colors to the default of black and white. With the foreground color now set to black, paint out everything but the shirt, and SAD will return to normal. Save your file!

Choosing between multiple layer masks and a clipping group. These diagrams show the difference between using duplicate layer masks applied to multiple layers (top), and the same mask applied to a Clipping Group made up of the exact same layers and layer sequence (bottom). The left column is zoomed way in, capturing a tiny area just under the statue's nose and a bit of the lip. Note the single pixel edge along the mask in the top rectangle. The right column shows the noticeable difference in the blend of the face into the background.

Another blue layer set to Overlay mode gives everything behind the Orange Fish layer a common color cast.

The Mask to the right was used to blend the statues, the stripes on the statue, and an Adjustment Layer into the background.

6 **Making the car and sand look "right."** There is still quite a lot of color and tonal variation throughout the image. To address this, choose Layer > New > Layer and fill it with the blue color that should still be your foreground color. Now set the Blend mode to Overlay. Click on the name of the layer and drag it out of the SAD Group, placing it immediately below the Orange Fish layer.

The car appears dark and inconsistent with the rest of the picture. Everything you do to the car in this step needs to be contained within the Clipping Group to allow every layer to share the same mask. Start by selecting the Car layer and then press Ctrl-G/⌘-G to place it in a Group Folder. Ctrl-click/⌘-click on the Car layer's layer mask thumbnail, making it an active selection. Click on the Group folder you just made and press the Layer Mask button at the bottom of the Layers palette to mask the group.

Now throw away the layer mask on the Car layer by clicking on its thumbnail and dragging it onto the trash can icon on the Layers palette. Choose Delete, *not* Apply, from the pop-up menu.

The front of the car appears closer to the viewer than the back of the car, and all of it falls behind SAD. The farther

The car is first faded to match the haze at the farthest point from the viewer.

The car is brought back by duplicating the Car layer, adding a layer mask with a gradient and reducing the opacity to 40%.

away it gets, the less clear and more uniform in color it should become. To fade the car gradually, you will fade the parts of the car farthest away to visually match elements equally as far away, then gradually return the front clarity.

Start this effect by shifting the color first to a hue that matches the background. In Step 5, you created a layer and filled it with blue. Duplicate this layer by first selecting it on the Layers palette and then dragging it onto the New Layer button. Click and drag the new duplicate layer into the car's clipping group, setting it just above the Car layer. Change the Blend mode to Soft Light and return the Opacity to 100%. The car is now very dark, but the hues are similar to the rest of the image.

Choose Layer > New Layer and then press Shift-F5 to bring up the Fill dialog. Use the pop-up menu to select white as the fill color. Leave the Blend mode at Normal and reduce the Opacity to 13%. Click this layer on the Layers palette and drag it to between the blue layer you just made and the Car layer. Now the car looks like it belongs, but it lacks a sense of dimension.

Use the Layers palette to duplicate the Car layer by dragging its Layer Preview onto the New Layer button.

Select and drag it to above the blue layer and reduce the Opacity to 40%. Choose Layer > Layer Mask > Reveal All to make a layer mask. Select the Gradient tool (G); then click and drag from the front-left headlight, parallel to the chrome strip down the length of the car. This may take a few tries to get the gradation to look right.

You'll add two more layers in this step to add shadows and smooth the sand. First, click on the Lake Bottom layer and choose Layer > New > Layer. Reduce the layer's Opacity to 75%; then select the Brush tool. Hold down the Alt/Option key and sample the blue at the same place as before, near the top. Press F5 to open the Brushes palette and select the Soft Round 200 brush. Paint over the sand, leaving the rocks alone.

The car's shadow is added by making another new layer, then setting its Blend mode to Multiply. Sample the gray-blue on the underbelly of one of the two fish on the Two Fish layer using the same method you employed to select the blue in Step 5. Right-click/Ctrl-click on your image to access the Brush Controls and use the Master Diameter slider to reduce the brush size to 125. Freehand draw the shadow and save your document.

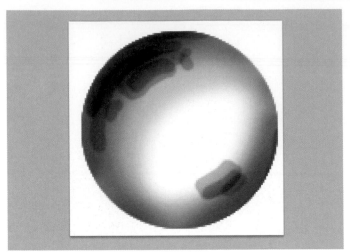

The custom Bubble Brush is created as a negative. When used, the blacks and grays on the brush fill with the foreground color (right).

The Bubble Brush is used at a size of 60 pixels and 35 pixels. The bubbles scatter due to the Scattering setting on the Brushes palette.

7 Painting bubbles. Painting all of those bubbles looks like a monumental task, but it's surprisingly easy. A custom brush and a new layer are all that's required. To make the bubble brush, you need to create a grayscale document. Choose File > New, set the Width and Height to 70 pixels and set the Color Mode to Grayscale.

Now comes the trickiest part of the entire exercise for some: drawing one bubble! To make a round selection to shape the bubble, select the Elliptical Marquee tool. Holding down the Shift key to constrain the shape, click and drag from the top-left corner to the lower-right corner.

Press the D key to return the foreground color to black. Paint along just outside of your selection, allowing the brush's side to creep into the active area. The darker you paint, the lighter and more reflective the final painted bubbles will become. Optimally there should be little, if any, solid black around the edges unless you want a spectral highlight on the side of your bubbles. You may find it easier to perfect your bubble by setting the Opacity slider on the Options Bar to 20 and the Mode to Multiply. Paint your stroke all around the sides of your selection, heaviest at the top-left and bottom-right edges.

8 Casting a bit of light on the subject. Since there are a lot of reflections and shadows, it makes sense to add a few rays of light to penetrate the depths you've created. To do this, you'll add two very similar layers.

First, click the New Layer button and move this layer below the Blue Fish layer. Press the F5 key and choose the Soft Round 200 brush, then press and hold the Alt/Option key and sample a light yellow-green color from the shirt. Return the brush Opacity to 100% on the Options Bar and press and hold the Shift key as you paint five or six parallel lines from the top of the image to the bottom. Choose Filter > Blur > Gaussian Blur, set the Radius to 40 and press Enter/Return.

Press Ctrl-T/⌘-T to free transform the layer. Before moving any corners, press and hold the Ctrl/⌘ key. Select and drag the individual corners until it appears that the strokes emanate from the top-left to the bottom-right. Drop the Opacity to 23 on the Layers palette.

Repeat this step, this time moving the layer below the SAD group and setting the Opacity to 50%. Save your file!

To paint light reflections in the bubbles, choose a smaller brush and paint black wherever you wish these

Using free-transform and holding down the Ctrl/⌘ key allows you to pull the anchor points individually, including the middle anchors.

The Smart Blur filter removes leftover photographic detail, as shown in this before (top) and after (bottom) comparison.

highlights to appear. Select the Hard Round 13 variant and paint the details on the bubble, setting the Opacity slider to 75 on the Options Bar.

When you're happy with your bubble, save your file, calling it *Bubble Brush*. Choose Edit > Define Brush Preset and name the new brush Bubble Brush. This new variant appears at the end of the list on the Brushes palette, but it is not quite ready for use. Select the Bubble Brush and click on Brush Tip Shape on the Brushes palette. Set the Spacing to 150%; then click on the boxes in front of Shape Dynamics and Scattering to turn them on. Now click on the words *Shape Dynamics* and set the sliders as follows: Size Jitter: 75%, Minimum Diameter: 35%, and Roundness Jitter: 16%. Click on Scattering and set Scatter to 340% and Count to 2.

Choose the top layer on the Layers palette and click on the New Layer button. Click on the Foreground Color box and use the Color Picker to select white. Click the Brush Preset Picker to scale your brush to 60 pixels and start painting. Scale to 35 to add smaller bubbles when the bigger ones are done. And, as always, save your file!

9 **Blurring away the fingerprints.** Finally, the image looks close to finished. Everything below the bubbles could use simplifying to eliminate leftover noise.

A neat trick enables you to merge your visible layers although keeping them at the same time. Start by turning off the layer(s) you don't want included in the merged image. The only layer you are worried about here is the Bubbles layer, so turn it off by clicking the Eye icon in front of its name on the palette.

Select the Orange Fish layer immediately below and press Ctrl-Alt-Shift-E/⌘-Shift-Option-E to merge all of the visible layers on a new layer. This layer will always fall above the layer currently selected on the Layers palette. If you were to choose another visible layer before merging, the resulting layer would be identical, but it wouldn't be on the top, thus affected by each layer above.

To globally simplify the leftover noise and detail in the merged layer, choose Filter > Blur > Smart Blur. Set the Radius slider to 7 and the Threshold to 19, and choose High Quality from the pop-up menu.

Finally, click the Bubble layer back to visible on the Layers palette, save your document, and you're finished!

Wood, Sea, Sky

A Painter's Sense of Composition

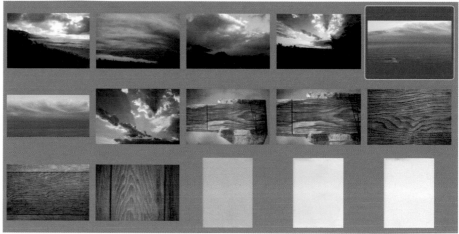

With collages in mind, I shot photographs of skies at different locations, at different times of day. I also took photos of wood and made scans of colored art papers.

A composition tells a story. In the collage *Wood, Sea, Sky*, space is expansive, and elements have natural textures and painted planes of color.

With Photoshop and Painter, it's possible to create a wide variety of compositions, collages and montages. This project focuses on creating a collage in Photoshop by incorporating photographs and scans, and combining them with Painter brushwork.

On several different photography excursions, I shot photos of interesting landscapes, including ocean scenes, and found elements such as used, weathered wood. Back at the studio, I scanned my favorite colored art papers to use as a painting surface.

To shoot the wood items outdoors, I set up the Canon 5D on a tripod, with a Canon Macro lens EF 100mm f/2.8. I used Aperture Priority mode with apertures between f/2.8 and f/5.6, ISO 200 and shutter speeds ranging between 1/125 to 1/200. As the lighting changed with passing clouds, I checked the light meter and adjusted the exposure accordingly.

I also scanned a variety of art papers for *Wood, Sea, Sky*. Pieces of chosen photographs were used to design the composition and then the Mixer in Painter was used to build a color palette. Chalk and pastel brushes were then used to paint over the scanned paper and collage elements, focusing on atmosphere,

color and texture. Three areas of detail—the sunlit area in the clouds, the set of waves on the sea and the organic lines in the wood texture—invite the eye to travel the composition.

For inspiration before shooting photos and painting, look at the collage work of the American pop artist Robert Rauschenburg, including *Pilgrim*.

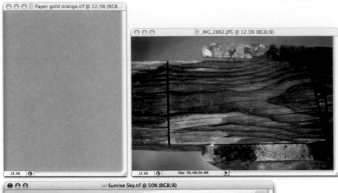

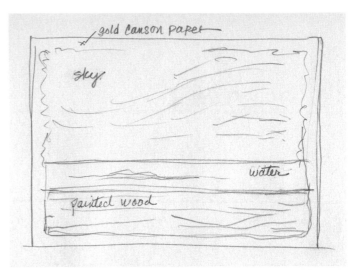

The chosen collage elements have rich color and texture. The organic lines of the wood grain complement the free curves in the wispy clouds.

Sketching with pencil and paper helps to organize ideas. One of the early rough sketches drawn with pencil and paper.

1 **Conceiving the composition.** Before you begin, think about what *picture format* will work best for your idea—horizontal, vertical or square, depending on the elements that you have in mind for your composition. The picture format is the shape or proportions of the *picture plane*. The picture plane is the two-dimensional area where artists sketch and photographers compose the image. This collage uses a horizontal format.

Now that you have decided on your picture format, think about where to position the main elements, for instance, a horizon line and possible center of interest. At this point, make some preliminary decisions about the size of elements. Your composition may have more interest if you divide it up unequally, for instance, one-third/two-thirds, or one-fifth/four-fifths, rather than into equal halves, which can be static. This is just a guideline, however, because a symmetrical composition may be the right choice for certain subject matter. (Both Photoshop and Painter offer grid features that can be helpful for laying out compositions. Painter's Divine Proportion and Layout Grid features are especially useful. See page 221 for information about Painter's Layout Grid feature.)

This project uses chalk and pastel brushwork (in Painter) over colored art paper. Choose an 8.5 x 11-inch piece of pastel paper (try Canson Mi-Teintes paper). Place it on your flatbed scanner and set up your scanning software to scan at 100% (full size) with a resolution of 300 pixels per inch. Save the file in TIF format.

Next open all of the elements in Photoshop and size them small on the screen to make them easy to study. Eliminate any unneeded candidates and then get out your sketchbook and make a rough composition sketch.

When you've settled on your concept, open a new file. The file for this project is 4368 x 2912 pixels, measuring 17 x 11 inches at 240 pixels per inch. Save your composition file by choosing File > Save As. (This project uses *Wood, Sea, Sky 01.psd*.)

The preliminary layout of the sky, ocean and wood elements shows general proportions and size relationships.

A detail of the early composition shows how the organic lines in the wood grain complement the natural lines and texture in the ocean and sky.

2 Assembling elements. You will paint over the photo elements with layered brushwork. The layout stage can be accomplished in Photoshop (used here) or Painter. Keep in mind the following important themes regarding the composition. First, you need to consider maintaining good white space (or the space around elements). You need to consider size relationships. You also want to

create movement for the eye to follow. Last, you want to consider adding repetition of texture and color.

Open all of the source elements that you want to use. To isolate an element in a source file, use the Lasso tool to make a loose selection around the area that you'll use. Next give the selection a soft transparent edge by feathering it. Choose Select > Modify > Feather and type a number in the field. (The amount of feather depends on the size of your file. This project uses 3 pixels.) Copy items from the source files and paste them into the composite

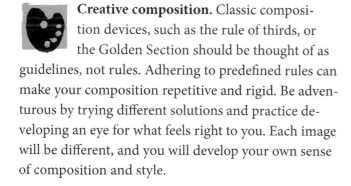 **Creative composition.** Classic composition devices, such as the rule of thirds, or the Golden Section should be thought of as guidelines, not rules. Adhering to predefined rules can make your composition repetitive and rigid. Be adventurous by trying different solutions and practice developing an eye for what feels right to you. Each image will be different, and you will develop your own sense of composition and style.

 Using the Layout Grid. The Layout Grid in Painter is helpful for planning your composition. Choose Window > Show Layout Grid to open the palette, and then select the Enable Layout Grid check box. Next, choose the number of divisions. An odd number such as 3 or 5 will yield more interesting results than a space with even divisions.

Painting the layer mask with a large, soft brush and black paint.

The layer mask on the wood layer reveals the wood that will be seen.

file as layers. When you have the elements selected and pasted into the working file, try out composition ideas. To easily select elements on each layer, click on the Move tool in the Toolbox and then make sure that the Auto-Select check box in the context-sensitive Options Bar is selected. Auto-Select allows you to select elements on underlying layers. To become more comfortable with the composition elements, try moving them around in the image with the Move tool. Try different size relationships. Select a layer in the Layers palette and then choose Edit > Free Transform. To size the item proportionally, press the Shift key and then drag a corner handle. When the item is scaled as you like it, press the Enter/Return key to accept the transformation.

To hide a portion of a layer, do so nondestructively, using a layer mask. Target the layer, click the Add Layer Mask button on the Layers palette. A mask filled with white appears. Click on the layer mask to select it and use a

The Gray Wood layer mask is active.

brush, painting with black color to hide areas and white to reveal. When your layout is ready, save the file.

Composing in Painter. To organize collage elements in Painter, create a new file and then choose File > Place to place each item into the working collage file. Each placed image will appear as a named reference layer in the Layers palette. Then you can use the Layer Adjuster tool to position and scale the items without loss of quality, because they are in a "reference state." If you attempt to paint on the reference layer, or add a layer mask and then paint the mask, a Commit dialog prompts you to commit it into an image (or standard) layer. Click Commit if you're ready to accept. It's a good idea to make all scaling decisions before painting on the reference layers. To use a layer mask in Painter, click on a layer you want to mask and then click the Create Layer Mask button on the Layers palette. A mask filled with white appears. Click on the mask to activate it and then paint black to hide a portion of the layer or white to reveal.

The scan of golden-orange art paper, rotated to horizontal format.

The paper image with the clone source set and Tracing Paper enabled.

3 Prepping files for painting and opening in Painter.
Next, for the best performance during the sketching and painting process, make a new version of the file in Photoshop format with the Wood and Sky layers merged with the Background choose File > Save As, and give the file a new name. (This project uses *Wood, Sea, Sky 02 flat. psd.*) Now choose Layer > Flatten Image. Save the file.

Next, open the scan of the art paper that best fits your design. The scan of golden-orange paper is in portrait mode, and for the purposes of this image, it is rotated to horizontal format. To rotate the image, choose Image > Image Rotation > 90° CW and then choose File > Save As, to save a new version of the file in Photoshop format. (This project uses *Gold paper.psd.*) The proportions and

resolution of the scan of colored art paper will be similar to the resolution of the working composite file. Scale the paper scan so it has the same number of pixels as the working composite (*Wood, Sea, Sky 02 flat.psd*).

Resizing the paper scan to fit the composite.

Choose Image > Image Size. Deselect the Constrain Proportions check box in the Image Size dialog and type the exact number of pixels needed in the Width and Height fields at the top of the dialog. As you will see below, matching the pixel size of the two files aids in the painting process. To use the cloning and Tracing Paper features in Painter, the images must have the exact same pixel dimensions. When the sizing is complete, save the file, and close it and then close in Photoshop.

Now open Painter, and open the *Wood, Sea, Sky 02 flat.psd* file and the *Gold paper.psd* file. With the *Gold paper.psd* file active choose File > Clone Source, and from the File > Clone Source menu choose the flattened composite (*Wood, Sea, Sky 02 flat.psd*). To enable Tracing Paper, choose Canvas > Tracing Paper or press the Ctrl-T/⌘-T keys.

Using the Soft Cloner to paint imagery into the colored paper file.

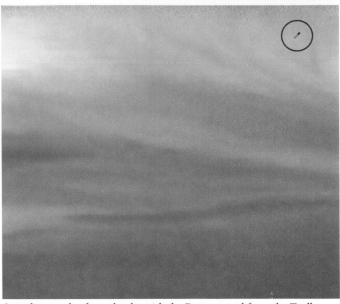

Sampling a color from the sky with the Dropper tool from the Toolbox.

4 **Painting photo imagery into the paper file.** In this step, you will use Painter to clone imagery from the composite file into the paper file.

Add a new layer for your painting by choosing Layers > New Layer. In the Layers palette, make sure that the Preserve Transparency check box is deselected. Now choose the Soft Cloner variant of Cloners from the Brush Selector Bar and use it to magically clone the photo imagery into the paper image, being careful to preserve edges of the orange paper. The cloned imagery will be a base for more painted brushwork, which uses color from the Mixer palette, Colors palette or color sampled from the image, painted with Chalk, Pastels and Blenders brushes.

Painting with color from the Mixer. To pick up color from the Mixer palette and apply it to your image, select the Sample Color tool on the Mixer palette (the Dropper). Choose a brush variant (such as the Square Hard Pastel variant of Pastels) and apply color to the image.

5 **Mixing a color palette in Painter.** Before beginning to paint over the cloned imagery, make a palette of colors to use while painting. So you can sample colors for the Mixer palette in this step, switch out of the Cloners brushes by choosing the Chalk category in the Brush Selector Bar. Now open the Mixer palette by choosing Window > Color Palettes > Show Mixer. Using the Dropper tool (Toolbox), click on a desired color from

The Mixer with the color palette for the Wood, Sea, Sky *image*

the reference image and apply it to the Mixer Pad using the Apply Color tool (the Brush) on the Mixer palette. Continue to sample color from the reference and apply dots of color onto the Mixer Pad. When you have the colors you desire, use the Mix Color tool (the Palette Knife) to blend the colors and values.

Painting over the cloned imagery and along the border of the image.

Using Blunt Chalk to paint more texture in areas of the sky.

6 **Setting up, painting and adding the border.** The cloned imagery serves as a base for more brushwork painted with the Chalk, Pastels and Blenders brushes. In the Layers palette, click on the layer with the cloned imagery. Now choose Rough Charcoal Paper in the Paper Selector in the Toolbox. Rough Charcoal Paper complements the art paper scan used here. Choose the Square Chalk variant of Chalk in the Brush Selector Bar. Square Chalk is a bold, expressive tool that paints broad, textured strokes. Additionally, Square Chalk reveals more paper grain if you paint using light pressure on the stylus and less grain with heavier pressure.

When painting the soft-textured border treatment, begin by painting with color from the clone source. With Square Chalk chosen, enable the Clone Color button on the Colors palette and make soft strokes along the edge of the image using a circular motion with your stylus. Paint over the cloned imagery and pull brushstrokes out into a textured border. When the border is laid in, deselect Clone Color in the Colors palette, sample color from the image and add fresh, new strokes of color.

7 **Painting with chalk and pastel.** The cloned sky and water imagery is painted over with hand-drawn, brushstrokes so that the image does not look cloned. Photographic detail is only retained on the wood. Do not focus on details at this point, but on basic forms, lighting and patches of color. The style of the image is expressive and modern. Color is sampled from the Mixer palette, or from the cloned imagery (using the Dropper tool in the Toolbox), and then painted using Square Chalk. Brushstrokes are applied using crisp short strokes. Avoid "scrubbing," or rubbing back and forth with the stylus.

For areas where you want broad textured strokes, try the Blunt Chalk variant of Chalk. Choose color from the Mixer and apply it using a light pressure on the stylus. With very light texture, Blunt Chalk will apply color only to the peaks of the paper texture. For a softer application of paint, try the Square Soft Pastel variant of Pastels. This brush is ideal for painting water reflections and for smoother paint application. The Square Hard Pastel and Round Hard Pastel brushes paint textured strokes, with more sensitivity and size variability than Blunt Chalk.

Using the Rubber Stamp tool to paint source material over the cut lines.

Painting short, diagonal strokes on the clouds.

8 **Removing the dark, saw-cut lines from the wood.** At this stage, your entire image should be painted over with Chalk strokes. This is a good time to step back and take a good look at your image and also to make a proof print.

In the case of this image, the dark, saw-cut lines on the wood distract from the wood texture and the overall painted image, so the cut lines are retouched using the Cloner and Rubber Stamp tools in the Toolbox. To select the Rubber Stamp tool (nested under the Cloner tool), click the Cloner tool (the brush with the circle icon) in the Toolbox and hold to reveal the Rubber Stamp tool. The Rubber Stamp tool repairs by painting imagery over an area that needs retouching. The Rubber Stamp tool can be used with a Soft Mode or Hard Mode, chosen in the Property Bar. For repairing detailed wood grain, select the Hard Mode. To set a source point for cloning, Alt-click/Option-click in an area that you want to use as a source and then paint over the area that you want to retouch. The source point is identified by a crosshair cursor as shown in the illustration above.

9 **Adding fresh, layered brushwork and details.** The areas are now repaired, and the cloned imagery is painted over with chalk and pastel.

Now it's time to paint fresh, light strokes over the wispy cloud, and sky. When working on this step, for the most accurate view of the brushwork, view your image at 100% while painting. Choose the Square Chalk variant of Chalk and press Alt/Option to temporarily switch from the Brush tool to the Dropper tool to sample a color from the sky. Release the Alt/Option key to switch back to the Brush tool and paint more crisp strokes. Continue the process of sampling color and painting as you work.

For the water, choose the Round Soft Pastel variant of Pastels. The reflections in the water and the wind texture are mostly horizontal patches of color. As you pull strokes with the Round Soft Pastel, pull them horizontally. Sample color from the image with the Dropper tool as you paint, as is shown in the image above.

In areas where you want more texture, for instance, the highlights, switch to the Round Hard Pastel or the Square Hard Pastel brush variant. Viewing your image at 100%,

Painting horizontal strokes over the water with a Round Soft Pastel.

Adding highlights to the white water using a Square Hard Pastel.

Experiencing Real Hard Media. New in Painter 11, the Real Hard Media brushes, such as the Real Soft Pastel (Pastels), Real Hard Chalk (Chalk) and Real 6B Pencil (Pencils), offer an amazingly realistic painting experience as they incorporate tilt, bearing and velocity. When holding your stylus upright, these brushes make narrower strokes, and when the stylus is laid over on its side, the stroke is wider, just like when you tilt a conventional pencil to shade with the side of the pencil. If you have Painter 11, in Step 9 of this project, try using the Real Soft Pastel instead of the Round Soft Pastel, and the Real Hard Pastel instead of the Square Hard Pastel.

Real Hard Pastel. Holding the stylus vertically (left) to make a narrow stroke and tilting the stylus to make broader strokes (right).

carefully analyze the form that you are painting, and its highlights and shadows. Sample color from the image and apply the color using short, dabbing strokes that follow the direction of the forms. To paint the details, for instance, the white water highlights on the waves shown here, size the brush smaller (try 5–10 pixels), sample a very light color from the image and paint the highlights—all the while letting your brush follow the direction of the moving water forms. For the shadows, sample color from the image and paint using a small brush. Continue to sample and paint as you work over the details.

Step back and take a final look at your image. Do any areas need to be blended or finessed? To blend, switch to the Blenders category in the Brush Selector Bar and choose the Grainy Water variant. The Grainy Water blends paint while preserving some of the paper texture. Apply the blender as you would a paint brush, allowing your strokes to follow the forms. When you've finished finessing the details, your project is complete. You have learned how to compose a collage, and have painted with dry media and blenders.

Index

A

abstract art, 190–203
  mixed media, 198–203
Accented Edges filter (Photoshop), 34
acrylic and oil-painted looks
  acrylics, 148–155
  oils
    with Chiaroscuro lighting, 156–167
    from photos with noise, 168–179
    Old Masters style, 180–189
Acrylics brushes (Painter)
  Artists' Oils, combining with, 167
  Captured Bristle, 49–50
Add Layer Mask button, Layers palette
    (Photoshop), 59, 66
Add Noise filter (Photoshop), 174, 179
Adjust Colors effects (Painter), 90
Adjust Dye Concentration effect (Painter), 61
Adjustment Layers (Photoshop), 7–8
  Curves, 145, 179
  versus dynamic layers (Painter), 166
  Hue/Saturation, 64, 96–97, 197, 211, 213
  Levels, 43–44, 70–71
Adjustments palette (Photoshop), 7
Adobe Bridge, raw files, 13
Adobe Photoshop. *See* Photoshop
Afternoon Light and Shadow Play, 4, 38–39
Agent Don Gets Wet, 206–208
Airbrush brushes, Digital Airbrush (Painter),
    52–53, 167
ala prima brushwork, 81
Aligned check box, Clone Stamp tool
    (Photoshop), 112, 159, 200
All, Select menu command
  Painter, 71
  Photoshop, 210
Amount setting
  Painter
    Apply Surface Texture, Using Paper
        effect, 114
    Image Luminance, Glass Distortion
        effect, 61
    Surface Lighting command, 21
  Photoshop, Unsharp Mask filter, 59
Anchor setting, Canvas (Photoshop), 129
Angle setting (Photoshop)
  Brush Tip Shape controls, 9
  Lens Correction filter, 172
Aperture Priority mode camera settings,
    31–32

Apple Cinema Display, 2
Apply Color tool (Painter), 224
Apply Surface Texture (Painter)
  Using Image Luminance effect, 122
  Using Paper effect, 111, 114, 122
Arches papers, 3, 127
Arrange Palettes commands (Painter)
  Default, 17, 24
  Save Layout, 24
Art History Brush (Photoshop), 6, 8, 10, 81,
    85–87, 101, 103–104
  with brush presets, 9
  controls, 105
  history state, 106
  Spatter brush tip, 85–87
Artistic filters (Photoshop)
  Dry Brush, 58, 63, 65
  Film Grain, 174–175, 179
  Paint Daubs, 33
  Palette Knife, 39–40, 42–43
  Watercolor, 40, 43–44, 175
Artists' Oils brushes (Painter)
  Blender Bristle, 183, 188
  Blender Brush, 160, 165, 181, 183,
      187–189
  Blender Palette Knife, 160, 163, 165,
      183–184, 186–189
  Bristle Brush, 183
  combining with other brushes, 167
  Dry Brush, 160, 183, 187
  Dry Palette Knife, 183, 188–189
  Oil Palette Knife, 160, 162–164
  Oily Bristle, 167–168
  Property Bar settings, 162
  Tapered Oils, 164
  Wet Oily Palette Knife, 160–162
art papers, scanning, 219, 223
Art Pen (Wacom), 2
artwork
  Afternoon Light and Shadow Play, 4, 38–39
  Agent Don Gets Wet, 206–208
  Blooming Purple, 192
  Carpenteria Shore, 126–127
  Children of Tuileries, 10, 100
  Danubis Afterglow, 3, 27, 180–181
  Impression: Peace, 23, 46–47
  Jovial Street Musician, 11, 80
  The Mail Boat, 60–61
  Maine Day in May, 54
  Moon Over Lennox, 24, 26, 148–149
  Night on the Seine, 10, 168, 178
  Pie, Please, 30
  Pink Ginger Sky, 22, 110
  Rachel, 18, 156
  Sanctuary in Morning Light, 8, 62–63
  Shower at Sunset Point, 21, 198–199, 203

  Summer Afternoon Play, 88–89
  Thoughts Hidden in Blue, 136, 139, 141, 143
  Torch Ginger Study, 118
  Wood, Sea, Sky, 19, 218–219
Auto Levels Adjustments command
    (Photoshop), 41
Auto-Painting palette (Painter), 23, 47, 185
  medium strokes, 51
  rough strokes, 49–50
  Short Dab strokes, 50
  small strokes, 51
Auto Select commands, Using Image
    Luminance (Painter), 77

B

Background Color (Photoshop), 6–8
backgrounds
  busy, subduing, 81–87
  sepia-toning, 97
Banana Flower No. 1, 119
barreling, 171–172
Basic panel menus/sliders, Camera Raw
    dialog
  Blacks, 13
  Brightness, 13, 56, 60, 120, 128, 138, 158,
      194
  Clarity, 14
  Contrast, 13, 56, 60, 90, 120, 128, 158, 200
  Exposure, 13, 56, 60, 102, 138, 194
  Fill Light, 13, 150, 158, 182
  Recovery, 13, 158
  Saturation, 14, 32, 82, 90, 128, 138, 150
  Tint, 90
  Vibrance, 14, 82, 90, 102, 128, 138, 150,
      182
  White Balance, 13, 138
Basic Paper (Painter), 130–132
Basic workspace (Photoshop), 11
The Beach at Trouville, 89
Beach at Valencia, 89
Bicubic interpolation (Photoshop), 5
black and white
  textured look, 118–123
Black Edge setting, Woodcut effect (Painter),
    37, 61, 76
Black Input setting, Levels Adjustment Layer
    (Photoshop), 71
Blender Bristle Artists' Oils brush (Painter),
    183, 188
Blender Brush Artists' Oils brush (Painter),
    160, 165, 181, 183, 187–189
Blender Brush Cloner (Painter), 184–185,
    187

Blender Palette Knife Artists' Oils brush
(Painter), 160, 163, 165, 183–184,
186–189
Blenders brushes (Painter), 127
Flat Grainy Stump, 116
Grainy Blender, 116
Grainy Water, 116–117, 133, 135, 227
Just Add Water, 92–93, 135
Oily Blender, 93
Oily Bristle, 92–93
Round Blender, 121, 123
Round Blender Brush, 203
Smooth Blender Stump, 92
Smudge, 116
Soft Blender Stump, 92
Blend modes (Photoshop), 8
Hard Light, 34
Lighten, 44, 58
Lighten Blend, 59
Luminosity, 34
Multiply, 45, 216
Normal, 34, 35, 58, 195, 212
Overlay, 94–95, 212, 214–215
Screen, 44, 45
Soft Light, 34, 213, 215
Vivid Light, 35
Blend setting, Artists' Oils brushes (Painter),
162
Blooming Purple, 192
Blue/Yellow Fringe Chromatic Aberration
setting, Lens Correction filter
(Photoshop), 171
Blunt Chalk brush (Painter), 20, 225
Blur filters (Photoshop)
Gaussian Blur, 59, 216
Lens Blur, 81, 84–85
Smart Blur, 217
Blur Focal Distance setting, Lens Blur filter
(Photoshop), 84
Blur tool (Photoshop), 6
Border, 49, 81, 87, 89, 91–92, 115, 117, 123,
135, 225
Bridge, raw files (Adobe), 13
Bright Beach, 149
Brightness setting, Dynamic Plugins
(Painter), 166
Bristle Brush Artists' Oils brush (Painter),
183
Broad Water brush (Painter), 130–132, 134
Brush Controls
Painter
Artists' Oils settings, 162
Impasto, 21
Show Color Variability, 50
Water, 203
Photoshop, Soft Round 200 brush, 215

Brush Creator settings (Painter), 20
Artists' Oils, 162
Brush Detail setting (Photoshop)
Dry Brush filter, 58, 65
Watercolor filter, 43–44, 175
Brushes palette (Photoshop)
brushes
active brush tip shape, 9
adding/loading to palette, 105–106, 139
naming, 174
pixel sizes, 83
resizing, 175
saving variations, 106
using new, 139
using with tool presets, 9
Bubble Brush, 216–217
Chalk 36, 27
Chalk-Light, 107–108
Dry Media Brushes, 106, 139
Natural Brushes 2, 106
Oil Medium Wet Flow, 109
Oil Medium Wet Flow brush, 27
Old Medium to Large Tip, 174–175
Painting workspace, 11
Pastel Medium Tip, 109, 139, 142, 144
Wet Media Brushes, 9, 106, 174
Brush Preset Picker (Photoshop)
Charcoal Flat, 10, 107–108
Clone Stamp tool, 200
Hard Round
#13, 208, 217
#19, 104, 113, 195
New Brush Preset, 106
Smudge, 175
Soft 65, 66
Soft Round
#27, 57
#65, 105, 108, 210
#200, 104, 108, 216
#300, 212, 215
Spatter, 85
#39, 27
#59, 142, 144
32 Oil Medium Wet Flow, 178
Brush Selector Bar (Painter), 17
Acrylics
Artists' Oils, combining with, 167
Captured Bristle, 49–50
Airbrush, Digital Airbrush, 52–53, 167
Artists' Oils
Blender Bristle, 183, 188
Blender Brush, 160, 165, 181, 183,
187–189
Blender Palette Knife, 160, 163, 165,
183–184, 186–189

Bristle Brush, 183
combining with other brushes, 167
Dry Brush, 160, 183, 187
Dry Palette Knife, 183, 188–189
Gouache, combining with, 167
Oil Palette Knife, 160, 162–164
Oily Bristle, 167–168
Property Bar settings, 162
Tapered Oils, 164
Wet Oily Palette Knife, 160–162
Blenders, 127
Flat Grainy Stump, 116
Grainy Blender, 116
Grainy Water, 116–117, 133, 135, 227
Just Add Water, 92–93, 135
Oily Blender, 93
Oily Bristle, 92–93
Round Blender, 121, 123
Round Blender Brush, 203
Smooth Blender Stump, 92
Smudge, 116
Soft Blender Stump, 92
Chalk, 224
Blunt Chalk, 225
Blunt Chalk 30, 20
Real Soft Chalk, 27
Square Chalk, 225–226
Charcoal
Charcoal, 119, 123
Soft Charcoal, 119, **121–122**
Soft Charcoal Cloner, 121
Cloners, 113
Soft Cloner, 93, 133, 224
Digital Watercolor, 127, 129, 133
Broad Water, 130–132, 134
Coarse Mop, 130–131
Dry, 134–135
Flat Water Blender, 134
Gentle Wet Erasers, 135
Real Filbert, 27
Round Water Blender, 130–132,
134–135
Salt, 127, 131, 135
Simple Water, 130–132
Soft Diffused, 131–132
Spatter Water, 131
versus Watercolor, 130
Wet Erasers, 131, 135
Gouache, combining with Artists' Oils, 167
Impasto
Palette Knife, 21
Round Camelhair, 21
Smeary Round, 21
Thick Bristle, 21

Oils
    Artists' Oils, combining with, 167
    Opaque Round, 203
    Round Camelhair, 167
    Smeary Bristle Spray, 203
Pastels, 130
    Real Soft Pastel, 19
    Round Hard Pastel, 117
    Round Soft Pastel, 226–227
    Square Hard Pastel, 115–116, 224, 226–227
    Square Hard Pastel *versus* Blunt Chalk, 225
    Square Pastel Cloner, 116–117
    Square Soft Pastel, 225
Pencils, 130
Real Bristle Brushes, 199
    Real Blender Flat, 152–154, 202–203
    Real Blender Round, 152–154, 203
    Real Blender Tapered, 154
    Real Blend Flat OR, 202–203
    Real Fan Short, 151, 155
    Real Fan Soft, 151, 155
    Real Flat, 152, 154–155
    Real Flat Opaque, 154
    Real Oils Short, 24, 154
    Real Round, 152, 154–155
    Real Tapered Bristle, 27, 155
Real Hard Media
    Real Chalk, 22
    Real Hard Pastel, 227
    Real Pastels, 22
    Real Pencils, 22
    Real Pens, 22
Restore Default Variant, 115
Save Variant, 115
Watercolor
    versus Digital Watercolor, 130
    Smoothy Runny Bristle 30, 203
Brush Size setting
    Auto-Painting palette (Painter), 23, 50–51
    Dry Brush filter (Photoshop), 58, 65
Brush Strokes filters (Photoshop)
    Accented Edges, 34
    Ink Outlines, 34
    Spatter, 63, 65–66
Brush Tip Shape controls (Photoshop), 9, 142
Brush tools
    Painter, 16, 20
    Photoshop, 6
        with brush presets, 9
        Large Texture Stroke, 109
        Oil Medium Wet Flow, 109
        Pastel on Charcoal Paper, 109
        Soft 65-pixel tip, 66

Brush Tracking Preferences, Corel Painter or Edit menu commands (Painter), 16, 151
Brush Type pop-up menu, Simple, 33
Bubble Brush (Photoshop), 216–217
burning and dodging, 35, 94–95
The Burning of the Houses of Parliament, 199
Burn tool
    Painter, 16
    Photoshop, 6, 9, 94–95

C

Camera Raw dialog. *See also* Photoshop Camera Raw
    Basic panel menus/sliders
        Blacks, 13
        Brightness, 13, 56, 60, 120, 128, 138, 158, 194
        Clarity, 14
        Contrast, 13, 56, 60, 90, 120, 128, 158, 200
        Exposure, 13, 56, 60, 102, 138, 194
        Fill Light, 13, 150, 158, 182
        Recovery, 13, 158
        Saturation, 14, 32, 82, 90, 128, 138, 150
        Tint, 90
        Vibrance, 14, 82, 90, 102, 128, 138, 150, 182
        White Balance, 13, 138
    clipping warnings, 13
        Highlights and Shadows check boxes, 13, 32, 48
    Crop tool, 120, 182
    Detail panel tabs/sliders
        Noise Reduction, Color, 14, 56, 170
        Noise Reduction, Luminance, 14–15, 158
        Sharpening, 158
        Sharpening, Amount, 14, 170
        Sharpening, Detail, 170
        Sharpening, Masking, 14, 170
        Sharpening, Radius, 14
    Histogram, 13
    HSL/Grayscale panel menus/sliders
        Convert to Grayscale, 120
        Hue, 194
        Luminance, 56, 170, 194
        Saturation, 194
    Image Size check boxes
        Constrain Proportions, 194
        Resample Image, 194

Lens Corrections panel menus/sliders
    Chromatic Aberration, 15, 102
    Defringe All Edges, 15, 102
    Defringe Highlights Edges, 15, 158
    Red/Cyan setting, 102
Main control buttons, 13
Open Image *versus* Open Copy, 82
Preferences window, 13
Preview window, 13
Rotate Image 90° Clockwise, 82
Save Image, 13
Temperature, 90
Tone Curve panel tabs/sliders, 158
    Parametric, 14
    Parametric, Highlights, 158
    Point, 14
Tool Bar, 13
Zoom controls, 13
cameras. *See also* cameras/lenses; tripods
    Canon Digital Rebel, 208
    Canon EOS 5D, 2, 81, 157–158, 181, 199, 219
    Canon EOS 20D, 2, 32, 63
    Canon Rebel XT, 2
    Nikon D200, 2, 55, 169
    Sony Cybershot DSC-F505V, 47, 127
cameras/lenses. *See also* cameras; tripods
    avoiding shaking, 32
    Canon 5D camera
        17–40mm f/4 L lens, 81, 181, 199
        f/1.4 fixed focal length lens, 157
        Macro lens EF 100mm f/2.8, 219
    Canon 20D camera, 18–55mm zoom lens, 149
    Canon Rebel 6-megapixel camera, 207
    Canon Rebel XT camera, 70–200mm lens, 137
    Sony Cybershot DSC-F505V camera, Carl Zeiss zoom lens, 47
    lenses only
        55–200mm lens, 193
        80–400mm lens, 101
        Nikon 80–400mm telephoto lens, 171
Camille at the Beach at Trouville, 89
Canon Digital Rebel, 208
Canon EOS 5D camera, 2
    17–40mm f/4 L lens, 81, 181, 199
    f/1.4 fixed focal length lens, 157
    Macro lens EF 100mm f/2.8, 219
Canon EOS 20D camera, 2, 32, 63
    18–55mm zoom lens, 149
Canon Rebel XT camera, 2
    70–200mm lens, 137
Canon's CRW and CR2 raw formats, 12
Canson Mi-Teintes paper, 220

Canvas menu commands (Painter)
    Canvas Size, 91, 123
    color combining with layers, 36
    Resize, 5
    Set Paper Color, 113
    Surface Lighting, 21
    Tracing Paper, 223
Canvas Size
    Canvas menu command (Painter), 91, 123
    Image menu command (Photoshop), 87,
        128, 173
Captured Bristle brush (Acrylics) (Painter),
    49–50
Caravaggio, Michelangelo, 157
Carl Zeiss zoom lens, 47
Carpenteria Shore, 126–127
Cézanne, Paul, 39
Chalk 36 brush (Photoshop), 27
Chalk brushes (Painter), 224
    Blunt Chalk, 225
    Blunt Chalk 30, 20
    Real Soft Chalk, 27
    Square Chalk, 225–226
Chalk-Light brush (Photoshop), 107
    versus Charcoal Flat brush, 108
Channels palette
    Painter, 17
    Photoshop
        Lightness channel, 15
        Quick Mask, 83–84
Charcoal brushes (Painter)
    Charcoal, 119, 123
    Soft Charcoal, 119, 121–122
    Soft Charcoal Cloner, 121
Charcoal Flat brush (Photoshop), 107–108
    versus Chalk-Light brush, 108
Charcoal Paper texture (Painter), 114, 121
Charrette Corporation, 3
Chiaroscuro lighting, 157–167
Children of Tuileries, 10, 100
chromatic aberration, 102, 171–172
Chromatic Aberration settings, Lens
    Correction filter (Photoshop), 171
Cintiq tablets/pens, Cintiq 21UX, 2
The Cliffs of Etretat, 63
Clipping Groups (Photoshop), 212–213
    versus layer masks, 214
clipping masks, 97
clipping warnings, Camera Raw dialog, 13
    Highlights and Shadows check boxes, 13,
        32, 48
Clone Color check box, Colors palette
    (Painter), 50, 115, 121, 183
Clone command (Painter), 48, 91, 183
Cloners brushes (Painter), 113
    Soft Cloner, 93, 133, 224

Cloner tool (Painter), 16, 23, 113, 159, 226
Clone Source command (Painter), 49, 93
Clone Stamp tool (Photoshop), 6
    with brush presets, 9
    Hard Round 19 brush, 104–105
    Old Medium to Large Tip brush, 174
    retouching, 159, 182
    sampling
        all layers, 104, 174
        current layer, 112, 200
CMYK color mode, 5
CMYK preview (Photoshop), 177
Coarse Cotton Canvas paper (Painter), 24
Coarse Mop Digital Watercolor brush
    (Painter), 130–131
cold press watercolor paper, 127, 130, 139, 140
collages, 219–220
Color, Main and Additional (Painter), 16, 18
Color and Tone workspace (Photoshop), 11
Color Bar (Photoshop), 7–8
Colorize check box, Hue/Saturation
    Adjustment Layer (Photoshop), 97, 211
Color palette (Photoshop), 7–8
    Clone Color check box, 50
    Grayscale setting, 145
    Painting workspace, 11
Color Palettes commands, Show Mixer
    (Painter), 224
Color Picker, sampling colors (Photoshop),
    106
Color Sets palette (Painter), 17
Color slider, Hue/Saturation Adjustment
    Layer (Photoshop), 213
Colors palette (Painter), 16–19, 36
    black and white, 52
    Clone Color option, 115, 121
    cloning color, 224
    Hue Ring, 74
    paper colors, 113
    Rubber Stamp tool, 50, 115
    viewing, 73, 145
Color Swap icon (Painter), 18
Color Variability setting, Captured Bristle
    brush (Painter), 49–50
composite layers (Photoshop), 59
    color layers, 207–217
Composite Methods (Painter)
    Default, 18, 72
    Gel, 134
    Hard Light, 37
    Multiply, 61, 72–73, 75, 76–77
    Overlay, 36, 77
    Saturation, 77
    Screen, 77
    Soft Light, 77

composition and collaging
    with painter's composition sense, 218–227
    simulating reality, 206–217
Concorde Rag papers, 3
Cone Editions Inkjet Mall, 3
Cone Editions Press, 3
Constable, John, 149
Constrain Proportions check box, Image Size
    command (Photoshop), 223
Content selectors (Painter), 17
Contrast setting
    Painter
        Dynamic Plugins, 166
        Underpainting palette, 90
    Photoshop
        Grain filter, 179
Convert for Smart Filters command
    (Photoshop), 57
copying/pasting selections, 104
Corel Painter menu commands (Painter),
    Preferences
        Brush Tracking, 16, 151
        General, 152
Correct Colors effects (Painter), 90
Courbet, Gustave, 63
Create a New Layer button (Photoshop), 33
Create Layer Mask button (Painter), 52–53
Create New Adjustment Layer button
    (Photoshop), 43
Create New Fill or Adjustment Layer button
    (Photoshop), 70
Crop tool
    Camera Raw dialog, 120, 182
    Painter, 16
    Photoshop, 4
        defaults, resetting, 40
        proportion, constraining, 70, 103
        resolution settings, 57, 103
        rotating corners, 194
        "rule of thirds," 172–173, 221
        scaling images, 57
        width and height settings, 57, 103, 172
Crop tool, Camera Raw dialog, 120, 182
CRW and CR2 raw formats (Canon), 12
Cursors, Photoshop Preferences command,
    11
cursors, preferred painting (Photoshop), 11
Curves Adjustment Layer (Photoshop), 145,
    179
Custom Palettes commands, Organizer
    (Painter), 24

D

Dab Color swatch, Pop Art Fill effect (Painter), 36
Danubis Afterglow, 3, 27, 180–181
Darkness setting, Photocopy filter (Photoshop), 35, 41
da Vinci, Leonardo, 157
Davis, Jack, 169
Default, Arrange Palettes command (Painter), 17, 24
Default colors (Photoshop), 6
Default Composite Method (Painter), 72
Define Brush Preset command (Photoshop), 217
Define Pattern command (Photoshop), 138
Demuth, Charles, 137
Depth slider, Impasto brushes (Painter), 21
Derry, John, 60
Detail panel tabs/sliders, Camera Raw dialog
   Noise Reduction
      Color, 14, 56, 170
      Luminance, 14–15, 158
   Sharpening, 158
      Amount, 14, 170
      Detail, 170
      Masking, 14, 170
      Radius, 14
Detail setting, Photocopy filter (Photoshop), 35, 41
Diameter slider, Brush Tip Shape controls (Photoshop), 9
Diffuse Digital Watercolor, Layers palette (Painter), 135
Diffusion setting (Painter)
   Digital Watercolor brushes, 131
   Round Water brush, 134
Digital Airbrush brush (Painter), 52–53, 167
Digital Art Supplies, 3
digital photographer's studio setup, 2–3
digital printmaking studios/service bureaus, 3
Digital Watercolor brushes (Painter), 126–137
   Broad Water, 130–132, 134
   Coarse Mop, 130–131
   Dry, 130–131
   Flat Water Blender, 134
   Gentle Wet Eraser, 135
   Real Filbert, 27
   Round Water Blender, 130–132, 134–135
   Salt, 127, 131, 135
   Simple Water, 130–132
   Soft Diffused, 131–132
   Spatter Water, 131
   versus Watercolor brushes, 130
   Wet Eraser, 131, 135

Direction setting, Image Luminance, Glass Distortion effect (Painter), 61
Dirty Mode setting, Artists' Oils brushes (Painter), 162
Distort command (Photoshop), 128, 129
Distort filters, Lens Correction (Photoshop), 171
Divine Proportion tool (Painter), 16, 47, 220
docking palettes (Photoshop), 11
Document sizes (Photoshop), 7
Document window (Painter), 17
Dodge tool
   Painter, 16
   Photoshop, 6, 9, 94–95
dodging and burning, 35, 94–95
Drawing mode icon (Painter), 17
Dropper tool (Painter), 16, 77, 117, 187
Dry Brush Artists' Oils brush (Painter), 160, 183, 187
Dry Brush Digital Watercolor brush (Painter), 130–131
Dry Brush filter (Photoshop), 58, 63, 65
Dry Digital Watercolor, Layers palette (Painter), 134–135
Dry Media Brushes (Photoshop), 106, 139
Dry Palette Knife Artists' Oils brush (Painter), 183, 188–189
Duplicate Layer command
   Painter, 71
   Photoshop, 58
Dust & Scratches filter (Photoshop), 58, 211
dynamic layers (Painter) *versus* Adjustment Layers (Photoshop), 166
Dynamic Plugins (Painter), 18, 166–167

E

Edge Brightness setting, Accented Edges dialog (Photoshop), 34
Edge Effect, Jagged Vignette setting, Underpainting palette (Painter), 49
Edge Effects, Underpainting palette (Painter), 90
Edge Width setting, Accented Edges dialog (Photoshop), 34
Edit menu commands (Photoshop)
   Define Brush Preset, 217
   Define Pattern, 138
   Fill, 195
   Transform
      Distort, 128, 129
      Free Transform, 145, 150, 210, 216–217, 222
   Undo Brush tool, 178

Edit menu commands (Painter), Preferences
   Brush Tracking, 16, 151
   General, 152
Edit Smart Object command (Photoshop), 57
Effects menu (Painter)
   Adjust Dye Concentration, 61
   Esoterica, Pop Art Fill, 36
   Fill, 77
   Focus, Glass Distortion, 61
   Surface Control
      Apply Surface Texture, Using Image Luminance, 122
      Apply Surface Texture, Using Paper, 111, 114, 122
      Woodcut, 37, 61, 69, 71–74, 76
   Tonal Control
      Adjust Colors, 90
      Correct Colors, 90
Efficiency information (Photoshop), 7
Elliptical Marquee tool (Photoshop), 150, 216
Enable Brush Ghosting command (Painter), 152
Enable Layout Grid check box (Painter), 221
Enhanced Brush Ghost command (Painter), 152
Epson papers, 3
   Ultrasmooth Fine Art Paper, 3
   Velvet Fine Art Paper, 3
   Watercolor Paper Radiant White, 3
Epson Stylus Photo 1400 printer, 3
Epson Stylus Pro 4880 printer, 3
equipment. *See* cameras; cameras/lenses; tripods
Eragny and Eragny-sur-Epte, 47
Eraser tool
   Painter, 16, 67
   Photoshop, 6, 67
Erosion Time/Erosion Edge settings, Woodcut effect (Painter), 37, 61, 72, 76
Esoterica effects, Pop Art Fill (Painter), 36
Essential workspace (Photoshop), 7
Expand, Select menu command (Photoshop), 209
ExpressKeys, Intuos4 M tablet, 25–26
Eyedropper tools (Photoshop), 6, 57, 178

F

Faster option, Lens Blur filter (Photoshop), 84
Feather command (Photoshop), 96–97, 100, 221
Feature slider, Real Blender Flat brush (Painter), 202

File Handling Preferences command
  (Photoshop), 11
  JPG format, opening using Camera Raw, 83
File menu commands (Painter)
  Clone, 48, 91, 183
  Clone Source, 49, 93
  Open, 48
  Place, 222
  Quick Clone, 49, 113
  Revert, 152
  Save As, 48
File menu commands (Photoshop)
  Open, 32
  Photoshop Preferences, Cursors, 11
  Save As, 32
Fill command (Photoshop), 195
Fill effect (Painter), 77
Film Grain filter (Photoshop), 9, 174–175, 179
Filters menu commands (Photoshop)
  Artistic
    Dry Brush, 58, 63, 65
    Film Grain, 9, 174–175, 179
    Paint Daubs, 33
    Palette Knife, 39–40, 42–43
    Watercolor, 40, 43–44, 175
  Blur
    Gaussian Blur, 59, 216
    Lens Blur, 81, 84–85
    Smart Blur, 217
  Brush Strokes
    Accented Edges, 34
    Ink Outlines, 34
    Spatter, 63, 65–66
  Convert for Smart Filters, 57
  Distort, Lens Correction, 171
  Noise
    Add Noise, 174, 179
    Dust & Scratches, 58, 211
  Pixelate, Mezzotint, Fine Dots, 179
  Render, Lighting Effects, 10
  Sharpen, Unsharp Mask, 59
  Sketch, Photocopy, 35, 41
  Stylize, Find Edges, 34
  Texture, Grain, 179
Find Edges filter (Photoshop), 34
Finger Painting setting (Photoshop)
  Old Medium to Large Tip brush, 174
  Smudge tool, 87
Flat Grainy Stump Blenders brush (Painter),
  116
Flatten Image command (Photoshop), 105
Flat Water Blender Digital Watercolor brush
  (Painter), 134
Float command (Painter), 71
Focus effects, Glass Distortion (Painter), 61
Foreground Color (Photoshop), 6–8

Free Transform command (Photoshop), 145,
  150, 210, 216–217, 222
Full Size Brush Tip, Painting Cursors
  (Photoshop), 11

G

Gaussian Blur filter (Photoshop), 59, 216
Gel Composite Method (Painter), 134
General section, Brush Controls (Painter), 20
Gentle Wet Eraser Digital Watercolor brush
  (Painter), 135
ghosted images, 196
Glass Distortion effect (Painter), 61
glazing, 127, 134
Golden Section, 47, 221
Gouache brushes, combining with Artists'
  Oils (Painter), 167
Grabber Hand tool (Painter), 16, 92
Gradients Selector (Painter), 16
Gradient tool (Photoshop), 6
Grain filter (Photoshop), 179
Grain settings
  Painter brushes
    Artists' Oils, 162
    Digital Watercolor, 131
  Photoshop filters, Film Grain, 174–175, 179
Grainy Blender brush (Painter), 116
Grainy Water Blenders brush (Painter),
  116–117, 133, 135, 227
Grayscale mode (Photoshop), 216
  Color palette, 145
  scanning watercolor paper, 145
Green Flash Photography, 3
The Grotto of the Loue, 63

H

Hahnemuehle papers, 3
hand-rendered effect
  Painter, 60–61
  Photoshop, 55–59
Hand tool (Photoshop), 6, 159
Hanks, Steve, 137
Hansen, Ken, 193
Hard Light Blend mode (Photoshop), 34
Hard Light Composite Method (Painter), 37
Hard Mode, Rubber Stamp tool (Painter), 159
Hardness slider (Photoshop)
  Brush Tip Shape controls, 9
  Hard Round 13 brush, 208
  Hard Round 19 brush, 104
  Soft Round 65 brush, 108, 210

Hard Round 13 brush (Photoshop), 208, 217
Hard Round 19 brush (Photoshop), 104, 113,
  195
Healing Brush (Photoshop), 6
Heaviness setting, Woodcut effect (Painter),
  37, 61, 72
height and width (Photoshop)
  Canvas, 87, 129
  Crop tool, 103
  Image Size, 223
  New File, 216
Height slider, Texture Channel, Lighting
  Effects filter (Photoshop), 10
The Herald, 68
Highlight anchor point, Curves Adjustment
  Layer (Photoshop), 179
Highlight setting, Film Grain filter
  (Photoshop), 179
Histogram, Camera Raw dialog, 13
History Brush (Photoshop), 6, 8, 10, 106–107
  with brush presets, 9
History command (Photoshop), 11
History palette (Photoshop), 8, 86
  Art History Brush, 106–107
    settings, 10
  History Brush, 106–107
  New Snapshot, 106
  Painting workspace, 11
  undoing work, 178
history state (Photoshop), 8, 10, 106
Hockney, David, 31
Homer, Winslow, 55, 127
Hopper, Edward, 137
Horizontal, Perspective slider, Lens
  Correction filter (Photoshop), 171–172
"hot pixels," 170
HP Photosmart DesignJet 130 printer, 3
HP Photosmart Pro B8850 printer, 3
HSL/Grayscale panel menus/sliders, Camera
  Raw dialog
  Convert to Grayscale, 120
  Hue, 194
  Luminance, 56, 170, 194
  Saturation, 194
HSV color slider (Painter), 18
Hue Ring (Painter), 17–19, 74
Hue/Saturation Adjustment Layer
  (Photoshop), 64, 96–97, 197, 211, 213
Hue setting
  Color Variability (Painter), 49–50
  Hue/Saturation Adjustment Layer
    (Photoshop), 97, 211

I

Image Luminance setting (Painter)
Glass Distortion effect, 61
Pop Art Fill effect, 36
Image menu commands (Photoshop)
Adjustments
Auto Level, 41
Curves, 145, 179
Hue/Saturation, 197
Canvas Size, 87, 128, 173
Image Rotation, 90° CW, 223
Image Size, 5, 138, 223
Invert, 41
Mode, Lab color, 15
Image Rotation commands (Photoshop), 90°
CW, 223
images, resolution
ppi (pixels per inch), 4
for printing, 4
Image Size check boxes, Camera Raw dialog
Constrain Proportions, 194
Resample Image, 194
Image Size command (Photoshop), 5, 138,
223
Impasto brushes (Painter)
Palette Knife, 21
Round Camelhair, 21
Smeary Round, 21
Thick Bristle, 21
Impressionist looks
Painter, 46–53
Photoshop, 38–45
Impressionist masters, 39, 47, 63, 89, 111
Impression: Peace, 23, 46–47
Ink Outlines filter (Photoshop), 34
Innova papers, 3
Input box (Photoshop)
Curves Adjustment Layer, 179
Levels Adjustment Layer, 43
Intensity setting (Photoshop)
Film Grain filter, 179
Grain filter, 179
interpolation, Bicubic interpolation
(Photoshop), 5
Inverse command (Photoshop), 210
Inverted check box, Image Luminance, Glass
Distortion effect (Painter), 61
Invert Image command (Photoshop), 41

J–K

Jagged Vignette Edge Effect, Underpainting
palette (Painter), 49
Jitter settings, Shape Dynamics, brushes
(Photoshop), 217
Johns, Jasper, 31
Jolley, Donal C., 137
Jovial Street Musician, 11, 80
JPG format, 208
opening in Camera Raw, 83
versus raw format, 12
Just Add Water Blenders brush (Painter),
92–93, 135

L

Lab Color Mode command (Photoshop), 15
LaCie 22 Electron Blue with hood, 2
LaCie Big Disk Extreme 500 GB or 1 TB hard
drive, 2
Large Texture Stroke brush (Photoshop), 109
Lasso tool (Photoshop), 6, 96, 178, 221
Layer Adjuster tools (Painter), 16, 222
layer masks. *See also* layers (Painter);
layers (Photoshop); Quick Masks
(Photoshop)
Painter, 18, 52–53, 167, 222
Photoshop, 8
applying masks, 59, 66, 104, 108, 142,
215
versus Clipping Groups, 214
color layers, 207–217
versus Eraser tool, 67
hiding, 179
isolating image elements, 208–210
previewing, 209
layers (Painter). *See also* layer masks; layers
(Photoshop)
adjusting, 222
Commit dialog, 222
duplicating, 71, 104
dynamic layers *versus* Photoshop's
Adjustment Layers, 166
floating, 36
hiding/showing, 18, 73
naming/renaming, 72
new, 49
opening, 36
transparency, 72, 75
layers (Photoshop). *See also* layer masks;
layers (Painter)
active, 8
adding, 66, 67
Adjustment Layers *versus* dynamic layers
(Painter), 166
color layers, 207–217
combining, 64
composite layers, 59
constraining proportion, 210
creating new, 8
deleting, 8
duplicating, 58, 104
grouping, 8
hiding, 41, 210
hue/saturation, 64, 96–97
images
flattening, 105, 223
rotating, 210
locking/unlocking, 104
Master Layer, 173
merging, 105
naming
descriptive names, 33
renaming, 58
opacity, 105, 109, 139, 143, 144, 215
positioning, 66
Smart Objects, editing, 57
styles, 8
transparency, 45, 174, 224
Layers palette (Painter), 17–18. *See also*
Composite Methods (Painter); layer
masks; layers (Painter)
Diffuse Digital Watercolor, 135
Dry Digital Watercolor, 134–135
Dynamic Plugins, 166–167
Opacity setting, 75
Overlay mode, 145
Pick Up Underlying Color check box, 21
Layers palette (Photoshop), 7–8. *See also*
Adjustment Layers (Photoshop); Blend
modes (Photoshop); layer masks;
layers (Photoshop)
Clipping Groups, 212–213
versus layer masks, 214
Painting workspace, 11
Layout Grid features (Painter), 220–221
Length setting, Auto-Painting palette
(Painter), 23, 51
Lens Blur filter (Photoshop), 81, 84–85
Lens Correction filter (Photoshop), 171–172

Lens Corrections panel menus/sliders,
 Camera Raw dialog
  Chromatic Aberration, 15, 102
  Defringe All Edges, 15, 102
  Defringe Highlights Edges, 15, 158
  Red/Cyan setting, 102
Levels Adjustment Layer (Photoshop),
 43–44, 70–71
Lichtenstein, Roy, 36
Lighten Blend mode, 44, 58, 59
Lighting Effects filter (Photoshop), 10
Lightness channel (Photoshop), 15
Lightness slider, Hue/Saturation Adjustment
 Layer (Photoshop), 197, 211
line drawing, 37
Load Brushes, Brushes menu command
 (Photoshop), 105
Looks Selector (Painter), 16
Luminosity Blend mode (Photoshop), 34

M

Macintosh G5 computers, 2
Macintosh platform, photographer's studio
 setup, 2
Mac Pro computers, 2
Magic Wand tool
 Painter, 16
 Photoshop, 6, 209
Magnetic Lasso tool, 96
Magnification (Photoshop), 76
Magnifier tool (Painter), 16, 92
The Mail Boat, 60–61
Main control buttons, Camera Raw dialog, 13
Maine Day in May, 54
Manfrotto 3437 tripod head, 3001B Pro legs,
 32
Manual mode camera setting, 111, 119
Marquee Selection tool, 173
Master Diameter slider (Photoshop),
 176–177
 Brush tool, 196
 Hard Round 19 brush, 104
 Old Medium to Large Tip, 174–175
 Pastel Medium 29 brush, 139, 142
 Pattern Stamp brush, 143
 Soft Round 200 brush, 104
 Soft Round 300 brush, 215
 Spatter 59 brush, 142, 144

Master Layer, Layers palette (Photoshop),
 173
Menu Bar
 Painter, 17
 Photoshop, 7
Mezzotint filter (Photoshop), 179
Minimum Diameter Shape Dynamics setting,
 Bubble Brush (Photoshop), 217
Min Size section, Brush Creator (Painter), 20
Mix Color tool (Painter), 224
Mixer palette (Painter), 16–18
 color cloning, 224–225
 using Dropper, 154
 using sampled colors, 155
Mode setting (Photoshop)
 Art History Brush, 10
 History Brush, 10
 Image menu commands, Lab color, 15
Modify commands (Photoshop)
 Expand, 209
 Feather, 96–97, 150, 221
Monet, Claude
 The Beach at Trouville, 89
 Camille at the Beach at Trouville, 89
 Still Life with Pears and Grapes, 39
Moon Over Lennox, 24, 26, 148–149
Move tool (Photoshop), 6, 104, 222
Multiply Blend mode (Photoshop), 45, 216
Multiply Composite Method (Painter), 61,
 72–73, 75–77
Multiply mode, Pastel Medium Tip brush
 (Photoshop), 142
Museo papers, 3

N

Natural Brushes 2, 106
Navigation icon (Painter), 17
NEF raw format (Nikon), 12
negative space, 31
New Brush Preset, 106, 174
New Layer button (Painter), 18, 49
New Liquid Ink Layer button (Painter), 18
New Snapshot, History palette (Photoshop),
 86, 106
New Watercolor Layer button (Painter), 18
Night on the Seine, 10, 168, 172, 178
night photography, 169
Nikon 80–400mm telephoto lens, 171
Nikon D200, 55, 169
Nikon's NEF raw format, 12

90° CW Image Rotation menu command
 (Photoshop), 223
noise
 enhancing oil techniques, 179
 "hot pixels," 170
 oil emulation, 170
 suppressing, 56
 testing settings, 173–174
  selecting from tests, 175
Noise Amount setting, Lens Blur filter
 (Photoshop), 84
Noise filters (Photoshop)
 Add Noise, 174, 179
 Dust & Scratches, 58, 211
Nor'easter, 127
Normal Blend mode (Photoshop), 34, 35, 58,
 195, 212
Nozzles Selector (Painter), 16

O

Oil Medium Wet Flow brush (Photoshop),
 27, 109
Oil Palette Knife Artists' Oils brush (Painter),
 160, 162–164
Oils brushes (Painter)
 Artists' Oils, combining with, 167
 Opaque Round, 203
 Round Camelhair, 167
 Smeary Bristle Spray, 203
oil treatments
 with Chiaroscuro lighting, 156–167
 from photos with noise, 168–179
 Old Masters style, 180–189
 Realist style, 62–67
Oily Blender brush (Painter), 92
Oily Bristle Artists' Oils brush (Painter),
 167–168
Oily Bristle Blenders brush (Painter), 92–93
O'Keeffe, Georgia, 111
 Banana Flower No. 1, 119
 Pink Roses and Larkspur, 111
 White Camellia, 111
Old Masters style, 181–189
Old Medium to Large Tip brush
 (Photoshop), 174–175

Opacity settings
  Painter brushes
    Artists' Oils, 162
    Round Water, 134
    Simple Water, 131
    Soft Cloner, 133
  Painter Layers palette, 75, 107, 108
  Photoshop brushes
    Art History Brush, 10
    Hard Round 13, 217
    History Brush, 10
    Soft Round 200, 216
  Photoshop Layers palette, 139, 143, 197, 215
    Eye icon, 197
    Options bar, 105
    Pastel Medium Tip brush, 109
    Pastel on Charcoal Paper brush, 109
    Spatter brush, 144
Opaque Round Oils brush (Painter), 203
Open command
  Painter, 48
  Photoshop, 32
Open Image *versus* Open Copy, Camera Raw dialog, 82
Options Bar (Photoshop), 6–7
Organizer, Custom Palettes command (Painter), 24
Output Black setting, Woodcut effect (Painter), 72–74, 76
Output box, Curves Adjustments (Photoshop), 179
Output Color check box, Woodcut effect (Painter), 37, 61, 72–74, 76
Overlay Blend mode (Photoshop), 94–95, 145, 212, 214–215
Overlay Composite Method (Painter), 36, 77

P

Paint Bucket tool (Painter), 16
Paint Daubs filter (Photoshop), 33
painterly brushwork, 81–87
The Painter Wow! Book, 3, 20
Painting Cursors, Full Size Brush Tip (Photoshop), 11
painting for non-painters
  hand-rendered effect
    Painter, 60–61
    Photoshop, 54–59
  Impressionist looks
    Painter, 46–53
    Photoshop, 38–45

Pop Art look
  Painter, 36–37
  Photoshop, 30–35
  Realist style, 62–67
  woodcut look, 68–77
Painting workspace (Photoshop), 11
Palette Knife, blending colors and values (Painter), 224
Palette Knife filter (Photoshop), 39–40, 42–43
Palette Knife Impasto brush (Painter), 21
palettes
  Painter, 19
  Photoshop, 11
paper/paper manufacturers, 3. *See also* Tracing Paper (Painter)
  art papers, scanning, 219
  paper color, 113
  paper textures, adding, 24
  pastel paper, 220
  watercolor paper
    cold press, 127, 130, 139, 140
    scanning, 145
Paper Selector (Painter), 16
  Basic Paper, 130–132
  Charcoal Paper, 114, 121
  Coarse Cotton Canvas, 24
  Rough Charcoal Paper, 225
Pastel Medium Tip brush (Photoshop), 109, 139, 142, 144
Pastel on Charcoal Paper brush (Photoshop), 109
pastel painting, textured look, 110–117
pastel papers, 220
Pastels brushes (Painter)
  Real Soft Pastel, 19
  Round Hard Pastel, 117
  Round Soft Pastel, 226–227
  Square Hard Pastel, 115–116, 224, 226–227
    versus Blunt Chalk, 225
  Square Pastel Cloner, 116–117
  Square Soft Pastel, 225
pasting selections, 104
Patch tool (Photoshop), 6
Path Selection tools (Photoshop), 6
Pattern Library (Photoshop), 138
patterns (Photoshop)
  Define Pattern command, 138
  Pattern Stamp tool/brush, 139, 143, 144
  Preset Pattern Picker, 139
Patterns Selector (Painter), 16
Pattern Stamp tool (Photoshop), 6, 139, 143, 144
  with brush presets, 9

Pencils brushes (Painter), 130
Pencil tools (Photoshop), 6
  with brush presets, 9
Pen tool
  Painter, 16
  Photoshop, 6
Perspective Grid tool (Painter), 16
Photocopy filter (Photoshop), 35, 41
photographer's studio setup, 2–3
Photo-Painting system (Painter), 16, 23, 161, 185
Photoshop, opening raw files, 13
Photoshop Camera Raw. *See also* Camera Raw dialog
  file formats
    JPG, 83, 128
    multiple versions of, 103
    TIF, 12
    .xmp, 103
  raw files, opening
    with Adobe Bridge, 12
    Open Image *versus* Open Copy, 82
    with Photoshop, 13
Photoshop Preferences commands (Photoshop)
  Cursors, 11
  File Handling, 11
Pick Up Underlying Color check box, Layers palette (Painter), 21, 49, 115, 121, 153–155, 161, 164
picture plane shape or proportion, 220
Pie, Please, 30
pincushioning, 171–172
Pink Ginger Sky, 22, 110
Pink Roses and Larkspur, 111
Pissarro, Camille, 47
Pixelate filters (Photoshop), Mezzotint, Fine Dots, 179
pixels, 4
  grid of, 5
  interpolation, 5
  resizing *versus* resampling, 5
Place File menu command (Painter), 222
Play/Stop buttons, Auto-Painting palette (Painter), 50–51
Pointillism, 47
Pop Art Fill effect (Painter), 36
Pop Art look
  Painter, 36–37
  Photoshop, 30–35
ppi (pixels per inch), 4
Prefer Adobe Camera Raw for Supported Raw Files check box, File Handling Preferences (Photoshop), 13

Preferences, Corel Painter or Edit menu commands (Painter)
  Brush Tracking, 16, 151
  General
    Enable Brush Ghosting, 152
    Enhanced Brush Ghost, 152
Preferences menu commands (Photoshop)
  Cursors, 11
  File Handling, 13
    JPG format, opening using Camera Raw, 83
Preferences window, Camera Raw dialog, 13
Preserve Transparency check box, Layers palette (Painter), 49, 224
Preset Pattern Picker, Pattern Stamp tool/brush (Photoshop), 139
Pressure Expression, Brush Creator (Painter), 20
Pressure setting, Auto-Painting palette (Painter), 23, 50, 51
Preview window, Camera Raw dialog, 13
printers/printing, 3
  digital printmaking studios/service bureaus, 3
  papers/paper manufacturers, 3
  resolution
    for inkjet printing, 5
    for offset and screen printing, 4
  RGB and CMYK color modes, 5
Proofing workspace (Photoshop), 11
Proof Setup, View menu commands, Working CMYK (Photoshop), 177
Property Bar (Painter), 16–17
Property Bar settings, Artists' Oils brushes (Painter), 162
Proportions setting, Image Size command (Photoshop), 138
PSD (Photoshop) file format, 32

Q

Quick Clone command (Painter), 49, 113
Quick Curve tool (Painter), 16
Quick Masks (Photoshop), 6, 83–84. *See also* layer masks

R

Rachel, 18, 156
Radial pop-up menu, Touch Ring, Intuos4 tablet, 26

Radius setting (Photoshop)
  Dust & Scratches filters, 58
  Unsharp Mask filter, 59
Randomness setting, Auto-Painting palette (Painter), 50, 51
Rauschenburg, Robert, 219
raw files, opening in Photoshop, 13
Real Blender Flat brush (Painter), 152–154, 202–203
Real Blender Round brush (Painter), 152–154, 203
Real Blender Tapered brush (Painter), 154
Real Blend Flat OR custom brush (Painter), 202–203
Real Bristle Brushes (Painter), 149, 199
  Real Blender Flat, 152–154, 202–203
  Real Blender Round, 152–154, 203
  Real Blender Tapered, 154
  Real Blend Flat OR (Painter), 202–203
  Real Fan Short, 151, 155
  Real Fan Soft, 151, 155
  Real Flat, 152, 154–155
  Real Flat Opaque, 154
  Real Oils Short, 23, 154
  Real Round, 152, 154–155
  Real Tapered Bristle, 27, 155
  sensitivity, 151
Real Fan Short brush (Painter), 151, 155
Real Fan Soft brush (Painter), 151, 155
Real Filbert, Digital Watercolor brush (Painter), 27
Real Flat brush (Painter), 152, 154–155
Real Flat Opaque brush (Painter), 154
Real Hard Media brushes (Painter), 22
  Markers, 22
    Flat Rendering Marker, 22
  Real Hard Chalk, 227
  Real Hard Pastel, 227
  Real Soft Chalk, 22
  Real Variable Width Pen, 22
  Real 6b Soft Pencil, 22, 227
Real Hard Pastel (Painter), 227
Real Soft Pastel (Painter), 227
Realist style, 63–67, 89, 127–135, 207
Real Oils Short brush (Painter), 23, 154
Real Round brush (Painter), 152, 154–155
Real 6b Soft Pencil (Painter), 22
Real Soft Chalk (Painter), 27
Real Soft Pastel (Painter), 19, 227
Real Tapered Bristle brush (Painter), 27, 155
Real Variable Width Pen (Painter), 22
Red/Cyan Fringe Chromatic Aberration setting, Lens Correction filter (Photoshop), 171

reflections
  Art History Brush, 107
  Charcoal Flat *versus* Chalk-Light brush, 108
  painting water, 135, 176
Relative, Canvas Size command (Photoshop), 87, 128–129
Rembrandt van Rijn, 157
Remove Distortion slider, Lens Correction filter (Photoshop), 171–172
Render filters, Lighting Effects (Photoshop), 10
Resample Image check box, Image Size command (Photoshop), 5, 138
  Bicubic interpolation, 5
Resat slider, Real Blender Flat brush (Painter), 202
Resize, Canvas menu command (Painter), 5
Resolution settings, Crop tool (Photoshop), 103
Restoration palette (Painter), 185
  Soft Edge Cloner brush, 93, 186, 188–189
retouching images
  Painter
    Cloner tool, 113, 159
    Rubber Stamp tool, 23, 113, 120, 121
      Hard or Soft Modes, 159
  Photoshop, Clone Stamp tool, 112, 159
Reveal All, Layer Mask command (Photoshop), 104
Revert command (Painter), 152
RGB color mode, 5
RGB color slider (Painter), 18
RIF format, 48, 130
Rotate Image 90° Clockwise, Camera Raw dialog, 82
Rotate Page tool (Painter), 16
rotating images, 57
Rotation setting, Auto-Painting palette (Painter), 23, 50, 51
Rough Charcoal Paper (Painter), 225
Round Blender Brush, Blenders (Painter), 121, 123, 203
Round Camelhair, Impasto brush (Painter), 21
Round Camelhair, Oils brushes (Painter), 167
Round Hard Pastel brush (Painter), 117
Roundness Jitter Shape Dynamics setting, Bubble Brush (Photoshop), 217
Roundness slider, Brush Tip Shape controls (Photoshop), 9
Round Soft Pastel brush (Painter), 226–227
Round Water Blender, Digital Watercolor brush (Painter), 130–132, 134–135

Rubber Stamp tool (Painter), 16, 23, 50
   Soft or Hard Modes, 226
      painting from clone source, 115
      retouching, 113, 120, 121, 159
"rule of thirds," 172–173, 201, 221

S

Salt Digital Watercolor brush (Painter), 127,
   131, 135
Sample All Layers check box, Clone Stamp
   tool (Photoshop)
   Hard Round 19 brush, 104
   Old Medium to Large Tip brush, 174
Sample Color tool (Painter), 224
Sample Current Layer check box, Clone
   Stamp tool (Photoshop), 112, 200
sampling colors, 109
   Painter
      Cloner tool, 23
      Colors palette, 224
      Dropper tool, 16, 77, 117
      Mixer palette, 224
      Rubber Stamp tool, 23
   Photoshop
      Clone Stamp tool, 112, 182
      Color Picker, 106
      Eyedropper tools, 57, 178
   resizing *versus* resampling, 5
Sanctuary in Morning Light, 8, 62–63
Sargent, John Singer, 181
Saturation Composite Method (Painter), 77
Saturation setting
   Painter
      Color Variability, 49–50
      Underpainting palette, 90, 185
   Photoshop, Hue/Saturation Adjustment
      Layer, 64, 97, 211
Saturation/Value Triangle (Painter), 17–19
Save As commands
   Painter, 48
   Photoshop, 32
Save Image, Camera Raw dialog, 13
Save Layout, Arrange Palettes command
   (Painter), 24
Save New Brush Preset, Brushes palette
   (Photoshop), 106
Save Selection command (Photoshop), 84
Scale slider
   Painter, 17
   Photoshop, Bubble Brush, 217
scaling images, 57
Scattering setting, Bubble Brush
   (Photoshop), 216

Scratch sizes (Photoshop), 7
Screen Blend mode, 44, 45
Screen Composite Method (Painter), 77
sculpted effect, 76–77
Selection Adjuster tool (Painter), 16
selections (Photoshop)
   constraining, 150
   Elliptical Marquee tool, 150, 216
   Lasso tool, 6, 96–97, 178, 221
   Magic Wand tools, 6, 209
   Magnetic Lasso tool, 96
   Marquee Selection tool, 173
   modes, 6
   Selection tools, 6
Selection tools (Painter), 16
Select menu commands (Painter)
   All, 71
   Auto Select, Using Image Luminance, 77
   Float, 71
Select menu commands (Photoshop)
   All, 210
   Inverse, 71
   Modify, 150
      Expand, 209
      Feather, 96–97, 150, 221
   Save Selection, 84
sepia-toning backgrounds, 97
service bureaus/digital printmaking studios,
   3
Set Paper Color, Canvas menu command
   (Painter), 113
Shadow Intensity slider, Watercolor filter
   (Photoshop), 43–44, 175
Shape Dynamics setting (Photoshop)
   Brushes palette, 139
   Bubble Brush, 217
   Hard Round 19 brush, 195
Shape tools (Photoshop), 6
Sharpen filters (Photoshop), Unsharp Mask,
   59
Sharpen tool (Photoshop), 6
Sharpness setting, Paint Daubs filter
   (Photoshop), 33
Shine setting, Apply Surface Texture, Using
   Paper effect (Painter), 114
Short Dab stroke styles (Painter), 50
Show Auto-Painting command (Painter), 48
Show Brush Controls commands (Painter),
   162
  Show General, 20
Show Brush Creator command (Painter), 162
Show Channels command (Photoshop), 84
Show Colors Window menu command
   (Painter), 73
Show Color Variability, Window command
   (Painter), 50

Shower at Sunset Point, 21, 198–199, 203
Show General Brush Controls command
   (Painter), 20
Show Grid box, Lens Correction filter
   (Photoshop), 171–172
Show Layers command (Painter), 36
Show Layout Grid command (Painter), 221
Show Mixer command (Painter), 224
Show Restoration command (Painter), 93
Show Underpainting command (Painter), 91
Shutter Priority mode camera setting, 101,
   137
Simple Brush Type, 33
Simple Water brush (Painter), 130–132
Size Jitter Shape Dynamics setting, Bubble
   Brush (Photoshop), 217
Size section, Brush Creator (Painter), 20
Size setting
   Painter
      Artists' Oils brushes, 162
      Digital Airbrush brush, 52
      Real Blender Flat brush, 202
      Soft Cloner brush, 93
      Square Hard Pastel brush, 115
      Square Pastel Cloner brush, 117
      Wet Oily Palette Knife brush, 162
   Photoshop, Show Grid box, Lens
      Correction filter, 162
Sketch filters (Photoshop), Photocopy, 35, 41
Smart Blur, Underpainting palette (Painter),
   23, 48, 90, 91, 120, 130, 151–152, 161,
   201, 217
Smart Filters (Photoshop), 57
Smart Layers (Photoshop), Painter, lack of
   support, 57
Smart Objects (Photoshop), 57
   Edit Smart Object, 57
Smeary Bristle Spray Oils brush (Painter),
   203
Smeary Round Impasto brush (Painter), 21
Smooth Blender Stump brush (Painter), 92
Smoothness setting (Photoshop)
   Accented Edges dialog, 34
   Spatter filter, 65–66
Smoothy Runny Bristle 30 Watercolor brush
   (Painter), 203
Smudge Blenders brush (Painter), 116
Smudge tool (Photoshop), 6, 9, 174, 175, 178
   Finger Painting, 87
Soft 65-pixel tip, Options bar (Photoshop),
   66
Soft Blender Stump brush (Painter), 92
Soft Charcoal brush (Painter), 119, 121, 122,
   123
Soft Charcoal Cloner brush (Painter), 121
Soft Cloner brush (Painter), 93, 133, 224

Soft Diffused Brush (Painter), 131–132
Soft Edge Cloner brush, Restoration palette (Painter), 93, 186, 188–189
Soft Grain Type mode setting, Grain filter (Photoshop), 179
Soft Light Blend mode (Photoshop), 34, 213, 215
Soft Light Composite Method (Painter), 77
Soft Mode, Rubber Stamp tool (Painter), 159
Softness setting, Image Luminance, Glass Distortion effect (Painter), 61
Softness setting, Palette Knife filter (Photoshop), 42
Soft Round brushes (Photoshop)
    #27, 57
    #45, 112
    #65, 105, 108, 210
    #200, 104, 108, 216
    #300, 212, 215
Somerset papers, 3
Sony Cybershot DSC-F505V camera, 47, 127
    Carl Zeiss zoom lens, 47, 127
Sorolla y Bastida, Joaquin, 89, 149
Spacing settings (Photoshop)
    Brush Tip Shape controls, 9, 142
    Bubble Brush, 217
Spatter, Art History Brush (Photoshop), 85–86
Spatter brush (Photoshop), 85
    #39, 27
    #59, 142, 144
Spatter filter (Photoshop), 63, 65 66
Spatter Water brush (Painter), 131
Sponge tool (Photoshop), 6, 9
Spray Radius setting, Spatter filter (Photoshop), 65–66
Square Chalk brush (Painter), 225–226
Square Hard Pastel brush (Painter), 115–116, 224, 226–227
    versus Blunt Chalk, 225
Square Pastel Cloner brush (Painter), 116–117
Square Soft Pastel brush (Painter), 225
Standard workspace (Photoshop), 11
Status Bar (Photoshop), 7
Steamer in a Snowstorm, 199
Still Life with Fruit, 39
Still Life with Pears and Grapes, 39
Stop/Play buttons, Auto-Painting palette (Painter), 50–51
straightening images, 57
Strength setting, Old Medium to Large Tip brush (Photoshop), 174
Stroke Detail setting, Palette Knife filter (Photoshop), 42
Stroke Size setting, Palette Knife filter (Photoshop), 42

Stroke styles (Painter), Short Dab, 50
studio setup, digital photography, 2–3
Styles setting (Photoshop)
    Art History Brush, 10
        Tight Short, 85, 87
    History Brush, 10
    Lighting Effects filter, 10
Stylize filters (Photoshop), Find Edges, 34
subject focus, 78–79
    backgrounds
        subduing, 80–87
    painterly brushwork, 80–87
    sharp focus, 88–97
Summer Afternoon Play, 88–89
Surface Control effects (Painter)
    Apply Surface Texture
        Using Image Luminance, 122
        Using Paper, 111, 114, 122
    Woodcut, 37, 61, 69, 71–74, 76
Surface Lighting, Canvas menu command (Painter), 21

T

Tapered Oils Artists' Oils brush (Painter), 164
Temperature, Camera Raw dialog, 90
Text tool (Painter), 16
Texture Channel menu (Photoshop)
    Grain filter, 179
    Lighting Effects filter, 10
textured look
    with Art History Brush, 100–109
    with black and white, 118–123
    with pastels, 110–117
Texture filters (Photoshop), Grain, 179
Texture slider (Photoshop)
    Dry Brush filter, 58, 65
    Watercolor filter, 43–44, 175
Thick Bristle Impasto brush (Painter), 21
Thiebaud, Wayne, 31
Thoughts Hidden in Blue, 136, 139, 141, 143
Threshold setting (Photoshop)
    Dust & Scratches filters, 58
    Unsharp Mask filter, 59
TIF format, 64, 189, 220
    versus raw format, 12
Tight Short Style, Art History Brush (Photoshop), 85, 87
Timing information (Photoshop), 7
Tolerance setting (Photoshop)
    Art History Brush, 10
    History Brush, 10

Tonal Control effects (Painter)
    Adjust Colors, 90
    Correct Colors, 90
Tone Curve panel tabs/sliders, Camera Raw dialog, 158
    Parametric, 14
        Highlights, 158
    Point, 14
Tool Bar, Camera Raw dialog, 13
Toolbox
    Painter, 16–17
    Photoshop, 6–7
Torch Ginger Study, 118
Touch Ring Intuos4 M tablet, 25–26
Tracing Paper (Painter). See also paper/paper manufacturers
    toggling off/on, 115
    turning off, 114
    turning on, 49, 113, 223
Transform commands (Photoshop)
    Distort, 128, 129
    Free Transform, 145, 150, 210, 216–217, 222
Trillium Press, 3
tripods, 207, 219. See also cameras; cameras/lenses
    advantages/disadvantages, 31, 157, 181, 219, 269
    Manfrotto 3437 tripod head, 3001B Pro legs, 32
    movement prevention, 35
Turner, Joseph M. W., 199
2 O'Clock Spotlight Styles setting, Lighting Effects filter (Photoshop), 10
Type tool (Photoshop), 6

U

UltraChrome K3 pigmented inkset (Epson), 3
Ultrasmooth Fine Art Paper (Epson), 3
undercolor, 175
Underpainting palette (Painter), 128, 129, 185
    Edge Effect, Jagged Vignette, 49
    Smart Blur, 23, 48, 90, 91, 120, 130, 151–152, 161, 201
Undo Brush tool command (Photoshop), 178
Uniform Color setting, Adjust Dye Concentration effect (Painter), 61
Unsharp Mask filter (Photoshop), 59
Using Image Luminance, Auto Select menu command (Painter), 77

V

Value setting, Color Variability (Painter), 49–50
van Rijn, Rembrandt, 157
Variance setting, Image Luminance, Glass Distortion effect (Painter), 61
Velvet Fine Art Paper (Epson), 3
Vertical Perspective slider, Lens Correction filter (Photoshop), 171–172
View from my Window, 47
View menu commands, Proof Setup, Working CMYK (Photoshop), 177
Vignette settings, Lens Correction filter (Photoshop), 172
Viscosity setting, Artists' Oils brushes (Painter), 162
Vivid Light Blend mode (Photoshop), 35

W

Wacom tablets/pens, 89
    Art Pen, 2
    Intuos4 M tablet, 23
        Grip Pen, Tip Sensor, 25
    Intuos4 tablet, 2
    retouching images, 112
    Wacom software
        Pen panel, 26
        Tip Feel control, 26
Walk on the Beach, 89
Warhol, Andy, 31
Water Brush Controls (Painter), 203
Watercolor brushes (Painter)
    versus Digital Watercolor brushes, 130
    Smoothy Runny Bristle 30, 203
Watercolor filter (Photoshop), 40, 43–44, 175
watercolor looks/techniques
    Impressionist (Photoshop), 38–45
    soft, diffused painting (Painter), 126–135
    realistic (Photoshop), 136–145
watercolor paper
    cold press, 127, 130, 139, 140
    scanning, 145

Watercolor Paper Radiant White (Epson), 3
Weaves Selector (Painter), 16
Wet Edges setting, Brushes palette (Photoshop), 139, 140
Wet Erasers Digital Watercolor brush (Painter), 131, 135
Wet Fringe setting, Digital Watercolor brushes (Painter), 131
Wet Media Brushes (Photoshop), 9, 106, 174
Wetness setting, Artists' Oils brushes (Painter), 162
Wet Oily Palette Knife Artists' Oils brush (Painter), 160–162
Wet paint, 127, 131–135, 202
White Camellia, 111
White Input setting, Levels Adjustment Layer (Photoshop), 71
White is High check box, Texture Channel, Lighting Effects filter (Photoshop), 10
width and height (Photoshop)
    Canvas, 87, 129
    Crop tool, 103
    Image Size, 223
    New File, 216
William Turner paper (Hahnemuehle), 3
Willows by the Stream, 149
Wind Direction dial, Smoothy Runny Bristle 30 Watercolor brush (Painter), 203
Window menu commands (Painter)
    Arrange Palettes
        Default, 17, 24
        Save Layout, 24
    Brush Controls
        Impasto, 21
        Show Color Variability, 50
        Water, 203
    Color Palettes
        Show Colors, 73
        Show Mixer, 224
    Custom Palettes, Organizer, 24
    Show Auto-Painting, 48
    Show Brush Controls, 162
        Show General, 20
    Show Brush Creator, 162
    Show Layers, 36
    Show Layout Grid, 221
    Show Restoration, 93
    Show Underpainting, 91, 129

Window menu commands (Photoshop)
    Brushes, 139
        Load Brushes, 105
    Color, 145
    History, 11, 86
    Show Channels, 84
    Workspace
        Painting, 11
        Save Workspace, 11
Windows platform, photographer's studio setup, 2
Wood, Sea, Sky, 19, 218–219
Woodcut effect (Painter), 37, 61, 69, 71–74, 76
woodcut look, 68–77
Working CMYK, Proof Setup, View menu commands, (Photoshop), 177
Workspace commands (Photoshop)
    Painting, 11
    Save Workspace, 11
workspaces
    Painter
        customizing, 24
        navigating, 17
    Photoshop, 7
        customizing, 11

X–Z

.xmp files (Camera Raw), 103

Zoom controls, Camera Raw dialog, 13
Zoom tool (Photoshop), 6